PAT
NIXON

MODERN FIRST LADIES

Lewis L. Gould, Editor

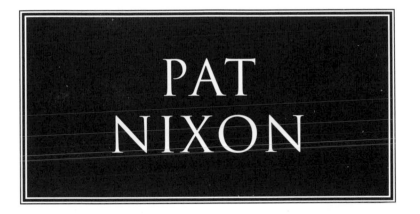

PAT NIXON

EMBATTLED FIRST LADY

MARY C. BRENNAN

UNIVERSITY PRESS OF KANSAS

© 2011 by the University Press of Kansas
All rights reserved
Published by the University Press of Kansas (Lawrence, Kansas 66045),
which was organized by the Kansas Board of Regents and is operated
and funded by Emporia State University, Fort Hays State University,
Kansas State University, Pittsburg State University, the University
of Kansas, and Wichita State University

Library of Congress Cataloging-in-Publication Data

Brennan, Mary C.
Pat Nixon : embattled first lady / Mary C. Brennan.
p. cm. — (Modern first ladies)
Includes bibliographical references and index.
ISBN 978-0-7006-1771-5 (cloth : alk. paper)
1. Nixon, Pat, 1912–1993. 2. Nixon, Richard M. (Richard
Milhous), 1912–1994. 3. Presidents' spouses—United States—
Biography. I. Title.
E857.N58B74 2011
973.927092—dc22
[B]
2010044916

British Library Cataloguing-in-Publication Data is available.

Printed in the United States of America
10 9 8 7 6 5 4 3 2 1
The paper used in this publication is recycled and contains 30 percent
postconsumer waste. It is acid free and meets the minimum requirements of
the American National Standard for Permanence of Paper for Printed Library
Materials Z39.48–1992.

For Brig and Patty
Two strong women who never let life's challenges
keep them down for long

CONTENTS

EDITOR'S FOREWORD

During her lifetime, polemics and politics shaped how the world viewed Thelma Ryan "Pat" Nixon. Admirers of Richard Nixon depicted his wife as the dedicated soul mate who stuck with her embattled husband through all of his political crises. Critics of the first lady found her a "plastic Pat" who endured a troubled marriage through a supreme act of will and emotional endurance. In the process, Mrs. Nixon became a caricature of a real person.

Mary Brennan has used the first lady's papers and the recollections of her friends and adversaries to provide a fuller and more nuanced account of how Pat Nixon emerged from a hardscrabble background to build a career and then a married life with Richard Nixon. With admirable balance and fairness, Brennan traces the evolution of Thelma Ryan into the Pat Nixon that the world first knew during the 1950s. Brennan's narrative of the Nixon marriage captures as well as any outsider could the genuine love at the outset of the relationship, along with the changes in the union that followed Richard Nixon's political rise. The reader sympathizes with Mrs. Nixon's capacity to overcome her husband's many deceits and broken promises regarding their future.

There are many strong points to Brennan's story—the brave performance of Pat Nixon in Venezuela in 1958, her emergence as an effective campaigner in three presidential election campaigns, and her genuine rapport with people before and during her White House years. Brennan has a good eye for the informative quotation, and she maintains an empathy for her subject while offering judicious appraisals of her positive and negative traits. Brennan's mastery of the Republican Party and her knowledge of conservative women in the 1950s and 1960s enable her to achieve a thoughtful and perceptive portrait of a woman who was at the center of national politics for two decades. No longer will Pat Nixon be an historical enigma.

Mary Brennan has moved beyond the oversimplified appraisals of this neglected first lady to provide a powerful study of a complex and fascinating presidential spouse.

—*Lewis L. Gould*

ACKNOWLEDGMENTS

When Lewis Gould contacted me in 2003 about writing a biography of Pat Nixon, I was not certain that I should agree. Although the idea intrigued me, I was in the middle of another project; I had a small child; I had departmental responsibilities; and I knew very little about the first lady except what I had read about her husband. To make matters worse, I discovered that many of the necessary documents were closed to researchers. Still, there was something about Pat's story that fascinated me. Like many women I have known, she faced her hardships head-on. She refused to give in to self-pity, and she persevered. She was neither the saintly victim nor the empty-headed cipher of legend. She was a woman with flaws who made choices and lived with the consequences even when she disliked the results of her decisions. I became determined to give Pat a voice and to let her story emerge without attempting to shape her image to fit the conventional stereotypes.

If I have succeeded at all, it was because of the extraordinary help I received along the way. I must begin with the archivists and staff of the Richard Nixon Library. From director Tim Niftali down through the ranks, everyone I encountered went out of his or her way to facilitate my research. In particular, I thank Gregory Cummings for sharing his research knowledge as well as coming in on a Saturday to allow me to conduct an interview; Ira Pemstein for computer assistance, insight into the "wilderness years," and lunch; Craig Ellefson for willingness to help out with my last-minute requests; Ryan Pettigrew for dealing so ably with my sometimes complicated picture requests; and Meghan Lee for her appreciation of Pat and her generosity and patience in guiding me through the Pat Ryan Nixon Collection. I also worked with some of Pat's first lady papers when they were still housed at the National Archives and Records Administration facility in College Park, Maryland. The archivists and staff there answered my many questions and helped me understand the often complicated system of files. Stephanie George and the rest of the staff of the Richard Nixon Oral

History Project at California State University, Fullerton, provided desk space and camera assistance during my time in their reading room. Finally, Margaret Vaverek, librarian extraordinaire of Alkek Library at Texas State University, San Marcos, worked her usual miracles in finding information quickly, and Mary Lou Bishop used her expertise to translate some of Pat's shorthand notes.

Two women played key roles in moving the project along. At a crucial point in the process, Julie Nixon Eisenhower intervened and facilitated the opening of the rest of her mother's papers. I could have finished without seeing those documents, but their inclusion certainly fleshed out my understanding of the first lady. Similarly, my conversation with Maureen Drown Nunn, daughter of Helene and Jack Drown, provided me with the human element missing from documents.

I also benefited from the support of the administration and my colleagues in the history department at Texas State University. Funds provided through the university's Research Enhancement Program allowed me to make numerous trips to California and Maryland. I also received a developmental leave, granting me the time necessary to travel and write. Throughout this long process, my colleagues listened, questioned, encouraged, and pushed me. I am particularly grateful to Vikki Bynum, Frank de la Teja, and Ana Romo, who read sections of the manuscript; to Lynn Denton and Ken Margerison, who let me talk through some trouble spots; and to Elizabeth Makowski, who, like the nuns she studies, is ever vigilant and hard-working, and who helped me stay on task. Shae Luther performed admirably as research assistant, hunting down articles in the library and on the Internet.

In addition, Irwin Gellman and Melvin Small improved the manuscript significantly through their careful readings. Both men offered valuable suggestions and thoughtful critiques of the chapters they read. Gellman knows more about the Nixons and the sources available than anyone else. I greatly appreciated his willingness to pay it forward. Small's comments served to tighten the arguments and clarify the characterizations. Any mistakes remaining are mine.

My thanks to the series editor, Lewis Gould, and the publisher, Fred Woodward, must also include a blanket apology. I do not think I met one deadline they established. I am certain that I sorely strained their patience. Yet they always remained polite and encouraging. I have learned a great deal during this process and I am grateful for their willingness to work with me. In addition, Lew provided the wonderful picture of Pat campaigning for chapter 3.

Finally, as always, I must acknowledge the contribution of my family. My sisters, Brigid Brennan and Patricia Dolezal, continually amaze me with their abilities to confront the obstacles life throws at them. I cannot thank them enough for their ever-present support and love. My husband, Alan Apel, pushes and challenges me to be more than I ever imagined I could be. And then there is my daughter, Riley, who helped me understand the sacrifices Pat made every time she had to leave her daughters.

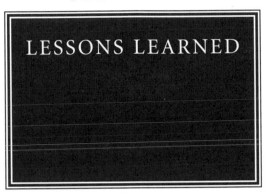

CHAPTER 1

LESSONS LEARNED

Throughout her long political career, Pat Nixon remained something of an enigma to the press and public. Was she the "plastic Pat" of legend? The woman with no personality of her own who stood behind her husband—literally and figuratively—during his many defeats and triumphs? Was she the warm, gracious woman who hugged children and remembered longtime supporters' names? Or was she the sharp-tongued politico who snapped at reporters who asked pesky questions? Republicans portrayed her as a paragon of traditional womanly virtue, while Democrats cast her as another of her husband's victims, a puppet wife. Many people, especially younger Americans, could not fathom that she chose to remain married to a man stubbornly pursuing a career and lifestyle she despised, that she overlooked his callous treatment of her, that she defended him despite evidence of wrongdoing. It was far easier for them to believe that her husband forced her into that position than to recognize her role in her own life. They, like so many other people, including at times her husband, underestimated her. They focused on her delicate appearance and missed the steel underneath.

If various public relations committees created the multiple images of first lady Pat Nixon, her family and childhood forged the reality. The daughter of an Irishman always looking for the pot of gold and a first-generation German immigrant determined to face life's tragedies and protect her children, Pat learned at an early age that life was hard. She understood that survival depended on everyone doing his or her part to keep the family afloat financially, emotionally, and physically. Orphaned by the time she was eighteen, she developed a deep sense of responsibility to others, a strong work ethic, and an empathetic nature. She also became skilled at protecting a part of herself from the outside world. Despite the difficulties of her youth, she retained a sense of adventure and curiosity. These lessons of her younger years gave her the tools she needed to navigate her life as a public figure.

The story of the future first lady's parents was the stuff of American legend. Her father, William Ryan, the son of first-generation Irish immigrants, spent much of his youth traveling and searching for a path to riches. He had sailed to the Philippines and braved the frigid wilderness in Alaska. He ended up in the gold mines of the Black Hills of South Dakota. There he met Katherine Halberstadt Bender, a widow with two young children. Kate had arrived in the United States from Germany as a child, accompanying a relative visiting her son. Around the turn of the century, she married Mathew Bender, who worked in the mines. After Mathew's tragic death in a flash-flood mine accident in 1905, Kate struggled to care for her young son and infant daughter. In 1909, she married Will Ryan, and together they left South Dakota to seek their fortune in the west. The new family first settled in Pioche, a small mining town in eastern Nevada that had once boasted a prosperous mine. A few years later, Will found better work in Ely, a slightly larger community about a hundred miles north of Pioche.[1]

During their relatively brief time in the Silver State, the family underwent several changes. Matthew Bender, Kate's son from her first marriage, went to live with his grandparents, who had moved to Los Angeles. The elder Benders' grief at losing their eldest son, combined with their prosperous circumstances, convinced Kate to allow Matthew to move in with his grandparents.[2] Although Kate missed Matthew, she had a growing brood to worry about in her own home. In 1910, William (called Bill) was born, followed the next year by Thomas. In 1912, early in the morning of 16 March, Kate delivered a girl whom she named Thelma Catherine. Will arrived home from the mines, and, overjoyed with his new daughter, he christened her his "St. Patrick's babe in the morning." In fact, he would insist on celebrating her birthday on the 17th instead of the actual date of her birth.[3] He also disliked the name his wife had chosen. He added "Patricia" to her name and refused to call her "Thelma." Most of the time, he called her "Babe." In fact, she would only be Thelma in school to her teachers and childhood playmates; her high school friends called her "Buddy."[4]

A little more than a year after their daughter's birth, Kate convinced Will to give up his mining job in Ely and move the family to booming Southern California. Kate had already lost one husband to the mines, and she did not intend to lose another. Will, who was always looking for the next opportunity, agreed to try something new. Although he initially knew nothing about farming, he packed up his family and bought land in Artesia, California.

The Ryans quickly learned that farming was a family endeavor. Will compensated for his lack of agricultural experience by reading every book he could get his hands on about crops, fertilizers, and soil. All of this study paid off, and he eventually became known as the "cabbage king," because he raised the biggest cabbages in the county. On numerous occasions throughout the planting, weeding, and harvesting cycle, Kate and the kids had specific jobs to do. Kate Ryan added to the family's financial stability with her egg money, earned from the chickens she tended. In addition, young Pat helped her mother keep the house "scrub clean."[5] With everyone's help, Will managed to keep his wife, stepdaughter, and their three children sheltered, fed, and clothed. The Ryans had no luxuries, but, even during the lean years of the 1920s, they had the necessities.

Most important, they had each other. Tall, lanky Will Ryan was a quiet man with a dry sense of humor. He had an endless supply of stories and jokes, which he delivered without ever cracking a smile. His daughter's friends marveled at his mustache as well as his ability to tell that they were up to something even though he was hard of hearing. Despite settling down as a farmer, Will never lost the curiosity that had driven him to travel so widely. He jumped into various money-making ventures even as he worked the farm. Most of his new adventures, however, now came vicariously through an endless supply of books about farming, oil wells, mining, or whatever other new opportunity sparked his interest. His baby girl spent hours on his lap listening to stories of his past journeys and future possibilities; his descriptions of a world beyond their farm, Artesia, and California whetted her curiosity about the bigger world.[6]

In contrast, short, plump Kate was all about home and family. Although the German accent flavoring her speech hinted at the stories she might tell of her own exploits as a young immigrant, Kate concentrated on the present, not the past or the future. She worked hard to keep her house neat and her children and husband happy. Years later, neighborhood children still remembered the smell of her cinnamon rolls wafting out of the kitchen, enticing them from their play or greeting them after school. Kate's busy-ness might have been her way of dealing with the losses she had experienced. After all, as a young child, she left her parents and siblings to travel to a strange new world; as a young wife, she lost her husband; as a young mother, she lived apart from her eldest son. Rather than complaining, she coped. She made a concerted effort to maintain contact with her first family. In fact, after the end of World War I, she secretly sent money to her desperate German relatives. Although she accepted that her in-laws could give Matthew material things she could not, her heart broke at the strained relationship she had with him. Again, she would not just let go. She insisted on taking the train into the city to see him whenever she could, often taking her youngest daughter with her.[7]

The Ryan children had one another and a solid group of playmates. With their chores completed, the children found plenty of activities to occupy their time. They rode the workhorses and their bicycles; actually, Pat and her friends, especially Myrtle and Louise Raine, had to "borrow" their brothers' bikes since they did not have any of their own. The borrowing often meant running away with them quickly before the boys noticed. The girls put on plays in the tank house between the Ryan and Raine properties. Creating costumes from whatever they could sneak out of their houses, they entertained themselves and sometimes a few of the neighboring children. They swam in the reservoir down the road, or they had their own little adventures in the cornfields or watermelon patches. One time they decided to get honey from a beehive. Pat told Myrtle to hit the hive with a stick and she would reach in and grab the honey. When the inevitable stings resulted, the girls ran to Mrs. Ryan's kitchen to get baking soda to treat their battle wounds.[8] Although life was far from idyllic, the Ryan household was generally happy.

Except, perhaps, when Will had too much to drink. In addition to showing her daughter how to keep house, Kate also taught Pat how to deal with a difficult husband. Will Ryan was a good provider and father. He could be "quite strict" with his children, but he never spanked Pat.[9] However, when he took to drinking, he could be loud and abusive. His children knew that at the very least, there would be shouting and stomping when he came home from one of his drinking bouts. In later years, Pat refused to discuss this aspect of her childhood or to dwell on it.[10]

The extent of Will's drinking problem cannot be determined by the available evidence. Other than a brief discussion with her daughter, recounted in Julie's memoir of her mother, Pat did not mention her father's behavior, nor do any of the available oral histories provide clues. Unlike other first ladies such as Eleanor Roosevelt and Betty Ford, whose fathers suffered from the psychological and physical symptoms of alcoholism, Pat's father did not show any other signs of the clinical disease. Whether he was a full-fledged alcoholic or simply a mean drunk, Will's actions still embarrassed and upset her years later.[11]

Clearly, her parents' behavior and relationship affected her and served to reinforce existing social norms. Their confrontations influenced her strategies for dealing with conflict. Following her mother's lead and emulating the women of that generation, throughout her life, she avoided arguments and pursued her goals by more indirect methods. Like her mother, she would not completely surrender her will to her husband. Unlike her parents, however, Pat refused to fight in front of her children. Additionally, neither Kate nor Will encouraged open displays of affection, even from their children. Both he and his wife expected their children to do whatever needed to be done, to face whatever joys or tragedies they must, and to continue to do their jobs without letting anyone know what they were thinking or feeling. In fact, toward the end of her life, Kate reinforced the lesson that women must keep part of themselves secret and private. She told her daughter that she had hidden a little of her chicken and egg money to keep as a cushion for Pat.[12]

Pat's childhood ended relatively quickly during her thirteenth year. Her mother got sick. Kate Ryan first refused to admit how ill she was. She eventually went to see the town doctor, who gave her the terrible news that she had Bright disease (a kidney ailment) and liver cancer. Less than six months later, on 18 January 1926, she died. For Pat, who was on the verge of womanhood, the loss was devastating. She and her mother had been close, and Kate's death shattered Pat's secure little world. Even as an adult, she did not like to think about those years.[13] She might have regrets about things she would never get to ask her mother about her family or her past, but taking her cues from her mother's example, she concentrated on going on. Years later, Pat told her own daughter, "When my mother died, I just took responsibility for my life."[14]

Barely a teenager, she took over the household management. She cooked and cleaned, and she kept her brothers and father presentable. Although her brothers helped with the work, even deigning to do "women's work" such as washing dishes, she still bore the burden of doing most of the cleaning and laundry. Her half-sister, Neva, who was going through nurse's training in Los Angeles, would occasionally come out on the weekends to help, but weekday chores fell to Pat. When her friends' mother died the year after Kate, the girls would help one another get the housework completed.[15]

Despite her additional responsibilities, Pat found time for social and school activities. She and her friends scandalized some of the neighborhood ladies by wearing their brothers' jeans as they went on their adventures in town and frustrated their fathers by "hooking" one of their brothers' cars for a ride to the beach.[16] Then there were her school commitments. By the time she was in high school, Pat was on the debate team, secretary of the student body, a member of the Filibuster Club "with the study of parliamentary law and public speaking as its purpose," vice president of Les Marionettes, a dramatic club, and an active participant in the school's dramatic productions.[17]

In fact, she excelled at theatrical productions, which allowed her to get outside of herself and live another kind of life. Pat appeared in many of the plays staged during her time at Excelsior Union High School, often with her brothers; in these productions, Pat built on the talents developed in her backyard. She earned rave reviews for her starring role in *The Rise of Silas Lapham* during her senior year. The *Excelsior Life*, the high school paper, noted that she was "going over big," and a later review commented on her "undeniable dramatic ability."[18] She certainly won over her costar, who took up an entire page in her senior yearbook to pledge his devotion to his "sweet Buddy with her perfect personality."[19]

Other friends noticed, however, that Pat was not all sweetness and light. She was, as one high school friend put it, "*very* ambitious. She was the type of person that would push to get where she wanted to go."[20] Others saw her behavior as determined rather than ambitious. Once she decided she was right, she could not be budged from that belief.[21] Added to this stubbornness was a fearsome temper. She would rarely let loose with her anger or frustration; even in high school, she exhibited the fierce control over her emotions that characterized her later. When she did let go, her temper was a terrifying thing. Moreover, her pique tended to be long-lasting. One of her friends explained that "when she was provoked, she was provoked for a while." Usually, however, she used more subtle means to let people know that she was upset or disagreed with them. She seemed so quiet that, according to another classmate, "you wouldn't know what was hitting you" until it was too late. By then, she had made her point, gotten her way, or let you know that she was mad as hell. This passive-aggressive behavior would remain very much a part of her personality.[22]

Another family crisis cast a pall over Pat's senior year in high school. The years in the mine began to catch up with Will, and his health suffered. A local doctor diagnosed tuberculosis. Thus, even as the three Ryans, who through a variety of circumstances were all in the same grade, prepared to graduate from high school in June 1929, they got jobs to help sustain them and pay their father's medical bills. Pat now added outside employment to her housework duties and her schoolwork. After graduation, Pat nursed her father during the day and took a shorthand course at night. When he moved to a sanitarium, she got a job at the First National Bank in Artesia. Four years after Kate's death, in May 1930, Will passed away, and the Ryans became orphans.[23]

Coinciding with the worst economic crisis Americans had ever experienced, their father's illness and death altered the college plans of the siblings. All of them won scholarships after graduation, but they decided that only Tom would take advantage of the opportunity. Although the student paper stated that Pat intended to go to Santa Ana Junior College, she and Bill delayed their chance for further education in order to care for their father and the farm. With farm prices plunging and their parents gone, however, Pat and her brothers rented out most of their land and concentrated on earning enough money for all of them eventually to go to college. To that end, Pat continued her work at the bank even as she enrolled in Fullerton Junior College in the fall of 1931.[24]

Two important symbolic events happened during Pat's brief time at Fullerton. First, she enrolled herself at the college as Patricia Ryan rather than Thelma Ryan. She told her daughters that she did it as a tribute to her father.[25] Although that might certainly have influenced the choice of the name, the action of renaming indicated, perhaps, that after years of taking care of other people, she was seizing control of her own destiny. Second, despite her burden of several part-time jobs as well as a full schedule of classes, Pat participated in the college's production of *Broken Dishes*. Whether she auditioned for the show because she just loved being on stage or she wanted to participate in the life of the college, her action reinforced her new independence and determination to do what she wanted to do.[26]

This independent Pat jumped at the chance to test her wings away from the security of her brothers and the limitations of small-town life. In 1932, an elderly couple hired her to drive them back East. Pat seized the opportunity to travel the width of the nation and to visit her father's relatives in Connecticut. She had not originally intended to stay in the East. In fact, the couple bought her a return ticket as payment; she planned to visit her father's relatives, see the sights, and then return to school. When her aunt, a Catholic nun, helped her get a job at Seton Hospital in New York City, however, Pat welcomed the excitement of new experiences almost as much as she did the employment at a time when jobs were scarce. She set to work as a secretary but eventually worked in numerous areas of the hospital, even training as a radiology technician. The fact that Seton specialized in the treatment of tuberculosis did not bother her at all. She claimed that it never occurred to her to be afraid of the disease. She seemed to be having too much fun. From attending conferences where the lectures were "most interesting" to playing hooky with the patients when they went sledding, she enjoyed all aspects of her time in New York.[27]

In addition to exploring New York and the surrounding areas, learning new skills, and spending time with the patients, Pat squeezed in a social life. By all accounts, she was a beautiful young woman with curling red-gold hair, warm brown eyes, an attractive figure, and an engaging personality; she attracted men of all ages and types. During

*Pat Ryan in Seton Hospital pharmacy, New York City, 1932. Richard Nixon
Presidential Library and Museum.*

high school, she had dated, but her brothers knew all of her friends.
Now, although she lived in a convent with a group of nuns who, she
wrote Bill, "were always hanging around," she had fun spending time
with a variety of men. Dr. Francis Vincent Duke, who headed up the
medical staff at the hospital, pursued Pat steadily. He was a nice man
(even her aunt, the nun, approved of him) with a great job, but Pat

continued to date other men. Dr. Duke, according to Julie's biography, "hinted at marriage," but Pat would have none of it. Watching the everyday reality of her parents' marriage might explain Pat's reluctance to commit herself too quickly to a relationship. More important, as she told Julie years later, there was too much she wanted to do to be tied down to a husband.[28]

After two years in New York, she realized she was ready to fulfill her dream of a college education. When Tom wrote her in the spring of 1934 that he had saved enough to get her back to California and help get her started with tuition, she willingly returned to sunny California and that fall enrolled in the University of Southern California. Although she majored in commerce, Pat took enough education classes to earn a teacher certificate as well. She graduated cum laude in three years.[29]

Pat accomplished this academic feat while juggling numerous part-time jobs. She started her time at USC with a research fellowship that covered her tuition and included a small stipend. In order to earn enough to pay her part of the rent in the apartment she shared with her brothers and to buy food and other necessities, Pat had to find additional work. As a result, she filled openings all over campus. Shakespearean scholar and professor Frank Baxter famously told a reporter in the 1950s that he ran into Pat everywhere: the cafeteria, the library, student research programs. The director of student teaching, Dr. W. G. Campbell, used her many jobs as an incentive for future school administrators by writing in a letter of recommendation that she brought "to the classroom a very rich background of practical experience in the various offices in the University."[30]

Two of Pat's college work experiences evidenced both her willingness to embrace new opportunities and her practical nature. The first involved her movie career. While she was working in New York, a professional talent scout for Paramount Pictures offered her the chance to pursue acting professionally. She was flattered but reluctant to give up a steady income for the "tough" life of an actress, with its low pay and immoral temptations.[31] When she returned to California, Hollywood beckoned once more. Pat and her friend Virginia Shugart enjoyed working as extras for $6 a day. The excitement of seeing themselves, even briefly, on screen and the thrill of catching a glimpse of famous actors and actresses could not outweigh the often tedious nature of the work or the instability of job prospects. Pat had firsthand experience with this when directors cut her one line from the 1935 movie *Becky Sharp.* When a studio offered her a contract, Pat turned down the chance at stardom. In addition to the uncertainty of employment, the subtle sexual harassment she had experienced during her brief forays into acting gave her an unwelcome taste of life as a starlet. Perhaps the final straw for Pat was the fact that a contract would put her destiny in the hands of a studio executive. She was determined to control her own fate as much as possible.[32]

The second experience resulted from her exploration of the possibilities surrounding her major in commerce. In late 1935, Pat won a position at Bullock's Wilshire department store in Los Angeles as what today would be a personal shopper. She enjoyed the work but found it exhausting. Although she had entertained thoughts of pursuing a career as a buyer, she realized that she would be stuck in a low-paying job for years as she tried to work her way up the bureaucracy.[33] She had spent too many years working to make ends meet; she wanted to travel; she wanted some security.

Teaching, she realized, would meet her needs. In addition to a decent salary and summers off for traveling, she discovered through her coursework that she was good at it. The students liked her, and she enjoyed the challenge. Her professors agreed that she would "enjoy a fruitful career" because of her "splendid attitude toward young people" and her resourcefulness. Dr. Campbell, director of student teaching, assured future employers that she could "handle any class situation that may arise."[34]

In the end, her background played almost as large a role as her credentials in landing her a position at Whittier High School. The district supervisor of Whittier High School at that time was David Stouffer, who had been principal of Excelsior High School while Pat attended classes there. According to his daughter-in-law's later reminiscences, Stouffer "greatly admired her" and supported her appointment. He recognized how hard she had to work "while raising her brothers after her mother died." Her character, combined with her degree from USC, earned her a place on the faculty.[35] In the fall of 1937, she began her first year of teaching shorthand and typing.

Pat intrigued her students from the start. She was young, beautiful, "charming," and "glamorous." Her "poise" and "reserve" were balanced with "a good sense of humor" and a generous spirit. Both boys and girls developed crushes on her as only teenagers can. They tried to follow her home and then loitered outside her room, waiting for a glimpse of her. One group of boys worked up the nerve to knock on the door of the apartment she shared with several other female teachers, only to be turned away with a polite but firm look of disapproval.[36] They apparently assumed that because she was so young, she would be a pushover. They were sorely mistaken. In fact, she turned out to be a "real disciplinarian" who would not tolerate tardiness or disruptive behavior.[37] She expected her students to work hard. As one former student recalled years later, "Miss Ryan followed the book. She allowed no compromises, no errors, no second-rate job."[38] She knew from personal experience that hardships could be overcome, but only through diligence, persistence, and effort.

Her difficult childhood might have made her value discipline and hard work, but it did not turn her into a humorless tyrant. In fact, it seemed to give her an understanding of the obstacles some students faced on a daily basis. For example, the children of migrant workers who attended Whittier High School often ran afoul of the truancy rules. According to Julie Eisenhower's biography, rather than reporting the absences, Pat would speak with the parents to explain the problem with keeping their children home for too many days in hopes that they could remedy the situation themselves. Even for students who simply faced the traumas of the teen years, she had words of encouragement. Margaret Langstaff Kaping remembered that Pat always told her students that they could "make anything" of themselves if they "set [their] heart[s] on it." She recognized that her family's support of her dreams had helped them become reality despite the financial and emotional hardships of her early years. Obviously, she wanted to pass that on to her students. Perhaps most importantly, during these years, Pat honed the trait that would serve her so well as first lady. As one former student put it, "She had the uncanny ability to always make you feel *you* were the most important 'Cog in the wheel.'" Pat made the person she was talking to feel as though she was totally focused on him or her.[39]

Despite her dedication to her students, Pat must have found life in Whittier somewhat restrictive. After all, she had lived in New York City and Los Angeles, both large, cosmopolitan cities offering much in the way of entertainment and activity. Even in Artesia, which could not really be called an urban area, she had found plenty to keep her busy. Perhaps the biggest change from Artesia, however, was the small-town, tightly knit community that existed in Whittier. As a young, attractive, and single woman, Pat must have felt the eyes of the town on her constantly. Teachers were expected to exemplify a moral, upright lifestyle. Pat certainly was no wild woman, but she did have a fierce sense of privacy and a determination to run her own life. She may not have wanted to go out partying every night, but she definitely did not want the good people of Whittier deciding that for her. Consequently, she spent most of her weekends in Los Angeles with her half-sister, Neva, and brother-in-law, where she could date whom she pleased without any prying eyes.[40]

Pat seemed to have two strategies when it came to men. She either dated a variety of men, as she did during her New York and Whittier years or, as at USC, she rarely went out at all. In both cases, she prevented any serious relationships from developing. She could have a good time but maintain her freedom. Pat found it important to establish herself, to ensure that she controlled her own destiny, and to make certain that she could protect herself from economic hardship.

All in all, Pat Ryan was in a good place in her life. She had a steady job that she found rewarding and that paid relatively well. Considering the economic climate of the nation, which was still struggling to recover from the financial disasters of the early years of the 1930s, Pat felt fortunate to be making as much as she was. The money allowed her to work only one job, definitely a luxury for her, and to live comfortably, if not lavishly. For once, she was not living paycheck to paycheck or worrying about paying off debt. Perhaps more important, the money and her work schedule allowed her to indulge her craving for travel and adventure. Granted, she took only small trips through California, but still, she must have loved the freedom to do as she wanted, when she wanted, without being responsible for or to another person. If occasionally she had to participate in some community events in Whittier, that was a small price to pay for her simple but fulfilling life.

From the moment Richard Nixon met Pat Ryan in early 1938, he threatened to disrupt her happy little world. They met at tryouts for a community theater production of *The Dark Tower*. Both were there for work-related reasons: school officials expected young faculty to participate in community events, so when a more senior teacher encouraged

Pat to audition, she felt she had little choice but to go. Considering her earlier theatrical efforts, her hesitation might have resulted from her being told what to do or to the potential drain on her time. Nixon, struggling to build his law practice in a small town, had joined the theater group as yet one more way to network and find clients; he had already joined most of the business and service clubs in town. According to Nixon, it was love at first sight. He asked her for a date that very night. She declined. By the third rehearsal, he told her that he was going to marry her someday. According to Pat, she thought he was nuts. Still, he was handsome and definitely persistent. Throughout the production's run, he drove her home and continued to ask her out. She kept saying no, even as she allowed him to drive her to Los Angeles to visit her sister (and go out on dates with other men!), even as she set him up with her best friend, and even as she accepted little gifts and notes from him.[41]

Perhaps Pat tolerated Dick's pursuit because she recognized the significant similarities in their backgrounds, their personalities, and their ambitions. Like Pat, Dick grew up in a working-class family. More important, he also had experienced familial tragedy as a young man. His parents, Frank and Hannah Nixon, were devout Quakers who ran a service station and market that required that their children work long hours. They always had enough food, but medical bills ate away at their income. In fact, Dick won a scholarship to Harvard but had to turn it down because he could not afford to live in Boston. Dick understood the gnawing fear of not being able to pay all his bills. He could relate to the embarrassment of working a menial job because there were no other options. He knew the panic associated with squeezing every penny and weighing every purchase.[42]

More importantly, he too had experienced tremendous personal loss as a youngster. His seven-year-old brother, Arthur, died of tubercular encephalitis when Dick was twelve years old. The family had already been struggling with their oldest son Harold's illness. Doctors diagnosed Harold with tuberculosis several years before Arthur's death, and the family spent years and a great deal of money trying to cure him. At one point, Hannah moved with Harold to a sanitarium, leaving her other children and husband to fend for themselves. Dick learned young to take care of himself.[43]

He also absorbed the message that public displays of frustration, of grief, or even of affection were bad. Quakers dislike confrontation of any kind, whether on a national or familial level. Frank Nixon, however, occasionally lost his fearsome temper. The fallout convinced young Dick that it was better to hold everything inside. Like the Ryans, the Nixons discouraged public displays of affection. In his memoirs, Dick relates the story of his baby brother asking permission to kiss him hello after a long absence. He comments that his brother "had acquired [the] family reticence about open displays of affection." Pat certainly could relate to that strategy.[44]

Still, she held him off. She told him she was not ready to settle down, that she wanted to travel and experience new places and people. He started calling her his "Irish gypsy." To reinforce her point, during the summer of 1938, she went to Michigan, drove back by herself, and did not get in touch with him when she returned. After six weeks, he broke down and wrote to her at school. She answered the letter, and they started dating again.[45] Throughout the autumn and into early 1939, he continued to woo her. He wrote her sweet love notes, including one transforming a Straight Note into a promise to pay her an exorbitant sum "every day, hour, minute, second or what you will."[46]

His strategy worked. By the summer of 1939, they were an item. They went dancing; they double-dated with her friends. Perhaps most important, the more they talked, the more they realized that in addition to similar backgrounds, they both wanted to go places. They might have started out in small towns with limited prospects, but they recognized in one another a kindred spirit of ambition and wanderlust. When Pat initially succumbed to Dick's persistence, it was to take drives out to the beach or to explore the small towns of southern California. They would sometimes take along their favorite books, drive to "their" beach, and sit in companionable silence reading together, separately. Pat must have found Dick's willingness to let her just "be" intriguing.[47]

After two years of courting, in March 1940, they got engaged; three months later, on 21 June, they married. It was a quiet, small ceremony with just the immediate families and a few friends present. Being the practical, adventurous sorts that they were, their honeymoon was hardly the typical romantic getaway. Instead, loaded with canned goods to save money on meals, they took off in Pat's car to tour Mexico. Their friends had removed all the labels from the cans as a joke, which added to the sense of mystery. They explored, sometimes slept in the car, and saw lots of sights. The whole trip cost them less than $200. Other people might see it as cheap and unromantic. They would miss the point. What was important to other people was not necessarily what was important to the Nixons. In fact, they so enjoyed their trip that they decided to live frugally and save their money for more such adventures in the future.

In addition to her new husband, Pat began the school year in 1940 with a freshly appointed assistant named Helene Colesie Drown. The administration assigned new faculty member Mrs. Drown to assist Mrs. Nixon with the pep squad. The two women hit it off immediately. Delighted to find that their husbands shared their feelings, Pat and Helene organized dinners, excursions, and sports outings for the two couples. As Helene wrote years later, they "all loved sports, music, and having fun."[48] Over the years, the couples would discover a mutual obsession with politics as well. For Pat, Helene would prove to be a rock she could depend on for support.

The newlyweds enjoyed their life but grew to realize that Whittier was too limiting. There were too many people who would be forever concerned with their lives and too few opportunities for advancement. Besides, with Europe already engulfed in war and America edging ever closer, they yearned to be where the action was. By October 1941, when an old professor of Dick's recommended him for a job with the new Office of Price Administration in Washington, D.C., they jumped at the chance to live in the East.[49] By the time they set off on what would be a "snowy and icy trip" across the country, America had formally entered the war against Germany and Japan, making Washington even more congested and crowded. Despite the chaos, the Nixons arrived safely, got Dick sworn in, and found an apartment, all on their first day in the city.[50]

Although their time in Washington was brief, working within the government bureaucracy affected their views on the federal establishment. The Office of Price Administration was one of a network of agencies created by Franklin Roosevelt to deal with the economic transition from peace to war. The OPA regulated prices and mandated rationing of some goods as a way to control inflation and keep the military supplied and the economy moving.[51] Because Pat found a job with the OPA as well, both husband and wife experienced the reality of working within a complex network of civil servants. Dick grew frustrated with what he saw as the extraordinary inefficiency and petty posturing rampant throughout the organization. He found many sincere, caring people working hard to help the American public. But it seemed to him that there were many, many others who seemed to thrive on causing more work for small business owners, who created mini fiefdoms and who gave little thought to the purpose of their jobs. Their experiences during this time would greatly influence their views on expanding government bureaucracy later on.[52]

With millions of Americans fighting the enemy, Dick found his desk job boring and frustrating. He longed to get more actively involved in the fight. He disliked going against his Quaker beliefs, but felt he had no choice but to combat the evil forces of Hitler and Emperor Hirohito. Consequently, despite the subtle but real disappointment of his parents, but with the loving support of his wife, in August 1942, he joined the navy and put in for active duty. It would take several years, but the navy finally assigned him to a transport and supply command in the South Pacific. In the meantime, he and Pat experienced life in the Midwest and on the West Coast.[53]

The war years were a time of mixed emotions for Pat. On the one hand, the letters she and Dick wrote to one another indicate the depth of their love and longing for one another. They missed each other intensely and worried about the other's safety and health. Because she spent most of her time without Dick in San Francisco awaiting his return, she was living alone in a city where she knew no one. She was lonely. On the other hand, these years allowed her to live out some of her fantasies. Within a few years, she had lived in various parts of the country and driven across it numerous times. She had gone back to work for the OPA in San Francisco, working her way up to the position of price analyst. By the end of the war, she was earning $3,200 a year— nice money for a woman. Moreover, as she herself explained to her husband, although she missed him desperately, "the many months you have been away have been full of interest." Under other circumstances, had she, for example, "been footloose," she would have been "extremely happy." Recognizing that his return would end this period of her life, she begged him "to love me lots and never let me change my feelings for you which has been so beautiful all these years." In this perhaps unintentionally self-aware letter, Pat seems to foretell her life. She understood that she could have a career, control of her destiny, financial security, and adventure if she were single. She was willing to give all of that up or share it with Dick because she was in love with him. If that love did not stay strong, she would then have to live with the regret of what she could have had.[54]

With Dick's homecoming in July 1944, the Nixons entered one of the happiest, most exhilarating periods of their lives. They spent time getting reacquainted; they learned they were going to have a baby; they did a little traveling; and they discussed what they wanted to do with the rest of their lives. Because Dick was still in the navy, at least until January 1945, they did as they were ordered to do and moved back East, first to New York, then Philadelphia, and finally Baltimore. These moves reinforced their desire not to return to small-town living; they enjoyed the conveniences and excitement of the big city. As they were debating what they would do next, Dick learned through a contact back in Whittier that a group of businessmen, community leaders, and interested citizens, eventually called the Committee of One Hundred, was looking for someone to challenge Democrat Jerry Voorhis, who had represented the twelfth congressional district in California for ten years.

While Dick had dreamed of a career in politics, Pat's interest and participation in the political system had been much more limited. As far back as eighth grade, Dick had written of his desire to run for office. Although Pat had not realized his plans for a political career began as early as they had, she must have sensed how central they were to his plans for the future. In fact, even though she might not have believed him that he wanted to marry her at their first meeting, she did tell her roommate that she thought he would be president someday.[55] Pat seemed to have no problem with this. She had, after all, campaigned for Al Smith while she was in high school and been a member of the Filibuster Club. In contrast to Dick's Republican affiliations, Pat registered as an independent in 1937.[56] Still, a life in politics might have seemed exciting to Pat. It promised travel and some financial rewards. She told a later biographer that she really did not care one way or the other about his choice of politics as a career. She believed that it was up to him to make up his mind, and then she would do what she could to support him.[57] She did, however, make two stipulations up front: she would never make a political speech, and their home must remain separate from politics.[58]

With Pat's blessing, Dick met with the Committee of One Hundred and laid out his plan for postwar America. Wearing his naval uniform because continuing consumer shortages made it difficult for him to find a civilian suit, he emphasized that the American public shared his frustrations with the Democratic administration and Congress. He and many other returning veterans, he implied, appreciated what the New Deal had done to help ease economic hardships during the Depression and applauded the Roosevelt–Truman handling of the war. But those times were over, and high prices, new regulations, and a dearth of consumer goods diminished public appreciation and support. Nixon's short speech to the Whittier business leaders laid out what would become his campaign message: the American people were ready for a change in Washington. Recognizing his considerable political skills as well as the appeal of his message, the Whittier group decided to back the young naval vet.[59] The Nixons' political odyssey had begun.

This first campaign offered many challenges. First there were the logistical difficulties. The couple needed to move back to Whittier quickly so that they could begin campaigning. They needed to set up living arrangements as well as a campaign office, and to find a staff. Pat had to organize the move, pack, and travel across the country at the same time that she prepared for the birth of her first baby. With housing in such short supply, they settled in Dick's parents' home. They had been there barely a month went Pat went into labor. Patricia "Tricia" Nixon was born as her father gave a campaign speech on 21 February 1946.

A second challenge involved money. The Nixons began the campaign with the money each had saved during the war years. Initially, they had assumed that this nest egg would serve as a down payment on a house. After some discussion, they agreed to put the money into the campaign because they would have no source of income while he was campaigning and she was pregnant. Moreover, Dick would get no money from the party until he won the primary. Even then, funds would be limited. They had no choice but to invest everything they had in the belief that Dick could win. At one point, Pat told an acquaintance, they "had spent all their money for campaign postage and they were down to their last fifty cents."[60] Eventually contributions began to come in. Pat felt gratified. For her, the donations indicated that people believed that "*we're* going to win" (italics added).[61] Obviously, most campaign staffers think of themselves as part of the candidate's team and use first-person pronouns when describing the campaign. In this instance, Pat knew that she was essential to Dick's success, and his victory would be hers as well.

Pat's participation in the 1946 congressional campaign went beyond financial backing. This original "Pat and Dick" team worked tirelessly side by side, handing out campaign literature, mailing postcards, distributing pamphlets by hand, writing thank-you notes, hosting teas, and giving informal talks. Six hours after giving birth to Tricia, Pat was sitting up in bed, doing research for Dick's speeches. Within a month, she left her newborn daughter with her mother-in-law to return to election headquarters and to hit the campaign trail with her husband.[62] Her help was vitally important for both practical and more abstract reasons. First, they needed the office help. They really could not afford a paid staff. Pat would drop baby Tricia off at her mother-in-law's and then go to the office to type letters, create pamphlets, run off copies, deliver material to the post office, and then be ready to accompany Dick to speeches and meetings. At the end of the day, she would pick up the baby crib and spend the evening running back and forth between the baby and the typewriter. Second, Dick found having Pat with him comforting and inspiring. She understood him in a way no one else did. She could bolster his ego when he needed it, but she also provided constructive criticism. After all, like her husband, she had been on the debate team when she was in school, and she was doing much of the research he used in his speeches.[63]

Pat was not the only woman with this expanded sense of familial responsibilities. In fact, despite the common perception of the postwar period as a time when women found themselves confined by the "feminine mystique," many housewives, mothers, and working women actively participated in the political process. Both the Republican and Democratic parties depended on women as their traditional male staffers found other jobs in the prospering economy. Women who had been fired from their wartime jobs joined younger women who espoused the ideal of the stay-at-home wife and mother to volunteer for

Mrs. Nixon campaigning during her husband's first campaign for national office, 1946. Richard Nixon Presidential Library and Museum.

political work. Telling themselves that their actions were just another means of protecting their families, these homemakers provided politicians with able volunteers to work elections, to educate the public, and to take care of the thousands of tasks necessary to get a candidate elected.[64]

Women volunteers were especially important to a relatively unknown candidate like Richard Nixon. The twelfth congressional district was huge, and most of its citizens had never heard of Dick Nixon. Considering his limited funds, he had to find an inexpensive way to meet lots and lots of people. The Nixon team, which included campaign manager Roy Day as well as Pat, decided that a series of house meetings would serve their purpose. A woman supporter would host a tea for the candidate. Dick would come and make a few remarks, then head out to another meeting, leaving Pat to answer questions and build goodwill. They hoped that at least a few of the guests would agree to host other gatherings and a network of volunteers and supporters would grow. In this way, Dick would go from an unknown entity to a recognizable commodity.[65]

Dick needed all the help he could get. Jerry Voorhis had served the district for ten years and had remained popular with Republicans as well as Democrats. Although Nixon benefited from the public's frustration with inflation, continued wartime regulations, and concern about corruption scandals, he feared that his limited experience would hurt him in the general election campaign. To overcome that, he challenged Voorhis to a public debate. He researched his opponent's record thoroughly and found what he hoped was a weakness he could use. Voorhis had won the endorsement of a political action committee with ties to the CIO. He had not asked for or accepted the endorsement. Nixon, however, caught Voorhis by surprise by producing a pamphlet showing the endorsement and proving the leadership of the PAC had leftist ties. Although the general disaffection with Democratic rule probably accounts for the election results as much as Nixon's tactics of stating that Voorhis was too left wing, the newcomer's willingness to engage in aggressive tactics shocked many people and laid the foundation for the legend of "Tricky Dick."[66]

Pat obviously played a key role in first the primary victory and then the general election campaign. Her clerical and organizational skills saved them countless dollars; her sincere kind-heartedness won over numerous potential volunteers; and her unquestioning belief in her husband convinced many doubting voters that Dick should be their representative. In his memoirs, Nixon admitted that "Pat was my best helper." He noted that she served as a thoughtful critic as well as a loyal cheerleader.[67] His success was also hers. Interestingly, Nixon claimed that of all his electoral wins, the one in 1946 was the sweetest. "Nothing," he wrote, "could equal the excitement and jubilation" of the news that they won. According to Nixon, he and Pat "were happier on November 6, 1946, than we were ever to be again in my political career."[68]

That statement was definitely true for Pat. For the young woman who had worried that her husband's return from overseas would spell the end of her independence and excitement, the campaign had validated her fears. Although she might have found the work exhilarating and interesting, she also realized that it was exhausting. And it was more than just the fatigue of dealing with a new baby who did not sleep through the night while trying to run an office by day. Even Pat, who boasted of her endless supply of energy, broke down occasionally under the strain of constant work and limited funds. At one point, after spending the day typing up political mailings, she realized that there was no money to mail any of it. She fell apart. Her temper flared when she learned that the group of "volunteers" to whom she gave piles of campaign pamphlets were really Democrats in disguise who destroyed the literature once they were outside. She never forgot this incident, even bringing it up to her daughters after the Watergate break-in years later.[69]

Moreover, for Pat, who was raised to value privacy and self-control, this first campaign introduced her to the difficulties she would face as her husband entered this new career. First, there was the constant strain of smiling and meeting new people. Pat had always liked meeting new people, but under different circumstances. In her old life, she met people because she was interested in them. Now, she had to work to get them interested in her. She would get better at this over the years, but, in 1946, she was unsure of herself, and her nervousness was readily apparent. In fact, Dick's campaign manager had to tell both young Nixons to look people in the eye and smile at them.[70] Second, there was the knowledge that even the most personal facts about their lives were now public knowledge. Tricia's birth became one more campaign tool, used to generate publicity for her father's congressional race. The fact that Dick was not there for the birth, even though the doctor had assured him that the labor would be a long one, also defined for her the priority family life would have for Dick.

Most importantly, as her daughter pointed out in her biography, the victory in 1946 created a shift in the balance of power within the Nixon marriage. Before, they had been partners, deciding together what steps they would take. Maybe Pat even had a little more power because she earned more than Dick did during the first years of their marriage and because he had pursued her so relentlessly. Now, however, he was the breadwinner and the one in the driver's seat, and her input seemed less valuable than it did before. If he had been asked, he probably would have said that his wife was still his best advisor, but as he was drawn deeper and deeper into Washington political circles, she would be more and more confined to the sidelines. He valued his wife's opinion, but he thought of politics as "man's work."[71]

One other repercussion of this campaign would plague Pat throughout her life and continue to obscure her image for the public. As with most candidates, the public got a glimpse of the inside of the

Nixon marriage. The legend would become a tale of a young woman dragged into politics by her autocratic husband. She becomes the helpless, passive victim, forced into a life she despises. This legend began during this period for several reasons. First, Pat admitted that she went along with her husband's choice of occupation despite her misgivings and lack of knowledge of the career move. Second, there were several incidents during which Nixon's associates, and the public by extension, got a glimpse of Nixon's temper and his treatment of his wife. At one point, Pat walked into a recording studio, and Dick yelled at her "as he would have a dog."

It is important to keep in mind that most women went along with their husband's wishes during this period. To have done anything else would have gone against the norms of society. Moreover, Pat had gotten to do things that she had wanted to because of Nixon's choices. When she went along with this initial decision, she did not know what the problems would be. Second, they had only been actually living together for a relatively limited period. They got married in June 1940; he went overseas in the summer of 1941 and was gone for three years. He returned in the fall of 1944. By the time the campaign started, they had lived together for only half of the time they had been married. In many ways, they were still getting to know one another. As for Dick's treatment of Pat, she seemed to not be unduly concerned. She had grown up in a household in which the man of the family occasionally exploded at his loved ones. She recognized the behavior. Although it might be true that Dick changed during the campaign, at least according to some of his old Whittier friends, they were also seeing a man who had been through many more real-life experiences since the last time they had seen him. Additionally, although the public occasionally saw Dick get angry, they rarely saw Pat's counterattacks.

Most importantly, she obviously made the choice to stay with him and to participate in his political life. She must either have liked the excitement of being part of the election process or she believed her place was beside her husband. Pat chose to participate. Having a newborn was a perfect excuse not to be as involved. That was not how Pat operated. She always believed that she should and could do whatever was necessary to help her family. To turn her into a passive figure denies her any control over her own life choices. She would never give that up without a fight.

Pat and Dick experienced the move to Washington in very different ways. For Dick, this was the beginning of a skyrocketing career. For Pat, who gave birth to their second daughter, Julie, in 1948, these years were a blur of endless activity as she once again found herself the primary caregiver for her children and her elderly in-laws. To complicate matters, she faced the daunting task of learning to deal with the Washington social circle with no one to guide her through the treacherous, gossip-filled waters. Their limited funds meant that she continued to have to scrimp to keep them properly outfitted and sheltered. These were stressful years for Pat.

Not so for Dick, who might have arrived in D.C. "the greenest" congressional representative of the 80th Congress, but who would not remain that way for long. His initial committee assignment, the Education and Labor Committee, introduced him to another freshman representative, John F. Kennedy. Although opponents from the beginning, their first dealings with one another were congenial even as they disagreed on the legislation that eventually became the Taft-Hartley Act.[72] Less than six months after taking office, he was more excited to discover that he had been appointed to the Herter Committee, a congressional delegation led by Massachusetts representative Christian Herter, charged with traveling to Europe to investigate circumstances there in connection with the foreign aid plan described by Secretary of State George Marshall. This trip encompassed many firsts for Nixon: first luxury cruise, first trip to Europe, first foray into foreign policy, and first meeting with foreign dignitaries. In his memoirs, Nixon did not focus on any one of these experiences. Instead, he concentrated almost entirely on this trip as his first exposure to the "true and brutal face" of communism.[73] He returned with a newfound respect for the dangers the Soviets posed in Europe and throughout the world and new insights into dealing with the Red Menace.

At this point in his career, however, it was the Reds at home who would bring him his first real taste of fame. In addition to the Education and Labor Committee, Speaker Joe Martin also appointed Nixon to the House Un-American Activities Committee. Martin hoped that Nixon would help to "smarten it up." The committee, under the leadership of Texan Martin Dies, was an embarrassment to many on Capitol Hill. Rather than seriously investigating radical activity, the committee engaged in racist, demagogic behavior, intimidating witnesses, ignoring proper procedure, and accomplishing nothing. Nixon, although the junior member, set an example for the senior members of the committee by treating witnesses with respect, doing careful research on the matters under investigation, and following the principles of due process.[74]

Martin and other Republican leaders wanted to relegitimize HUAC because they believed it could be an effective weapon in the battle against communist spies in America. This was an issue that had tremendous promise for the GOP in their quest to regain control of the national government. If they could show that the Democratic administrations of Franklin Roosevelt and Harry Truman had failed to take action to prevent or to stop the development of Soviet spy rings operating within the United States, they increased Republicans' chances at the polls. First, however, they had to convince the American public that there was a serious threat; then they needed an effective weapon to present their case to the people.[75]

The newly legitimized HUAC found the perfect case during the summer of 1948. Responding to the testimony of Elizabeth Bentley that an extensive spy ring had operated within the United States before and during World War II, HUAC subpoenaed Whittaker Chambers. Chambers admitted belonging to the Communist Party USA until he converted to Catholicism and renounced his membership. He was now a well-respected editor for *Time* magazine. A frumpy little man, he did not at first meeting inspire confidence in Nixon. Over the months, however, Nixon came to identify with this man who was disparaged as much for his appearance and background as for his testimony. The bond between the two men tightened when Chambers named Alger Hiss as an active party member during the 1920s and 1930s. Hiss epitomized the Eastern establishment. He had gone to the "right" prep school and then to Harvard University. After graduation, he worked for a Supreme Court justice and for various prestigious law firms before moving on to government service. He had been the State Department representative during the Yalta Conference and helped to create the United Nations. He went from there to the presidency of the Carnegie Endowment for International Peace. His background could not have been more different from Nixon's. And now Chambers said Hiss had not only been a communist, but an active agent.[76]

Because of the high-profile characters involved and the dramatic charges and countercharges, the case drew national attention. As Americans increasingly worried about Soviet behavior in eastern Europe, Hiss's presence during the Yalta talks took on new meaning. Had he promoted Soviet interests during the conference? The lack of clear evidence added to the controversy. Hiss sued Chambers for defamation of character. Chambers produced secret government documents he said Hiss gave him. The documents' dramatic exposure—they were hidden in a hollowed-out pumpkin on his farm—added to the excitement of the case. Because the statute of limitations had expired on espionage charges, the federal government charged Hiss, who claimed that he did not know Chambers, with perjury. Hiss's eventual conviction and jail term vindicated Chambers, cemented HUAC's new reputation as a legitimate Red-hunting weapon, and reinforced the Republicans' assertion of Democratic failures to deal adequately with the growing internal communist problem.

At the center of all this media attention was Richard Nixon, who realized that his national exposure presented him with an opportunity to enhance his position in Washington. He had easily won reelection to Congress in 1948, running ahead of the rest of the Republican ticket. By 1949, he realized that it would be years before he achieved real power if he remained in Congress. He decided, despite the dire predictions of failure from his political advisors, to run for the California Senate seat held by Sheridan Downey, a popular incumbent. When Helen Gahagan Douglas jumped into the race as well, challenging Downey in the Democratic primary, Nixon felt more confident of his decision to run. In fact, the damage the two Democrats inflicted on one another during the primary race certainly made things easier for Nixon. Douglas won, but Downey had used her liberal views to characterize her as the "pink lady."[77]

The Nixon–Gahagan contest of 1950 would further establish Nixon's reputation as "Tricky Dick." Echoing the accusations introduced by Downey, Nixon honed in on Douglas's liberalism. He used her voting record in Congress, her willingness to address groups listed on the attorney general's subversives list, and her own words in speeches to, as he put it in his memoirs, "question . . . her wisdom and judgement." He claimed that he "never questioned her patriotism." When she tried to argue that Nixon's voting record was more liberal than hers, the tactic backfired. Nixon put out a flyer listing the votes of

Douglas next to Vito Marcantonio, the only openly pro-communist member of congress. In a year in which Joe McCarthy's accusations against prominent Democrats rang in everyone's ears, Nixon's strategy worked. He won his Senate seat by a huge plurality.[78]

In the meantime, Pat's life was once again consumed by taking care of the needs of her family on a shoestring budget. Like those dark days after her mother's death, when her father was ill, Pat's time was not her own. With the birth of her second daughter, Julie, in 1948, Pat found herself with a toddler, an infant, elderly in-laws with health problems, and an increasingly busy and frequently absent husband. Her life revolved around pleasing everyone around her.

Like many other young families during the immediate postwar years, the Nixons struggled to reconcile their larger income with their rising expectations. Even though Dick earned more money than he ever had before, the family's expenses rose with their move to Washington, D.C. Neither had worked during 1946 because they had spent the year campaigning. A good part of the savings they had built up during the war had been spent during the primary campaign. Once Dick won the nomination, he did win over enough supporters to repay himself from the donations. The Nixons thus moved to D.C. with $10,000 in savings, a car, their furniture, and a life insurance policy.[79] They were clearly not destitute. These were two individuals, however, who had experienced financial hardship for most of their lives. Like many other Americans who had lived through the Great Depression or more personal economic catastrophes, Dick and Pat watched every penny even when they no longer had to be overly concerned. To put it nicely, they were frugal.

This attitude affected their lives when they moved to D.C. Housing was first scarce, then expensive. Consequently, the family lived in a crowded apartment until they finally bought a house in 1951. Even then, their new dwelling was a modest three-bedroom home. Still, Pat echoed the sentiments of many other middle-class housewives when she excitedly wrote her friend Helene Drown that it had an "electric kitchen with *dishwasher* and disposal." Over the next months, as the house was built, Pat worried about prices increasing as she chose draperies and carpeting and tried to fit her "California furniture" into their new home. She explained to Helene that "we feel we cannot sell and buy again." The costs continued even after they had moved in. Pat "had a little help from a decorator" but did most of the work herself. She would have liked a few more accessories, but she ran short of cash.[80]

Pat's thrifty nature affected other aspects of running the household as well. Obviously used to managing housewifely duties, Pat did most of her own cooking, cleaning, and child care. She, like many other wives, confronted the inflationary food prices of the immediate post-war years. Luckily for her, she claimed in an interview, Dick liked simple food that was inexpensive to prepare and did not overly strain her budget. He was not "a fussy eater" and would eat "ground round steak and spaghetti." She needed to watch her food expenses because new expenses were cutting into their income. Because of her social responsibilities as a congressional wife, Pat discovered that she had to hire at least some domestic help. She resisted doing this as long as she could, both because of the expense and because it was hard to find someone capable of meeting her expectations. At one point, she told Helene that she was tempted to send "Mary" to cooking school to improve the quality of the food. Other times, she complained that the new girl was impossible with the children. In fact, adequate child care was another of her continual headaches. The elder Nixons moved to a farm in Pennsylvania that made them more available for long-term babysitting, but that still left numerous evening obligations to attend. During campaign season, the problems intensified because they had to be away from the girls so much.[81]

Dick's career further strained their expenses. In addition to increased child care costs, Pat had to worry about having a wardrobe suitable for the various teas, luncheons, and formal dinners she needed to attend. Still, there were so many other things that seemed so much more important that she wrote Helene that her clothing needs were "about 8oth on the list." This was a problem that would plague Pat throughout Dick's career. She liked to look neat and stylish, but she hesitated to pay for too many new outfits. The ever-practical Pat tried to compensate by keeping careful track of what she wore to which event. This way she never appeared in the same outfit twice in the same place.[82]

As for their own entertainment budget, Pat frequently stated the Nixons' preference for informal gatherings of friends and family. The reasons for this varied. She explained in a piece she wrote for the *Satur-*

day Evening Post that they did not entertain much "because a senator's salary . . . runs out amazingly fast." Besides, she went on, they did not like to play bridge, and Dick in particular despised cocktail parties "as the greatest invention for wasting time." She added that because Dick was away from the girls so much, he liked to concentrate on them when he had time.[83] Once they had their house, the Nixons participated actively in the life of the neighborhood. Neighbors remember the couple taking part in neighborhood barbecues and small get-togethers.[84]

Perhaps Pat's biggest frustration in accepting their limited budget was the restriction on her ability to travel for fun. Certainly during campaign season, she logged thousands of miles of travel, but it was work, not recreation. When they were in Washington, Dick seemed to be always on the go, but not Pat and the girls. She tried on occasion to accompany him on his speaking trips, but as they paid for her expenses out of their pockets, she had to restrict the number of times she could do this. At various times, she would send Dick away to rest by himself. By the fall of 1951, for example, she worried that "Dick [was] more tired than [she] had ever seen him."[85] He was frequently too interested in what was going on in Congress to take advantage of her thoughtfulness.

His dedication to his responsibilities also kept him from fulfilling a promise he made to Pat soon after they moved to Washington. During his first trip abroad for the Herter Committee, he wrote Pat many letters vowing to retrace his steps through Europe with her.[86] Four years later, Pat was still waiting for what she referred to as "our big trip."[87] Her sarcasm was understandable, considering the fate of all of their other vacation attempts. Perhaps the most aggravating was the Caribbean cruise of 1948. They had already begun this long-anticipated vacation—in fact, they were already on the ship and out at sea—when revelations in the Hiss–Chambers case required Dick to fly home immediately. Pat soon followed.[88] Although they rarely got away as a couple, Pat insisted that the girls periodically needed a holiday. As a result, either she would take the girls alone or they would all go to the beach on occasion.[89]

Pat always felt she had too much to do to get away. In addition to overseeing her domestic help or doing the household work herself, she also had to deal with two small children. By the early 1950s, both girls attended some kind of school. Tricia, after an initial period of adjustment, did well in elementary school. Julie participated in a community nursery school that Pat helped to found. The "community" part meant that Pat had to take an active role in helping out with the children. Once they hired teachers, Pat's obligations eased and she found some "free time for errand-doing, shopping, etc."[90]

That free time could quickly be eaten up by the numerous visitors that descended on the Nixons. Their most frequent guests were Dick's parents. Although they both appreciated the help the elder Nixons provided with their willingness to babysit, their visits created additional work for Pat. The couple was getting on in years and suffered from various health issues. Pat once again had to play nursemaid. There were other visitors as well. Family members, friends from California, and political contacts taking in the sights in the nation's capital often assumed that they could bunk with the Nixons—or, at the least, that the Nixons could entertain them while they were in D.C. Pat welcomed and enjoyed some of the company; others were "musts" who could not be ignored. At times, she explained to Helene, they were "so swamped with visitors" that they could not "see even half of them."[91]

Pat dealt with many of these issues on her own, as did the wives of many other upwardly mobile men during this period. These women understood and by and large accepted the fact that the bulk of the household management would be their responsibility. They did, however, expect their husbands to participate in the family upkeep by taking on small repairs or by indulging in a little yard work on occasion. Even Senator Nixon earned blisters by pushing a lawn mower around. Pat wrote Helene that he had done it once (hence the blisters) and said "he'd take another try. I'll telegraph you when it happens."[92]

Again, Pat's sarcasm reveals an underlying tension at the situation. She willingly took on the major burden of running the household and keeping the family together; she had, after all, been doing that for most of her life. What she struggled with was the reality that she was doing it alone most of the time. That was fine when she was single, but she expected her marriage to be more of a partnership, as it had been in the early years. The six years Dick served in Congress, however, left her feeling many days as if she were a "widow."[93] As they had made the transition to Washington, she was the one who did the heavy moving. In a 1951 letter to Helene, Pat wrote, "I have moved so many times and the actual process has always been gruesome. Dick is always too busy, at least *his* story, so I do all the lugging, worrying and moving."[94] Perhaps subconsciously, Pat was referring to more than their physical relocations, although she had taken care of those. She moved them across the country when she was eight months pregnant. Then she moved them back with an infant. She settled them into their two-bedroom apartment and then into their first house.

But she might have been referring to the other transitions she oversaw mostly alone. While he traveled to Europe on a luxury liner, she only read about it in his letters home. Certainly he concentrated on how they would make the trip as a family "next year," checking out the "least expensive rooms" and assuring her that there was a nursery for Tricia, describing the many sights they would "see together," and detailing the gifts he purchased. He ended each letter by pledging his love.[95] The promised trip kept getting postponed. In the meantime, time passed and she coped with Tricia's adjustment to their new surroundings and to her parents' absence during campaign season. She took care of Dick's elderly parents and their increasingly bad health.

She finally told him how tired and alone she felt as she prepared for the birth of their second child. He promised to get her out of the city's heat and on a real vacation right after the baby's birth. Unfortunately for Pat, although they made it onto the ship for their aforementioned Caribbean cruise, a dramatic development in the Hiss case forced him to renege on his pledge.[96] They would not get to go away together for a real vacation until early 1952 when they went to Hawaii with the Drowns.

Of course, it was not all bad for Pat. She might not have gotten to travel as much as she wanted, but she was meeting many fascinating and important people, and she did get to spend some time with her husband. Occasionally she would accompany him on a speaking tour or meet up with him after one had concluded. If she met him in New York, they might catch a play or even go dancing. She went to cocktail parties, some of which had "most interesting guest" lists with people such as Hedde Messing, "the former communist," conservative writer Ralph de Toledano, author Clare Booth Luce, and Mrs. Theodore Roosevelt. For example, one weekend in early 1951, she and Dick went to a Broadway play, two cocktail parties, a dinner party, and had a "day in the country" at the estate of a millionaire. She wrote Helene that they "could hardly stumble back to Washington. . . . It was all so fantastic and fun!"[97]—and heady stuff for a small-town girl.

Unfortunately for the Nixons, most of the other aspects of their new life were not as thrilling. In fact, although Pat supported Dick in his quest for office, she was not as exhilarated by the job as he was. He seemed to feed on his growing prominence and power. She understood his motivations and his needs, but too frequently, she felt only the downside of their choices. She allowed his goals to become hers and subsumed her dreams to his. Consequently, she felt the pain and pressure, but only rarely the reward.

From their earliest days in Washington, Pat understood the serious nature of Dick's work. She was not a bubble-headed woman concerned only with fashion and housework. She wrote proudly to her mother-in-law that Dick "was one of the few [new representatives] who got an extra committee." She understood the significance of his getting the appointment as well as the important job with which the committee was charged, namely "cleaning up the Communistic forces."[98] Although she did not take an active role in any of the increasing number of anticommunist groups, some of her correspondents did. They wrote to her for advice, suggestions, or help gathering information.[99] During Dick's years of service in Congress and the Senate, Pat recognized the "seriousness of the tone of the country." She believed that generally Dick "spoke very sensibly" about the issues confronting the American people.[100]

Her own contributions tended to be more in line with helping Dick, whether through her work keeping his family life in order, or by going back to her secretarial days. Even in the midst of his love letters to her during the Herter Committee excursion, he told her to go to meet with some of the committee staff to see if they had resolved a scheduling conflict. If they had not, she had other instructions.[101] He eventually hired enough staff to get the office "really purring," as Pat told Helene.[102] That did not mean that she was off the hook, however. In a crisis, such as the furor over President Truman's firing of General Douglas MacArthur in early 1951, when Nixon received "approximately 6000 telegrams, 30,000 MacArthur letters, and 80,000 Fulton Lewis, Jr. poll letters," she would get "pressed into a six-hour non-paying job."[103]

During campaign season, she worked full time with her husband.

Her work during the first campaign in 1946 was invaluable, as previously mentioned. Never again would she have to serve as full-time office manager and secretary. In subsequent campaigns, Dick had a staff to take care of those more mundane tasks. Pat was promoted to the position of "candidate's wife," a role that required much more time and effort. Luckily, she eased into this role. She had learned some of the ropes in 1946. By 1948, she had some idea of what she was getting into. Fortunately for Pat, Dick's prominence and the continuing misfortunes of the Truman Democrats made his reelection practically a shoe-in; thus Pat, with a two-year-old and a newborn, had only limited obligations.

All of that changed in 1950, when Dick ran for the Senate, which required that they campaign all over the state. Dick expected Pat to accompany him on many of his speaking tours; she made shorthand notes on the itineraries with notes about his speeches and about the crowds and the reactions, and she kept track of thank-you notes she would need to write.[104] People noticed that she was always there, always smiling, always being supportive. Some constituents thought she did "outstanding work" in "ably assisting Dick." They recognized that her "moral as well as physical support . . . had a tremendous influence on the outcome" of the election.[105] Others were curious as to how she could listen to the same speech again and again or how she could leave her young children at home so much. She assured those who asked that she hated leaving the girls, but she thought that she and Dick were "really performing a duty for them [their daughters] and for all young Americans."[106]

Although she appeared smiling, happy, and fully supportive while on the campaign trail, there were definitely aspects of her new life in politics that required major adjustments for Pat. After all, this was Dick's dream, not hers. As she explained in an early magazine interview, however, fulfilling his dream was her ambition: "Dick is doing the thing he wants to do in the way that he believes he can best serve his country, and that is the kind of life I want the Nixon family to live."[107] Her use of *we* whenever she described Dick's position on a subject evidenced her ability to subsume her life into the one he chose. Additionally, his enemies became her enemies. Drew Pearson, Millard Tydings, and many others earned snide remarks in Pat's letters to Helene because of perceived animosity toward Dick. In fact, because Helene and

Jack were active in California politics as well, there was much gossip flowing between coasts as the women shared information about the movers and shakers of Golden State politicos.[108]

Harder for Pat to deal with were the slurs and epithets slung at her husband. Even in Dick's early career, he invited controversy. From the Hiss–Chambers controversy to the Douglas campaign, Dick proved to be a lightning rod for caricature and invective. Some of his old friends from Whittier thought politics hardened him and made him into someone they did not recognize. Certainly people across the country felt compelled to call him names and accuse him of unethical behavior. Fiercely loyal Pat reacted to all of the ugliness as if it were aimed at her. She could not believe that people were saying those things about her husband, and by extension about her.[109]

If Pat could suppress her own desires in order to fulfill Dick's dreams, she had a harder time with two ramifications of that decision. First, she was, as she admitted in a magazine article some years later, "what people call *reserved* by nature."[110] Although she liked people generally, she was uncomfortable being on display. Her parents had ingrained in her the importance of protecting privacy and keeping emotions hidden. Being in the political spotlight meant that the public had the right to invade that privacy, and they expected outward signs of positive emotion.

Pat's second trouble spot had to do with Dick's relationship with his family. Although Dick's letters home in 1947 indicated a man clearly in love with his wife and devoted to his baby girl, the reality of his new job threatened to undermine those feelings. The biggest problem was time. As Dick became involved in prominent and controversial matters, he spent more and more time at his office or on the road. His life increasingly revolved almost solely around politics; his family came in a distant second.[111] Pat was left with full-time parenting and household responsibilities. Certainly she was not the only wife of an ambitious man to face this reality. She was less worried about the amount of work she had to do than she was about the effect his absence could have on his relationship with his daughters and with her. She did not want to be left feeling as though she were one more staff member. She had warned him about her need for reassurance in the letter she wrote to him before his return from overseas.

Pat's natural reticence as well as descriptions of her as looking "absorbedly interested" in everything her husband said and "pleased and proud" of him laid the foundation for later press designation as plastic Pat.[112] In fact, just as this period saw the creation of the "Tricky Dick" label for Dick, the press and public also began pushing Pat into the mold of compliant, passive, adoring wife. Although this would become more pronounced during the vice presidential years, the image can be glimpsed periodically during the late 1940s and early 1950s.

CHAPTER 2

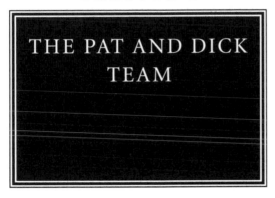

THE PAT AND DICK
TEAM

Her husband's terms as vice president of the United States from 1953 to 1961, particularly his first term, were in many ways Pat Nixon's happiest years in politics. Although they were considerably busier, both Pat and Dick still had time for one another and their daughters. Tricia and Julie were old enough not to need constant care, but young enough that they did not remember a time when their parents did not leave them on a regular basis. Letters to and from her friend Helene Drown indicate the Nixons remained a couple in every sense of the word. They shared an active interest in the political world; they spent time together away from business, enjoying one another's company; and they endured the hardships of their new life together. As she had all of her life, Pat juggled numerous responsibilities. She had always prided herself on her ability to do whatever needed to be done without complaint. Now, however, people marveled at her stamina, her capacity for hard work, and her talent for making it all look easy. Perhaps most important, these years brought financial stability, a new house and, best of all, travel. All of Pat's youthful wishing to visit far-off places and exotic locales came true as she toured the world.

But just as those imaginary visions did not always match the reality of the countries she visited, so the everyday grind of life as the wife of a powerful and famous government official undermined her happiness. The parts of politics that she hated as a congressional wife intensified as a senator's wife and occasionally threatened to consume her when she became the second lady. The loss of privacy, the ever-present prying eyes, and the attacks on her husband's character were challenges she managed to endure. The ever-increasing number of social obligations took her away from her children and even sometimes her husband. Complicating the situation was her sense that many of these meetings, parties, teas, and festivities were pointless. For someone who had always carried more than her share of the familial workload, she sometimes chafed at doing less than meaningful work. By the end of the eight years, much of the glamour had worn away and left behind just the work.

By the summer of 1952, despite having been in Washington for less than six years, the Nixons were a rising young couple. In a city where people boasted of thirty- or forty-year careers, they were babies. Still, they had been around long enough to learn some things. After all, Dick had gone from obscure congressman to national figure in a relatively brief period of time. His work on the Alger Hiss case guaranteed him news coverage in papers across America and transformed him into the rising star of the Republican Party. Democrats and more liberal-minded Republicans, however, focused on Dick's senate campaign against Helen Gahagan Douglas, with all of its name calling and mud slinging. Rather than Dick Nixon, boy crusader, they spoke of "Tricky Dick." For better or worse, everyone knew Dick Nixon's name and associated it with anticommunism. For her part, Pat had transformed herself from a "drab little wren" who needed to be coached not to wear too-bright lipstick into a well-dressed, confident young mother of two.[1] If Pat was not entirely pleased by her husband's choice of career, she accepted its importance to him and did her part to help him succeed.

Were it not for their prominence, the Nixons could have been any middle-class couple in many places across America. Like their counterparts around the country, the Nixons spent the postwar years having a family, buying their first house, establishing a career (for the husband), and setting up a household (for the wife). Taking advantage of the rising prosperity, they bought furniture, took their kids on vacations to the beach, and enjoyed the newest consumer gadgets and fads. They learned to negotiate the challenges created by his career, her frustration with rising prices, and their anxieties about the state of the world.[2]

Mrs. Nixon with daughter Julie on her lap and daughter Tricia, holding their dog's, Checkers, leash, September 1952. Richard Nixon Presidential Library and Museum.

And there was plenty to be anxious about. Less than five years after Americans proved their military superiority by winning World War II with a nuclear explosion, the Soviets exploded a device of their own, ending America's atomic monopoly. Many Americans rationalized that Soviet spies must have stolen the secrets and intensified their hunt for Red traitors in their communities. Meanwhile, in Asia the situation went from bad to worse. Communists in China, led by Mao Tse-tung, forced U.S.-backed Chiang Kai-shek into exile on Formosa. In Korea, the Soviet-backed government of the north invaded American-supported South Korea and threatened to win control of the peninsula. United Nations forces commanded by American General Douglas MacArthur pushed the enemy almost to the Chinese border, drawing the Chinese into the struggle. By 1951, the war had settled into a deadly stalemate with no end in sight.[3]

The Democratic administration of Harry Truman faced domestic crises as well as an unstable international situation. Although the economy boomed, many men and women, scarred by years of deprivation because of the Depression and war, lived with an underlying fear that the inflation of the immediate postwar years or the unemployment ghost of the 1930s would resurface. Minor fluctuations in prices could raise serious concerns among consumers, who were quick to blame the government. Many Americans found other reasons to dislike the Truman administration. Some people had never found him an adequate replacement for Franklin Roosevelt; he was too conservative, too unpolished, too ordinary. Ironically, others worried that he was too liberal, too soft on communists abroad and left-wingers at home. His willingness to establish an employee loyalty program to root out potential security risks struck anticommunist zealots as too little, too late, while liberals gasped at the infringement on civil liberties. He could not seem to please anyone. Exposure of corruption by his subordinates added to his troubles. Some Americans could not forgive him for firing General Douglas MacArthur back in 1951. Ever a realist, Truman realized that he could not run successfully for reelection in 1952. The Democrats would have to find someone else.[4]

For Republicans, shut out of the White House for twenty years, this situation presented an exhilarating opportunity. Thrilled with Truman's low popularity ratings, Republicans hoped for success. They could not afford to assume they would win, however. They had been stung in previous elections as sure-fire winners, most notably Thomas Dewey in 1948, lost the prize. In addition to overconfidence in their ability to win, Republicans recognized that their internal disunity undermined their chance for success. Conservative Midwestern, rural, and western Republicans wanted to eliminate the New Deal socioeconomic structure, focus on protecting American borders, intensify the hunt for domestic communist spies, and nominate Ohio senator Robert A. Taft for president. Eastern business leaders, however, more concerned about the international situation, acknowledged that the New Deal had become a part of the American government. They wanted someone who would protect their interests and, most importantly, win the election. Their candidate was General Dwight Eisenhower.[5] Well known for his role as supreme commander of the D-day invasion, Eisenhower combined fiscal conservatism with an internationalist perspective. His supporters believed that his popularity would lead to crossover Democratic voting and ensure their victory in November. Taft's backers disagreed, pointing out that such Eastern-wing candidates had failed every time they had run. The standoff between the two factions reverberated throughout the party ranks and threatened to undermine whatever advantage Truman's unpopularity gave them.[6]

For rising young politicians such as Richard Nixon, the key was to pick the right horse to back. Nixon's anticommunist work earned him a solid reputation with the conservative wing of the GOP, which should have put him in Taft's camp. When Taft came to get his support in early 1952, however, Nixon told him "with a great deal of sadness" that he could not back his candidacy because, as he explained in his memoirs, he "personally felt that international affairs would be more important for the next President" and Eisenhower was "the best qualified in that area."[7] An Eisenhower victory would also present a unique opportunity for the junior senator. Young Californian Dick Nixon, with his reputation as a fervent anticommunist, provided perfect balance to a ticket headed by a man whom the public perceived as an elderly moderate Midwesterner with little political experience. Although in his memoirs Nixon dismissed the idea that he sought the vice presidential nomination and was surprised by his inclusion on a list of potential candidates, scholars have pointed out that he was too politically astute not to have known which way the wind was blowing.[8]

Whether consciously or not, Nixon played his cards well. He made his support for Eisenhower public knowledge despite his pledge to back California governor Earl Warren as a favorite son candidate on the first ballot at the convention. In May, former GOP candidate Thomas Dewey invited Nixon to give the principal address to the New York state Republican Party's annual fund-raising dinner. This event provided the Californian with an opportunity to solidify his standing within the party as a whole, and more significantly, to meet many of the prominent men around the general. Nixon passed with flying colors and became a favorite with many important Republican leaders.[9] For his part, Nixon continued to deny that he was a potential candidate, preferring to play party loyalist.

As Pat prepared to attend the convention in Chicago, she must have had mixed emotions. On the one hand, her good friends the Drowns would be joining her for the convention, and that promised at least some fun.[10] On the other hand, she had heard the rumors circulating about her husband and the vice presidency. It had been in the newspapers; people were discussing it at parties. Moreover, Pat had to have known that he wanted the vice presidency. The night before Eisenhower won the nomination, Dick and Pat stayed up all night discussing the situation. Although most biographies of Dick emphasize her determination to keep him out of the race, that seems unrealistic.[11] That she might have argued against it; that she pointed out the pitfalls in terms of attacks on his character and the rigors of campaigning; that she emphasized the cost to their family, their marriage, and especially their daughters—all of that makes sense. For her to have assumed that she would be able to talk him out of such a significant opportunity seems out of character. She knew he was ambitious when they married; she was ambitious as well. That connection was part of what drew them together. When they called Murray Chotiner to come and offer them advice, she had to have known that Dick was leaning toward the nomination. She would have been naive or ignorant of her husband to have thought that he would turn it down. Perhaps she hoped the choice would not be offered.

When it was made, she was not there to voice an opinion. After the morning session of 11 July, during which Eisenhower won the nomination on the first ballot, Pat joined her friends Helene Drown and Phyllis Chotiner for a late lunch. Dick went back to the hotel room to take a nap. While he was drowsing, Herbert Brownell, one of Eisenhower's closest advisors, called and told him the general wanted to see him. Understanding what this meant, Dick and Murray hurried to Eisenhower's hotel suite. Pat continued her lunch. On the way to meet Ike, Dick told Murray to call Whittier and let his family know what was going on. By the time he got through, they already knew. The press had reported the news as soon as they saw Nixon arrive at the hotel suite. Nowhere in any of the memoirs is there any mention of Dick's attempt to notify his wife. She heard the news on a television at the restaurant. She and her companions hurried to the convention hall, where she joined the throng in the distinguished visitors' gallery to hear her husband be nominated by acclamation.[12]

Whatever doubts or concerns troubled Pat vanished in the excitement of the moment. Called to the rostrum by the convention chair, the Pat and Dick team made their way from the floor, swept up in the enthusiasm of the crowd. So caught up in the cheers and exhilaration of the moment were they that they did something they rarely, if ever, did in public: they kissed! All of the work and drudgery they had endured up to that point disappeared to be replaced by the exhilarating realization that they were on the platform with General Dwight Eisenhower, the hero of D-day. For two people who had struggled and worked hard all of their lives, the feeling at that moment must have been overwhelming. Friends, family, enemies, and millions of people they did not know shared their sense of wonder and amazement.[13]

Of course, they could not stay on the convention stage forever; the reality of life as candidate for the second highest office in the land began at once. A frantic call from Hannah Nixon resurrected all of Pat's concerns about the effect of the nomination on their family. The night of the nomination, reporters barged into the Nixon home back in D.C., frightening the girls with their questions. Six-year-old Tricia's response to her mother's announcement of Daddy's good news was disappointment in realizing that her parents would be campaigning again. Unlike in earlier campaigns, the girls were old enough to miss their parents in a way they had not been before and to express their anger, frustration, and fear.[14] Once at home, Pat realized that this campaign would invade the sanctity of their home in ways earlier campaigns had not. She added service as an adjunct secretary to her workload as she fielded calls from reporters and aides and collected telegrams.[15] The Pat and Dick team was back in business.

This time, however, Pat had to take on a much more public role. Few citizens care about the wives or husbands of potential senators or congress members; they do, however, pay close attention to the spouses of presidential and vice presidential candidates. Although she would always be uncomfortable being the center of attention and would refuse public speaking engagements, Pat proved herself to be a valuable member of the campaign. Her consideration and kindness won over Republicans and Democrats alike. For example, Pat's "friendly letter" so amazed St. Louis *Post-Dispatch* reporter Ed Harris that he assured her that he would vote for her "for anything you want to run for—including the Presidency." He still was not certain that he felt the same way about her husband![16]

Recognizing her value as a source of positive publicity, the Nixon people arranged for her to work with a reporter for the *Saturday Evening Post*. This article, entitled "I Say He's a Wonderful Guy," served at least two purposes. First, by telling the story of the struggles the young Nixons had faced as they tried to enter the political arena, it reinforced the Eisenhower–Nixon campaign strategy of contrasting their homespun, squeaky-clean image with the corruption scandals of the Truman administration. Pat explained that they came from "typical, everyday American families that have had to work for what they got out of life, but always knew there was unlimited opportunity for achievement in the United States." Filled with anecdotes about ordinary Americans donating time or their "hard-earned half dollar or perhaps a dollar" to the Nixon cause, the article succeeded in painting the vice presidential candidate as the ideal small-town politician just trying to do good for his community.[17]

Second, the article established what would become Pat's image as the perfect housewife/mother/wife. Although she claimed that her life was not that much different from that of any other housewife, she then went on to detail her workload:

> I run a suburban household, and by that I meant I do everything, because we've never had a fulltime maid until the week before the Chicago convention. I cook and wash dishes and do a lot of chauffeuring, and last year I went to school to learn how to make draperies and slip covers. Then I went to some other classes to learn how to make hats.[18]

In addition to these "everyday" chores, Pat, of course, had responsibilities as the wife of a candidate. She did not emphasize these other duties, but women reading the article would have recognized that she did all the work they did plus went out on the campaign trail with her husband and—judging by the information provided in the article—kept up with all of the political news as well. Pat had always been a hard worker and probably did feel a kinship with all of the other hardworking women in America. Unfortunately, this emphasis on her almost superhuman stamina would always be a double-edged sword: what made her seem sympathetic to some women turned her into an unrealistic caricature for others.

Last, through the article, Pat assumed a new role for her: conduit for placing Dick's agenda before a different audience. In earlier campaigns, Pat's reluctance to speak before large groups of people limited her ability to spread the Nixon message. This article, published in a mainstream magazine, showed Pat's potential value as a campaign weapon. Not only did the exposure bring favorable publicity to the Eisenhower–Nixon team, it also packaged the vice presidential candidate in the right form. The pictures of the couple with their adorable little girls established Dick as a typical young family man, the kind of guy who might live next door. Yet by alluding to her fears that people would only associate her husband with the Alger Hiss case, Pat not only reviewed his anticommunist credentials for the public, but she also listed his other achievements.[19] She proved herself to be an asset not just as tireless unpaid campaign worker, but also as symbol of Dick's wholesomeness. Although this would become important to Dick's career, Pat's shift away from substantive work foreshadowed Pat's underlying frustration with the path her life had taken.

Pat and Dick got a taste of the cost of that new life within a few short months of the nomination, when press discovery of Dick's alleged slush fund forced the Pat and Dick team into a humiliating fight for their political lives. Shortly after his Senate election, some of Dick's supporters began contributing to a fund to pay for his political traveling and other expenses. The fund, which was operated by a trustee, was neither illegal nor secret. In fact, numerous politicians, including Democratic presidential candidate Adlai Stevenson, kept such funds.[20]

The story of Nixon's fund emerged in mid-September as the Nixons set off on their first major campaign tour, a railroad trek along the West Coast. When the first reporter approached him about the information, Nixon answered questions and directed him to the treasurer of the fund, Dana Smith. Nixon thought little more about the story because, in his mind, there was no story. As the campaign train made its way up the California coast, however, unbeknownst to the isolated Nixon entourage, the little news item grew exponentially. The *New York Post* broke the story on 18 September with a sensational headline promising details about a "secret rich men's trust fund." Papers across the country picked up the story. Hecklers showed up at campaign stops; editorials appeared in major newspapers; politicians sent advice; but from General Eisenhower there was deafening silence. Eisenhower recognized that some Americans would use the controversy to accuse the Eisenhower–Nixon team of hypocrisy. The Republicans had been attacking the "mess in Washington" created by supposed corruption in the Truman administration. The allegations of a slush fund made Ike and Dick look just as sleazy. An increasing array of political operatives suggested that Nixon should resign from the ticket, but Eisenhower refused to rush to judgment.[21] As the news reached them, tension on the train mounted. Nixon realized that he would have to take the suggestion of former New York governor and Eisenhower protégé Thomas Dewey and plead his case before the American public. When Eisenhower finally called, he offered little comfort. Instead, he told his vice presidential candidate that he would wait and see how the public reacted to Nixon's explanation before making a decision.

Nixon went on television and gave the speech of his life. In it, he provided the audience with a "complete financial history," detailing "everything I have earned, everything I have spent, everything I own." Dick bared his assets and his debts, including an outstanding loan from his parents. He explained the fund, asked for the support of the American people, and got in a few jabs at Stevenson, "who inherited a fortune from his father." He did admit, however, that he intended to keep one gift from a constituent. A supporter in Texas sent his little girls a black-and-white cocker spaniel that Tricia named Checkers. Moved by Dick's honesty and touched by the Checkers story, three million Americans sent telegrams to the Republican National Committee or called the television station. The overwhelming numbers of supporters left Eisenhower no choice but to welcome Nixon with a hearty "you're my boy" as though nothing had happened and the campaign should just go on as normal.[22]

Pat played a vital role in this drama. Although her job on the campaign trip was "moral support and . . . candidate's wife," she twice provided her husband with the kind of tough love necessary to get him through the crisis. The first time occurred after he had read the editorials calling for his resignation. According to Dick's recollections in both his memoirs and in *Six Crises*, Pat refused to let him quit. She believed that it would be bad for the country because Eisenhower would lose the election. More important, he could not "simply crawl away" from the fight. If he did, she argued, he would be "marred" for life as would his family "and particularly, your daughters."[23] Days later, as they waited to go on the set for the television broadcast, Dick hesitated, doubting that he could go through with the speech. Pat assured him that he could, held his hand, and walked with him onto the stage.[24]

Her presence on the set also helped to move potential voters.

Throughout the speech, she sat watching him, supportively, loyally, sincerely. For the millions of viewers, her face, captured periodically by the roaming camera, epitomized the essence of what a wife should be. Some people trusted Dick because of Pat. One constituent explained that "no man can have his wife look at him like Pat is looking at Dick and be anything but the grandest guy alive."[25] Hundreds of people wrote to her after the speech. Some told her how proud they were of Dick; some wrote of how proud she must be of him. Many women wrote to her because they recognized that she had gone through the crisis along with him. Mrs. Roberta Wiley summed up the sentiments of many: "For surely his pain is your pain and his problem, your problem."[26]

Mrs. Wiley was more accurate than even she knew. The tension on the train was palpable, yet Pat had no release. The facade she presented to the public was supportive and loyal. To her good friends the Drowns, she raged at the unfairness of the accusations and the indifference Eisenhower had showed to them. Throughout this ordeal, she suffered from a painful stiff neck. Dick's speech could only have made certain aspects of the crisis worse for her. After all, to vindicate himself, he had to expose the meagerness of their lifestyle and their finances. While emphasizing the fact that she wore a "Republican cloth coat" rather than a mink helped his cause and endeared him to millions of middle-class Americans, it embarrassed her; it seemed to imply that she could never have one in the future.[27] In her own way, she was a proud, self-disciplined, and private person. She had been raised to believe that you did what you had to do without asking for favors or help. You did not let other people know that you were struggling. As a child, she had accepted a school demerit for being out of uniform rather than ask for special consideration of her circumstances. (She was out of uniform because she was so busy ironing her brothers' clothes that she did not have the time to do her own.[28]) Although she supported Dick's effort to fight the allegations of wrongdoing, she questioned the necessity of groveling before the accusers.[29]

She was not, however, without the means of making her feelings known. During the broadcast, she wore a dress that had been knitted for her by women back in Whittier. Although it certainly appeared as a simple, elegant dress befitting a candidate's wife, it might also have been her way of snubbing the Eastern establishment types who were trying to run the Nixons out of the campaign. Her frustration showed through more directly during the Nixons' first campaign stop with the Eisenhowers after the incident. Trying to make conversation, Mamie lamented that she did not know "why all this happened when we were all getting along so well." Pat let her know that whatever problems Mamie and the general had experienced diminished when compared with what the Nixons had gone through.[30]

The fund crisis permanently changed politics for Pat. She had been dealing with the nasty side of politics almost from the beginning of Dick's career. His campaign against Douglas included name-calling and innuendo, but she had grown to live with it. After the Hiss trials, she had become accustomed to seeing unflattering caricatures of her husband on the editorial page. But she believed in him; she thought he was doing important work. She could accept that some people might not understand that what he was doing was so critical. The fund crisis was different. This was not just about a political opponent; it was not about his work. The fund accusations attacked their family, their finances, and their integrity. To counteract the allegations, they had to expose themselves in a way Pat found humiliating. The thousands of Americans who admired her as she sat beside her husband supportively throughout the broadcast had no idea how much that smile cost her. Decades later, when her daughter questioned her about the fund issue for the biography Julie was writing, Pat refused to discuss it. Even after all that time, it was still too painful.[31]

Dick's reaction to the situation exposed a fissure in the foundation of the still-strong Pat and Dick team. Although he too was appalled at the idea of being forced to reveal all of their private financial dealings, in the succeeding years, he concentrated on the vindication the Checkers speech brought him. In fact, he continued to celebrate the anniversary of the speech for years and he proudly included it as one of the *Six Crises* he had faced and overcome.[32] For Dick, the positive result balanced out the pain of the situation. Perhaps because Pat did not get to make a speech explaining herself, or because she did not get the same elation from electoral victory, the result did not erase the cost.

Neither Pat nor Dick had time to ruminate on the costs of the fund crisis once it was resolved, however, because there was still an election to win. The six weeks remaining until the November vote sped past in a whirlwind of campaign stops, speeches, and appearances. Nixon stated in his memoirs that the couple traveled 46,000 miles and visited 214 cities. By Election Day, they were numb with exhaustion. In the end, the effort paid off: Eisenhower–Nixon won with 3.5 million votes to spare.[33] After two decades, the Republicans returned to the White House.

They returned to troubled times. In addition to ongoing police action in Korea, many Americans resented continued Soviet domination of Eastern Europe. Although Eisenhower managed to bring the stalemated Korean conflict to a close, he was less successful in fulfilling his promise to liberate the captive peoples of Eastern Europe.[34] Conservatives in particular increasingly found themselves frustrated by Eisenhower's approach to foreign policy. Although he was a fervent anticommunist, Eisenhower maintained a more sophisticated understanding of geopolitics than most Americans who saw the world in terms of black and white. The president worried that Americans would spend themselves into defeat by putting too much money into defense, especially the arms race.[35]

Some conservative Republicans found even more cause for concern with Eisenhower's domestic agenda. Having spent the first part of the decade searching for communist spies in the Truman administration, Republicans such as Wisconsin senator Joseph McCarthy had a difficult time accepting Eisenhower's more subtle approach to redhunting.[36] Moreover, despite his own fiscal conservatism, Eisenhower realized that he could not, as the right wing of his party desired, undo the New Deal. The socioeconomic framework of social welfare and regulatory legislation had become too much a part of the American way of life. There was no going back. Instead, he tried to limit expansion of existing programs and moderate the creation of new ones. Although he called his program "modern Republicanism," some conservatives within the party saw him as a traitor to everything the GOP held dear.[37]

The internecine fighting among Republicans spelled both opportunity and trouble for Vice President Richard Nixon. On the one hand, because of his strong anticommunist record, he could serve as a sounding board for disgruntled conservatives. Although they did not trust him completely, they recognized that he was closer to their perspective than was Eisenhower. On the other hand, he was part of an administration that continued to support legislation they found objectionable. For their part, more liberal Republicans applauded his efforts to carry the administration's message in speeches throughout the nation as well as his handling of his responsibilities during Eisenhower's illnesses. In fact, in part as a result of Eisenhower's heart attack, colon, and stroke problems, Nixon gained much valuable experience during his tenure as vice president. Unlike some of his predecessors who saw the job as a wasteland, Nixon traveled extensively throughout the nation and the world spreading the Eisenhower message, meeting with world leaders, and making contacts for future visits.

While Dick adjusted to his new role, Pat worked to maintain a comfortable, stable home for her daughters and husband. From 1951 to 1957, the family lived in the modest seven-room house on Tilden Street that they had purchased, then they moved into a larger home on Forest Lane. Although she hired a series of housekeepers, she cleaned, sewed, ironed, and cooked for the family whenever necessary or possible. A talented seamstress, she sewed curtains for their homes as well as clothes for the girls.[38]

Most important, she wanted the girls to be as unaffected by the vice presidency as possible. She did not let them become spoiled by their father's status. (In fact, she would not take them to the White House during the first year because she did not want them to have privileges their friends did not.[39]) Along with other children in their neighborhood, the girls attended Horace Mann Elementary School, an integrated public school. They switched to Sidwell Friends School, a private Quaker school, in 1958 when Tricia graduated from Horace Mann. Pat insisted on the move because she feared her daughters were falling behind academically.[40] Despite her own hectic schedule, she participated in their school lives, helping them with homework and organizing little parties with their friends. Although she had to spend many evenings away, she tried to make certain that they had a fairly consistent routine and that she was a part of it. She made sure that they got a vacation even if Daddy could not join them.[41] For the first years of the vice presidency, she continually hoped that they would be able to take a real family vacation. Fatalism replaced hope as the years went by, however, with no family trip in sight. As early as 1955, she wrote Helene, that although "Dick still mentions Europe," she had "learned better" and was not counting on it.[42]

Pat's responsibilities as second lady complicated her efforts to keep the girls on a regular schedule. Her only official job as the vice president's wife was to head up the Ladies of the Senate Club, an organization of the wives of senators which met monthly and did charity work during the year. Pat jumped into her role and reported to Helene that, at least in the beginning, the women were being "very sweet . . . and complimentary." She recognized that they could have easily been the opposite and so was grateful especially as she adjusted to her new position's "terrific" pace.[43] In addition to these meetings, lunches, teas, dinners, and other social engagements increasingly filled Pat's days and evenings. She had at least three different schedules she had to consult: one from Dick's office with his, hers, and their commitments; another from Dick's office limited to her appointments; and one personal calendar that included the girls' school and play dates as well as the clothes she wore to various events.[44]

The vaguely defined role of second lady expanded during the Eisenhower–Nixon administration as a result of Pat's relationship with the Eisenhowers. Despite the tension surrounding the earlier fund crisis, Pat and Mamie got along well. From the beginning of their tenure in office, Mamie reached out to Pat. The first lady invited the second lady to explore the White House residence only two days after the 1953 inauguration. Dick would have to wait much longer to view the private quarters of the president. In fact, the first lady invited Pat to the White House for various functions at least five times in the first six months of 1953. The two women, who were from very different generations, respected one another and developed an affectionate relationship.[45]

In fact, Mamie and Pat had more in common than appeared on the surface. Both were frugal housekeepers who pinched pennies. Both understood the importance of dressing appropriately for the occasion. Both doted on the children in their lives and responded warmly to the youngsters they met in public. Both attempted to keep their private lives separate from their husbands' work. Finally, Mamie and Pat shared a respect for the American people that manifested itself in their dedication to their correspondence. During her years serving with Mamie, Pat followed her lead in penning personal responses to all the people who wrote to her. She would continue this practice once she became first lady.[46]

Mamie provided Pat with an example of an effective first lady. Having been a military wife for most of her life, Mamie was perhaps better prepared than most to assume the role of first lady. She understood how to delegate responsibility while keeping control in her hands. She managed to run a strict, somewhat formal household and yet maintain good relations with everyone on the staff. Ike trusted her to make decisions and did not challenge her authority over East Wing matters.[47] Pat would not be so lucky with her husband when she moved into the White House.

Various circumstances during Eisenhower's years in office forced Mamie to delegate some of her responsibilities to Pat. Mamie had a heart condition and other ailments that sometimes left her unable to attend scheduled activities. Additionally, when the president was ill, Mamie stayed by his side. Her devotion to her husband meant someone else would have to cut the ribbon, or attend the meeting, or have lunch with the visiting dignitary. That someone was almost always Pat.[48] According to one news account, Washington correspondents marveled at the way Pat "stretch[ed] an already crammed schedule to take on extra duties and yet stay[ed] unruffled and serene." State Department personnel came to rely on the second lady to fill in for Mamie, even at a moment's notice. In addition to more appointments, Eisenhower's illnesses also increased the chaos of the Nixon household. With her husband acting as a temporary replacement for the president, Secret Service agents and reporters became a constant presence, turning their home, she wrote Helene, into a "madhouse." The extra people meant more cooking, cleaning, and arranging. Perhaps the worst part, however, was that the agents "prowl at night which is a little hard on light-sleeper me."[49]

Even without the occasional addition of Mamie's events, Pat's life was increasingly hectic. Plunged into the social whirl of D.C., Pat and Dick became partygoers and -givers. There always seemed to be, as she put it in a letter to Helene, "a new set of state visitors." In addition, especially after the move to their new home in 1957, the Nixons entertained a steady stream of visitors at home. During the first term, they had held the parties they were obliged to give at hotels or restaurants because of the limitations of their house. The new house provided them the room to invite officials, dignitaries, and even friends to parties at their house. This did not mean an open door, however, because the Nixons were particular about whom they invited to their engagements. They had long memories when it came to those who had snubbed them earlier; those people never got invited. Of course, all of these soirees, whether sit-down dinners for foreign diplomats or stag parties for Dick's cronies, meant work for Pat. For example, she explained to Helene in 1958 that they were hosting "a series of Christmas parties with over a hundred guests at each." When they had returned from England, her husband, who did not understand the amount of work that went into each affair, had "one or two such dinners, lunches, etc. daily!!"[50]

To help her deal with this hectic schedule and the ever-expanding amount of correspondence, members of Dick's office staff ably assisted Pat. The most important of these women was Rose Mary Woods.[51] Rose started working for Nixon during his Senate years and became not just an essential employee but a valuable member of the family. Rose and Pat were both dedicated to Dick and often ended up being the only women on some of the diplomatic junkets. They shared hardships, companionship, and even clothes. Others on the vice president's staff, such as Loie Gaunt and especially Elizabeth (Bessie) Newton and P. J. Everts, worked closely with Pat on issues of scheduling and mail. Although some decisions had to be cleared with the boss, as they all called him, Pat always controlled her own schedule and influenced the language of her correspondence.[52] She tried to answer as much of her mail personally as she could.

In fact, Pat's willingness to put herself totally into whatever task she faced earned her praise from all sides. Marie Norrie, general chair of the Goodwill Embassy Tour, found herself speechless in the wake of Pat's "magnificent gesture in greeting every single one of the thousands of visitors" who attended the event her organization sponsored. Whether she was shaking hands with the workers at the AC Spark Plug Division in Flint, Michigan, or lunching with the Aga Khan, Pat managed to make whomever she met feel welcomed and appreciated. Her hand-shaking abilities as well as her apparently tireless feet proved legendary.[53]

But it was more than her stamina that impressed those she met. Whether she was meeting a constituent on the campaign trail, the prime minister of a country, or a peasant in an African village, she treated every individual she encountered as though he or she were the only important person in the world. She treated people as individuals. She remembered names, faces, and interests. For example, one evening in 1954, as the Nixons exited a dinner at which President Eisenhower was going to speak, they came across an Indian woman sitting on a bench outside the banquet hall. Pat thought she recognized the woman and asked Dick if he did. When he said no, they continued down the steps. Halfway down, Pat remembered the woman and made her husband return to where the woman was sitting. Pat spoke with the woman and asked if they had not met previously. When the woman replied that they had, Pat asked about her stay in the United States and inquired what she was doing in the hotel hallway. The woman explained that she was returning to India in a few days and had hoped to catch a glimpse of the president before she went home. Pat then arranged for the woman to be given a seat at the dinner so that she could hear the speech as well as see the president. The Nixons then left the hall for their previous engagement.[54] Pat's willingness to go out of her way to provide a special experience for someone of no particular political importance typified her attitude toward the people she met on her travels or on the campaign trail.

Pat's connection with people made her an invaluable campaigner. After all, part of the vice president's job was to stump for the party in ways the president could not. Consequently, Pat once again joined Dick on the campaign trail. In all, she traveled over 125,000 miles during her years as second lady.[55] Although she generally refused to give formal speeches, she stepped up to the plate during extraordinary circumstances. For example, at a 1956 Oklahoma City rally, Pat "supplemented the talk of her husband" when illness forced him to cut short his speech. According to news accounts, she gave a two-minute "plea for all-out party activity at the grassroots."[56] This political speech was the exception, however. Most of the time, she preferred to chat with individuals or small groups. As she told one reporter, " 'I never discuss politics. . . . I just like to talk about my children and home life.' "[57] Pat's strategy was deceptively simple and amazingly effective. Without giving a typical stump speech, she managed to win support for her husband and her party.

This approach, which was strictly followed by Nixon's staff in arranging Pat's appearances, complied with the accepted place of women in politics during the 1950s.[58] Recognizing that the number of women voters had been steadily increasing, leaders of both parties attempted to appeal to these new voters. In addition to adding more women to the party structure to provide insight into this new constituency, Republicans and Democrats tried to find ways to entice women to support their candidates.[59] They assumed that the easiest way to get them to the polls was to appeal to their feminine interest in family and children. Journalist Nona B. Brown, in a piece for the *New York Times,* argued that women "like a political candidate who is a good family man." To that end, a candidate's wife became an essential part of the image. Brown concluded that "a charming, attractive . . . perfect helpmeet" added an "intangible dimension" to the candidate, a "phenomenon" which, the author wrote, Nixon completely understood.[60]

Perhaps that was the reason that press coverage of Mrs. Nixon emphasized her homemaking abilities. Journalists marveled at her stamina as she juggled her responsibilities as second lady with the normal duties of being a mother and housewife. Frequently, they reported, she took care of everything on her own without any outside help.[61] For many, Pat exemplified the perfect 1950s wife and mother. In fact, in 1953, the Homemakers Forum awarded her the title of the "Nation's Ideal Wife" because, as their spokesperson explained, she was "the kind of helpmate who doesn't try to compete with her husband, yet stands beside him when needed."[62] Many women across America identified with her and applauded her efforts. They addressed her as Pat, rather than Mrs. Nixon, because they felt that they knew her, some explained. Others reassured her that "underneath all the outspoken criticism there are many, many who feel real sympathy for your position."[63]

And there was criticism. Some, like the woman who wrote to reporter Inez Robb, resented what she called "Pat Nixon, Superwife." How could normal women complain about all they did when Pat was cooking, cleaning, ironing, sewing, tending children, traveling around the world, and having rocks thrown at her? Her strength seemed superhuman. Moreover, as Robb pointed out, the Nixons did have some housekeeping help. Lying about that fact and denying the help left a bad taste in the mouths of potential women voters.[64] The tendency of the GOP to play up Pat's remarkable stamina added to the image emerging in some circles that the second lady was cold, dull, and bitter. The stoicism Pat learned from her mother and her natural tendency to keep her feelings private, evidenced during the Checkers speech, fueled the development of the myth of "plastic Pat."[65]

The media swipes at her character irritated her but did not bother her as much as some of the other challenges she faced. Two in particular proved a constant source of tension. She had dealt with the first, the attacks on her husband, almost from the beginning of Dick's career. Still, as vice president, he was even more of a target. In addition, the girls were older and better able to comprehend what people were saying and writing about their father. Pat made it a practice to hide any newspaper containing a Herblock cartoon. She wrote Helene about an interview "in a labor magazine that related that [Drew] Pearson blamed Nixon for getting him off TV and radio." Dick did not "deserve the credit but . . . he is very glad to take it."[66] The struggle to ignore all of the name-calling and insults must have been constant. Second, Pat had a difficult time with her newfound fame. Everywhere she went, people stared and approached her. In 1953, she was not used to this yet. She wrote Helene about a trip she and the girls tried to take to the zoo and lunch. "You'd think I was one of the inmates . . . just a fish in a bowl. I'm going to practice to be a lion and growl some of them away."[67] She could not get away from prying eyes even when she was at home. Their house sat on a corner lot rather close to the street, and passersby would point and stare. Because in those days Secret Service coverage did not extend to the vice president's family, there was no way to prevent strangers from approaching Pat and the girls.[68] Although she did learn to cope over the years, she continued to find the constant "hounding," as she called it, aggravating.[69]

There were other difficulties as well. Perhaps from force of habit as well as the reality of the situation, Pat worried about money. She tried to economize where she could by doing her own grocery shopping, repairing the girls' clothes, and hunting for bargains in department stores.[70] But there were many new expenses. They had to give receptions and parties for visitors from around the world and the country. She had to have an appropriate wardrobe. To cut down on expenses, Pat kept careful track of which outfits she wore to which events so that she could rotate the same suits and dresses without insulting any hostess. Although she liked to look good, she found the process of finding the right dresses and suits annoying, time-consuming, and costly.[71]

Compounding the logistics of fulfilling all of her various roles, in the spring of 1958, Pat injured her back. Julie explained in her biography of her mother that Pat strained her back while lifting Julie to see a bird's nest. Another biographer claimed that the injury happened during the move to the house on Forest Lane. Whatever the cause, this in-

Richard and Pat Nixon with Jack and Helene Drown in the mid-1950s. Courtesy of the Richard Nixon Foundation.

jury flared up periodically for years. Although she tried to work through the pain, occasionally even she had to give in and rest.[72] Obviously, Pat was under a great deal of pressure from her husband, the party, the public, and, most significantly, herself.

Pat survived all of this pressure with the help of her friends and family. During the first term, the Nixons lived in the Spring Valley neighborhood, mostly surrounded by people who considered themselves friends. According to at least one neighbor, the second couple was very much a part of this community. They shared babysitting, barbecues, and evenings out with their neighbors. The neighbors, in turn, did what they could to protect the privacy of the Nixons and responded in outrage when a magazine reporter wrote that the neighbors disliked or were afraid of them.[73] She also could rely on the women in the vice president's office for help or support. They provided occasional babysitting as well as important clerical assistance.[74]

Most important, there was Helene, her confidante, advisor, and friend. Helene was perhaps the only person with whom she could really let her hair down and be herself. After all, Helene knew her from before all the fame, before the parties, before she had to be "on" all the time. With Helene, she could laugh and giggle and remember the old days when they were young marrieds who drank and smoked too much and did a wild hula. They shared not only a past, but also a wide circle of common acquaintances. Because of Helene's interest in Republican politics and her husband's involvement in various Nixon campaigns, she understood Pat's situation in ways that family members or other old friends did not. Helene's letters, her visits, and later her phone calls, never failed to lift Pat's spirits. When she needed a rest, Helene's busy household in Southern California was her favorite retreat. As Pat wrote Helene in 1959, "The days of relaxation did me a world of good and I have been back in the harness with a daily race schedule."[75]

Of all of her new tasks, the one she embraced most enthusiastically was the need to travel. From a young age, as she listened to her father telling stories of his adventures, she had longed to see the world. The vice presidency provided the couple with the opportunity to do just that. Although they could not take the girls and they had a restricted schedule, Pat could not help but be excited, especially in the beginning, about the places she would visit.

Their first big trip was a tour beginning in Asia and continuing to parts of the subcontinent during the fall of 1953. It would prove to be an eye-opening experience, especially for Pat. Although Dick had promised her a real family vacation, when the president asked him about plans for the summer, "Dick said he hadn't any definite ones yet." As a result, she wrote Helene, "the following day the President announced at a cabinet meeting that Dick was going to give up his vacation to go on a good will tour." Eisenhower had also told Nixon that he should "take Pat with you." She realized that it would be "work—though interesting."[76] Pat described the pending trip in almost exactly the same words in a letter she wrote Helene the next month. In that same letter, she revealed her determination to get some family fun time before the business trip. Not only were they planning to visit the New Jersey coast during the summer, but she hoped that the Drowns would meet the Nixons in Hawaii "as we'll need a vacation before or after the strenuous trip." After less than eight years in politics, she had already "decided in this game you can't make any personal plans."[77]

Although they did manage to meet up with the Drowns during their first stop in Hawaii, the rest of the trip was "strictly official and a working one."[78] Along with a minimal entourage that included a military aide, a State Department representative, a flight surgeon, three press representatives, two Secret Service agents, Nixon's administrative assistant, Christian Herter Jr., and his secretary, Rose Mary Woods, the Nixons embarked on their 42,000 mile journey. In just over two months, the group visited over fifteen countries, attended hundreds of state dinners, participated in innumerable ceremonies, and spoke with millions of people.[79] The State Department had briefed the group on the many countries and peoples they would be visiting. Pat took the briefings seriously, perhaps more so than anyone else. One member of the group told a reporter a few years later that Pat had served as the group's "walking encyclopedia."[80] Her husband concentrated on the larger mission of reassuring America's Asian allies and friends, clarifying Eisenhower's policies and assessing attitudes toward communism. Neither he nor Pat had ever been particularly interested in formal socializing, so he requested that official dinners be kept to a minimum so that they could meet with as many different peoples as possible in the countries they visited.[81]

Pat recognized that there was a "job to be done," as she wrote in the travel diary she kept during the trip, but she could not help but be caught up in the "thrill of traveling." Even her sadness at leaving the girls did not completely overwhelm her excitement.[82] The harsh reality of such extensive travel and a little girl's enthusiasm for seeing new and different sights leap off the pages of her diary. She gleefully recorded her initiation ceremony as she crossed the equator for the first time: "Dick acted as King Neptune and wore the crown as 'designed' by the crew. What fun!" She admitted attendance at a "female frolic" where

the hostess "arranged to have all male entertainment—Quite risqué."
On 14 October, she detailed their experience in a Maori village in New
Zealand where Dick had to take part in ritual dialogue and actions with
a native sentry. Both she and Dick then had to participate in the cus-
tom of nose rubbing. Although she "felt faint when some of the di-
sheveled oldsters lined up for a session of nose rubbing," the Nixons
wanted to "be good sports," so "we took it."[83]

In addition to the beauty of her surroundings and generosity of the
people they met, she also had to deal with the unpleasantness of traveling through numerous time zones and the sometimes not-so-nice aspects of encountering new and different cultures. The trip to the
Maori village included more than just the nose-rubbing challenge. Invited to lunch with King Koraki, Pat first visited with the women who
would be preparing their luncheon. The kitchen was "so unsanitary"
and the women in such "filthy clothes" that she ended up not being
able to "eat a bite!" By the end of the trip, she had learned to "put an or-
ange and potato peeling" over food that was inedible.[84] At one point,
they were so desperate for a break from the exotic food that they
begged off from dinner by saying they had had a "huge delicious
lunch" and ate K rations in their rooms.[85] Besides dealing with unusual
food, the troupe also had to deal with the effects of zipping back and
forth through various time zones. Their bodies were never sure
whether it was night or day.[86] When they did get a chance to sleep, the
accommodations were not always that comfortable. Years later, during
a series of oral history interviews, Richard Nixon told one of his former aides that they had air-conditioning at only one of their stops. The
rest of the time they dealt with the heat, humidity, and insects as best as
they could.[87]

Pat was also extremely busy. She wrote Helene that although the
"trip has been tremendously interesting," "the schedule [was] so
heavy" that she felt as if she were "campaigning again." Although she
attended formal dinners and official visits with her husband, Pat had
her own separate itinerary that went beyond just the government-
sponsored or -approved women's teas and socials. She made it a point
to seek out the institutions that affected women and children. Ever the
business teacher, Pat jotted her reactions to the sights and peoples she
met in shorthand on her official schedule. In Ceylon, she "went with
Mrs. DeSilva to see hospital and Sister Home for the aged." She com-

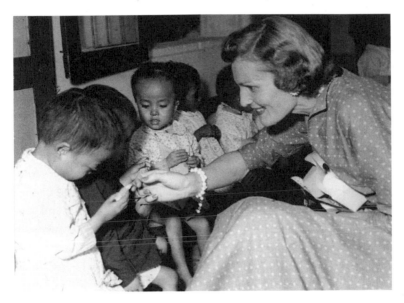

Mrs. Nixon distributes candy to children during a visit to an orphanage in Hanoi,
Vietnam, November 1953. Richard Nixon Presidential Library and Museum.

mented that the "old people [were] thrilled because nobody had been
to see them." In the Philippines, she visited an orphanage and a "training center for learning trades which can be done in the homes."[88] In
South Korea, she went to a Republic of Korea Division Hospital and
"gave out candy and cigarettes." Her brief comments indicated the
state of things: "In heat. Wounded on Army cots with Army blankets.
Soiled bed clothes."[89]

Occasionally, politics would force its way even into Pat's schedule.
In Burma, communists interrupted Dick's speech. Ever the proud wife,
Pat wrote, "Dick shook hands with them and completely demoralized
them." Sometimes women appealed to her directly for help with their
situations. In Teheran, a "mother with two children ran past guards to
plea[d] that other children could be with her." A group of Korean
women who had lost men when the Chinese invaded took a more
straightforward approach. They sent her a letter during her visit to
their country, appealing to her "tender heart" to "do something for us."
They wanted her to use her influence to make government leaders live
up to agreements to effect repatriation of their menfolk. Pat answered
the letter but explained that there was nothing she could do.[90]

After their trip, Pat took some time to jot down notes summarizing what she had seen and learned over the months. She was obviously impressed by the hard work of the people of the various countries as they tried to help their most needy. Although, she wrote, "aggressive communists can bring such misery to the innocent people," she took heart in the teamwork she saw displayed in the more than 200 institutions she had visited. They were promoting industry, training women to support themselves and their children, and setting up neighborhood kitchens and dispensaries. Because her group made unscheduled stops, she felt that they were able to "get a real picture." She concluded that "in general, people can sense when another [person] is friendly and genuinely interested." That is what they had tried to do: "to show them [the peoples they were visiting] that we were interested in them as people."[91] Pat took her role as official representative of the United States seriously; she saw herself as part of the team.

She certainly made something of an impression on the people she met. One constituent explained to Pat that her husband was on a round-the-world business trip and had run into "Pat Nixon's Trail." He wrote his wife that Pat "really rang a bell in this part of the world at a time when Americans are not very popular." An American couple living in India sent Pat a letter after her return, praising the couple for bringing a "fresh understanding of . . . America" to the people of India. President Eisenhower praised both Nixons for their work on the trip.[92] Even the American press noticed Pat's role on the tour. William Theis in the New York *Journal-American* explained that although she did not "make any speeches or carry on high policy discussions, . . . she bore her full share of the work load."[93] Her love for travel, her openness to new peoples and places, her quick smile, and her genuinely kind heart endeared her to the people she met and made her a wonderful unofficial ambassador for the United States.

This would prove to be the case on all of the overseas trips that the Nixons would make during the vice presidential years. Although their schedules were often crowded with official duties and the conditions could be challenging, Pat continued to be thrilled at visiting new countries. In early 1956, she and Dick attended the inauguration of a new Brazilian president, Juscelino Kubitchek, in Rio de Janeiro, "the most spectacularly beautiful city" she had ever seen where the "parties at the palace were fabulous" but the climate change required "a terrific adjustment."[94] In July, the Nixons set off on another whirlwind tour. She explained in a letter to Helene that this was "a fast and full trip . . . in the course of one day we were in three countries (Thailand, Pakistan and Turkey)." Although her husband met with government leaders, she again had her own schedule of events. In the end, she wrote, "it has left us dizzy but happy that in such a short time so much can be accomplished."[95] A year later, journalist Earl Mazo labeled her "this country's most effective female ambassador of good will" after accompanying Pat and Dick on a tour through Africa and Italy and watching as she "charmed peasants by the thousands and potentates by the dozens." Without talking politics, Pat managed to win over not only the "ragged women" in a Monrovian market but also Sultan Mohamed V, who granted her an unprecedented formal audience. Her goal, she told Mazo, was "to convince the people 'we enjoy being here and are genuinely interested in them.'"[96]

Not everyone could be convinced, as Pat found out firsthand during a trip to South America in 1958. In the spring of that year, the president asked Dick to attend the inauguration of President Arturo Frondizi of Argentina. The vice president, worried about the upcoming congressional elections, did not want to leave the country for what he perceived to be a "purely protocol trip" when he had much work to do at home. He could not refuse a presidential request, however, and the trip to Argentina quickly turned into a three-week South American goodwill tour.[97]

The trip was an avoidable tragedy of misperceptions. From Washington's perspective, this trip would show American support for the anticommunist efforts of men such as Frondizi. Many of the peoples of the countries the Nixons would visit did not see it the same way. Mired in poverty, living under the oppressive rule of dictators supported by the United States, and observing the privileges granted to American businesses while their peoples struggled to survive, a segment of the population hated what the Americans represented and turned to communism. Ironically, the democracy Nixon celebrated in his speeches throughout the tour came at the cost of real freedom for most peoples.

Although the first part of the trip went relatively smoothly, tensions heightened when they got to Peru and then exploded in Caracas, Venezuela. In Uruguay, Argentina, and Bolivia, friendly crowds greeted the Nixons, although they did encounter both protesters and critical questions during some of their stops. Nixon encountered more dissatisfaction when the couple arrived in Peru. In fact, a trip to San Marcos University had to be cut short as a result of the potential for riots, and Nixon faced another angry mob when he returned to his hotel. Pat endured a nerve-racking vigil as she watched out the hotel window as a frenzied crowd threw things at her husband as he entered the hotel.

The tensions in Peru hinted at what they would find in Caracas. Although the Secret Service had learned of a possible assassination attempt there, the group continued to Venezuela anyway. Tension filled the air as the Nixons stepped off the plane. A large crowd of demonstrators greeted them, shouting so loudly that the band playing the Venezuelan national anthem could not be heard. Dick decided that they should forego the ceremony at the airport and proceed to their cars. As they walked along the red carpet laid out for them, the band started playing the national anthem again. Out of respect, the Nixons stopped and waited. Unfortunately for them, they were forced to wait directly under an observation deck holding the demonstrators, who showered them with spittle. Pat's new red suit was covered in brown tobacco spit. In his book *Six Crises,* Dick wrote that although he "was horrified" that Pat had to endure this indignity, he "was proud that she was with me."[98] Despite the spit and the chanting and the insults, Pat stopped to smile at a young girl who gave her flowers and to shake hands with another young woman who was shouting insults at Dick.

The situation worsened once they were in their cars. Dick and the Venezuelan foreign minister rode in the first car and Pat and the minister's wife in the second. As they drove to the first stop on their schedule, a stalled truck blocked their path, and crowds attacked the cars. Desperate to get the vice president out of his car, the mob threw rocks, their signs, and anything else they could find at the car. The bulletproof glass shattered but did not break. Glass shards showered the occupants of the cars. As the Secret Service tried frantically to keep the crowd away from the car, the driver looked for a way out. After twelve long minutes, he finally found one. During that time, Pat sat calmly in her car watching as the out-of-control protesters tried to get at her husband. She comforted the wife of the foreign minister, who was afraid for her husband and embarrassed for her country.[99] Once they had driven clear of the danger, Dick sent his aide back to Pat's car to make certain that she was all right and to assure her that he was fine.[100] Rather than continuing on with the published itinerary, Nixon decided to go to the American embassy. After a night in the embassy, the Nixons attended a luncheon that Pat told Julie years later "seemed to last forever." The vice president and his wife then traveled back via the roads they had driven through the day before to get to the airport. This time, however, the streets had been ruthlessly cleared of all people.[101] They spent the night in Puerto Rico to allow time for an appropriate reception to be planned for their arrival in Washington. At their return, a huge crowd that included the president met them at the airport and expressed their admiration for the way they had handled the crisis.

The accolades rolled in not just for the vice president, but also for his wife. Radio personality Paul Harvey featured her on one of his programs. He praised not just her courage under extraordinary circumstance, but also her willingness "in the tedious years that reach out interminably ahead . . . always to share her husband with the ungrateful and the avaricious . . . and to keep so little for herself." J. Edgar Hoover sent her a copy of the Harvey broadcast along with his congratulations: "I think it very succinctly expressed what a tremendously brave person you are, and I use the term 'brave' in the fullest and broadest sense of the word." Journalists lauded her courage under fire. The military aide who had been riding with her claimed that she "had more guts than any man I've ever seen."[102]

Despite all of the praise, Pat's behavior presents an interesting problem. Her stoicism in the face of the danger makes sense. She was a woman who held herself under strict control. She would not break down in front of strangers. The question is her actions at the airport. Why would a woman, confronted by a spitting, jeering, potentially dangerous group of protesters, pause to hug a little girl or to reach between the bayonets to shake hands with a young woman hurling insults at her? Was she operating on instinct? Had she gone through the routine so many times that she acted without thinking? That might explain her response to the child bearing flowers, but what about the offensive demonstrator? Perhaps, she, like her husband, was a true believer. She told Julie years later that she was not frightened as much as she was angry. Here they were on a "goodwill" tour and a group of "communist-inspired hoodlums" ruined it. She believed in the importance of what she was doing; she thought perhaps that she was making a difference in the lives of people around the world.[103] Years later, she told a childhood friend that even though she occasionally felt inadequate to the task, that "she was only Pat Ryan from Artesia," the people she met were so gracious that she felt comfortable continuing the important work she and her husband were doing.[104]

Her belief in this principle continued even after the riot in Caracas as she embarked on the last big foreign trips of the vice presidential years. In November 1958, the couple traveled to London, where Pat "wow[ed]" much of the British press with her "natty" wardrobe and unspoiled manner. The left-wing *Spectator* took a different view, describing her as "a Republican Coppelia," a doll that "would still be smiling while the world broke."[105] The following year, they went to the Soviet Union and Poland. In Moscow, Dick confronted Nikita Khrushchev in the famous Kitchen Debate, during which the two leaders argued the merits of communism and capitalism in an exhibition of American consumer goods. Pat once again had her own agenda of visiting orphanages and hospitals. Dick might have gotten more headlines, but Pat's interactions with Soviet women and children also made a lasting impression. She told one reporter that she thought it helped "to have a woman along" on a diplomatic mission; they can make friends in ways different than men.[106] She was overwhelmed by the outpouring of cheers that greeted the Nixons as they traveled through the streets in Poland. Pat, who was not easily rattled, had to "fight back tears," according to one news account of their arrival in Poland.[107] Of all of her responsibilities as second lady, the travel not only fulfilled her childhood dreams, but also allowed her to feel useful and a necessary part of an important enterprise.

Pat was not alone in seeing the importance of her role. By the Soviet trip, the last of their vice presidential ones, Pat as ambassador of goodwill had won over even the *New York Times*. Calling her a "Diplomat in High Heels," the reporter described her as "self-possessed, self-made . . . orderly, [and] precise."[108] The Capital Press Club, an organization of African American news correspondents, presented her with its International Relations Award in 1957. Recognizing her "good will activities among the people of eight African countries," they chose her as "America's outstanding ambassador of good will."[109] Deputy Attorney General William Rogers wrote to Pat after a trip through Europe, during which he had been bombarded with requests for her presence on the next vice presidential trip. He praised her "important and significant role in public affairs."[110]

Even as her public role seemed to grow in importance, her relationship with her husband seemed to suffer from the tensions and pressures they both experienced. In 1953, she could still tell Helene about her "best time," a "jaunt" to New York City with Dick when they saw a Broadway show and later went out for dinner and dancing.[111] As the years went by, however, they spent less and less time together just as a couple. Certainly they spent time with each other during their trips, but these were almost always work related and included other people. Most married couples raising children and engaged in high-level careers experience the same pressures. The Nixons, however, could not afford to appear as though they were anything other than a happily married couple. To do otherwise would hurt his political image.

That image was important to Dick. He was an ambitious man. As he rose through the ranks of government service, he realized that he wanted the brass ring. He was aware that Pat did not share his enthusiasm for the game of politics. As early as 1954, he wrote up a list of reasons why he should get out of politics. One of those reasons was his wife. There were, however, more compelling reasons for staying in. He came to the conclusion that there was no reason to stay in the race unless you enjoyed it, needed the job, or the job needed you. He obviously believed that was true.[112] Whenever he faced a serious threat to his political career—such as the slush fund crisis—Dick fought to stay in the game. He talked occasionally about getting out but never seriously endeavored to do so.

Pat's feelings about politics, on the other hand, were complicated. On the one hand, she had been politically aware when she was single.[113] She had not run for office or marched for causes, but she had expressed enough of an opinion that others noted her interest. In addition, her best friend, Helene Drown, was actively involved in California Republican politics.[114] They shared many friends who were connected to the GOP. They gossiped frequently, especially during the vice presidential years, about those friends and acquaintances. They exchanged insights about the pecking order within the party, about who was snubbing or kissing up to whom, and who was getting their just desserts.[115] As a result, Pat kept up with election results even when Dick was not running and expressed "shock" and dismay when "we" did not

win. She obviously associated herself with the GOP. She frequently referred to the party in terms of "we" and "our."[116] Her willingness to express her opinions about political entities did not end with her discussions with her friend or husband. By 1954, she was letting President
Eisenhower know what she thought of some of the movers and shakers.[117] During the couple's trip to the Soviet Union in 1959, her pointed
questions to Nikita Khrushchev about his wife's absence from the festivities led to Mrs. Khrushchev's, as well as wives of other Soviet officials, unprecedented presence during the rest of the visit.[118] On the
other hand, she rarely, if ever, discussed issues, policies, or strategies.
Not only did she refuse to give political talks in public, but her correspondence offered no insights either.

For Pat, politics was her job, and one she did not always enjoy. Although on occasion she was proud of her work in helping to raise
funds for the party, she found many of her tasks frustrating and mind-
numbing. By the end of the first term, she expressed her jealousy of
her friend's reentry into the workforce: "I would like to do part time
work rather than all the useless gadding I am expected to do." The thrill
of meeting famous men and women and the glamour of white tie dinners at the White House wore off, leaving only the tiring routine of
constant evenings away from her girls and idle chatter with women she
did not always like.[119] For someone who had worked hard her entire
life, the situation could, at times, be intolerable. It was not the long
hours or the physical challenges that weighed her down. She resented
not being useful, not doing something meaningful. Perhaps that is why
the foreign travel appealed to her. During her trips overseas, she felt
that she was playing an important role; she was representing American
interests abroad.

Despite her dislike of aspects of her job, she chose to do it. She did
not have to. The wives of other politicians stayed home with their children or traveled with their husbands only when absolutely necessary.[120] Pat refused to take on that role. She had always been a doer; to
stay home would have been out of character. Additionally, although
she did not enjoy some of her tasks, she did believe she was doing some
good. She believed that she touched the "little people" she met. She
once justified her willingness to answer all of her mail by explaining
that she came from a small town and knew what a thrill it was for
someone to receive a letter from the White House. That sentiment

could apply to her determination to shake the hand of every person at the various functions she attended. Pat from Artesia understood that Pat the second lady could make someone's day by smiling at him or her. Perhaps those smiles made up for the snubs, insults, and challenges she faced the rest of the time.

As the end of Dick's second vice presidential term drew near, Pat had become both more polished and more cynical. She had fulfilled her desire for travel; in fact, she had seen the world. She had met world leaders and dined in the White House. She had also recognized that she would never have a normal life with a husband who worked from nine to five and barbecued on weekends. If she resented this, she buried her dissatisfaction the same way millions of women did theirs. Never one to argue in public (or private for that matter), Pat chose more passive-aggressive methods—venting to friends or making snide remarks to her husband.[121] She knew they were not done with politics yet.

CHAPTER 3

IN AND OUT OF POLITICS

The lessons Pat learned in her childhood help to explain her decisions and reactions to events of the 1960s. Family devotion, spousal loyalty, determination to face hardship, and a fatalistic attitude prepared her for the exhausting, stressful, and frequently heartbreaking experience of three major campaigns in an eight-year period. The brief respite between campaigns brought a different kind of frustration to a woman used to constant hard work. These years strained the Nixon marriage and challenged even Pat's legendary stamina. As a result, her husband's victory in 1968 was not as sweet as it might have been in 1960.

As the 1960s began, Pat greeted the new decade with a more realistic view of the world than she had had ten years earlier. Her girlhood dreams of travel had been fulfilled, but her rose-colored vision of the world had been dirtied, shattered, and spat upon. Her schoolteacher's wardrobe had expanded to include ball gowns and cocktail dresses. Major newspapers commented on her fashion sense. She had dined with kings, queens, and prime ministers. The president of the United States considered her a valuable member of the Eisenhower team. With Dick, she had faced mosquitoes, militants, and mobs. She had learned to share her husband with the world. She believed in him and his vision of the way things should be. She was ready to jump on the campaign wagon for him once more.

Although by the late 1950s the decision to run for the presidency had an aura of inevitability surrounding it, the couple had discussed their future on several occasions throughout the vice presidency. As noted earlier, in 1954, Dick had written a list for himself of reasons to get out of politics.[1] He believed the reasons to stay in outweighed the ones to choose another career. In fact, when Harold Stassen had pushed to eliminate Nixon from the ticket for the 1956 run, Nixon had clung to his position. Pat may not have "been keen" on the idea of staying in politics, but she did not want anyone else to make the decision for them. She supported her husband's determination to hold onto the vice presidency.[2] Still again in 1958, after Pat's back injury, Helene Drown wrote to Dick, urging him to "have a talk about the future" with his wife.[3] All of these talks and discussions appear to indicate that Pat remained ambivalent about her husband's career and that, despite his own occasional uncertainties, Dick never lost his desire for political office. Although Pat disliked certain aspects of politics, particularly the attacks on her husband and time spent apart from her girls, she never doubted that her husband had much to contribute to the country. Astute Washington observer Alice Roosevelt Longworth told one reporter that Pat was "ambitious for Dick, not to gratify her own ego." Many friends, acquaintances, and even strangers agreed with Whittier resident John Reilly, who asserted that "no one had more support by a woman than Pat gave Dick."[4]

And Dick needed her support more than ever in 1960, despite his advantages as a candidate. As the vice president, Nixon had built up a solid reputation as a party workhorse and a foreign policy expert, even substituting for the president on a number of occasions. His courage under fire in South America and his well-publicized Kitchen Debate with Nikita Khrushchev in the last two years of his term made him a household name and the front-runner for the Republican nomination in 1960. Still, Nixon knew better than anyone that there were no sure things in politics; he recognized the potential traps that lay in his paths. The lackluster economy, the continual talk about a missile gap, and dangerous internecine fighting within the GOP threatened his easy victory at the Chicago convention. Nixon confronted the party problems head-on by meeting with New York governor Nelson Rockefeller, leader of his Republican opposition. Although the gesture quieted the discontent on his left flank, it inflamed those on his right. Led by conservative Arizona senator Barry Goldwater, right-wing Republicans reluctantly agreed to support the vice president, but they vowed to win the nomination for one of their own in the future.[5]

With his party behind him, the Nixons faced a formidable opponent in Massachusetts senator John F. Kennedy. Backed by his father's millions, the handsome, charming senator beat out more experienced competitors such as Senate majority leader Lyndon Johnson and perennial candidate Adlai Stevenson. To Pat's surprise, Kennedy followed his party nomination by confronting his apparent disadvantages of Catholicism and youth head-on. First, he walked into the lion's den of the Greater Houston Ministerial Association to challenge the religious prejudice he feared would undermine his candidacy in the predominantly Baptist South. He reassured the ministers and their parishioners that he was the Democratic candidate, not the Catholic one. Second, he challenged his opponent to a series of debates. Although Nixon was only four years older than Kennedy, the Massachusetts senator realized that he appeared both younger and more inexperienced.[6] The debates would give him a chance to show he could hold his own against a man many perceived to be more knowledgeable.[7]

For his part, Nixon relished the challenge of the campaign. He agreed to the debates, feeling that he had more experience with the medium of television but recognizing his opponent's oratorical skills. Anticipating that it could be a close race, he promised at the convention to campaign in every state. He believed that he had the best strategy and the best chance of winning.[8]

A small accident early in the campaign led to big problems for Nixon's well-laid plans. While getting into a car in Greensboro, North Carolina, he bumped his knee. The minor injury became infected and forced Nixon off the campaign trail and into the hospital. When the doctors released him, he was underweight, pale, and way behind in his schedule to visit all fifty states. He refused to go back on his pledge, however, and so continued to maintain a grueling pace. In addition to the physical strain, his determination led to further weight loss and pallor that affected the reaction of television viewers to his debate performance. In contrast, Kennedy appeared tanned, fit, and, as it turned out, amazingly telegenic. The Republican candidate and his wife confronted a serious challenge. As a result, Nixon would need all the help he could get to win the election.[9]

Pat was ready in 1960 to provide that help. Despite her dislike for campaigning and politicking, Pat recognized that she was a valuable and necessary member of the Nixon campaign crew. The voters elected not just a man, according to Pat; they elected a team. She explained her views on the subject late in the 1960 campaign to an interviewer who asked her for advice for the wives of young politicians entering the field. Emphasizing the importance of working together, Pat stated that "the decision should be made before the couple enters politics, because it takes the work of two people."[10] She saw politics as her job as much as it was her husband's. This was the way the Nixons had operated throughout their marriage, particularly once he started running for office.[11]

From the beginning of the race, GOP leaders recognized Pat's value to the campaign. In fact, according to one strategist, they realized that although "the serious issues and international situation" would decide the election, "the nation's admiration for Pat Nixon could swing enough votes to tip the scales to our side."[12] As a result, after the Republican National Convention meeting in Chicago, the Republican National Committee and the Nixon staff organized a "Pat for First Lady" campaign. Complete with her own buttons, banners, and song, the Pat for First Lady operation led to numerous teas, socials, and women's club appearances and culminated in a Pat Nixon Week in October. Pat, who preferred not being in the limelight, vowed to "be out working . . . until the last votes are counted."[13]

Pat's specialty, and a large part of what made her participation so valuable, was her genuine interest in meeting and getting to know people. Because she believed that it was the obligation of her husband's team to "represent the voters," she felt an obligation to know them. "Knowing them" was the only way, she asserted, to "truly represent them."[14] She told reporter Christine Hotchkiss that she "like[d] people." They "fascinate[d]" and "stimulate[d]" her. She went on to explain that she liked "to be *there* [italics in the original], completely present, as to give [her] entire attention to the person momentarily before [her]."[15] At first glance, this kind of comment might be written off as trite politicking. Evidence from numerous sources, however, indicates that Pat lived up to her words. From the daughter of her closest friend to a constituent who approached Pat and the girls in a department store, people found her gracious, kind, and fun. Reporters who expected the always smiling, rigidly controlled wife of the vice president expressed amazement at the "vibrancy of youth" exuded by the private second lady.[16]

Through her many trips with her husband, she had become, as reporter Ruth Montgomery put it, "the symbol of the 'All-American housewife and mother.'" In a later article, Montgomery enthused that "no other woman in the world can count so many admiring friends on four continents."[17] Her ready smile and quiet beauty won over some, while her courage in the face of violent mobs in South America and her willingness to travel outside the sheltered walls of the embassies to visit orphanages and hospitals earned her a level of respect not usually accorded housewives and mothers.

Interestingly, Pat, who rarely if ever gave political speeches or commented on campaign issues, would share her views when it came to her travel overseas. In particular, the reactions of the crowds in Eastern Europe overwhelmed her, forcing her to break her usual silence. She told one reporter that during their trip through Warsaw, people lined the streets and covered their cars with, as she emphasized, "their own flowers, not government issue." She thought their actions were a tangible sign that "those unhappy Communist-dominated people" longed "for closer ties with the U.S. and freedom." On several other occasions, when reporters asked her the number one concern of women everywhere, she always answered "peace." "The people," she explained, "want peace. It's only the leaders who get us in trouble."[18]

Republican leaders were not alone in emphasizing the importance of the first lady question. In fact, newspapers and magazines featured numerous stories analyzing the candidates for the role. Although the stories tended to focus solely on issues of fashion, they inadvertently included some more substantive concerns. For example, Jacqueline Kennedy responded to criticism that she was spending a fortune on clothing by Paris designers by contending that Pat probably spent more because her clothes came from Elizabeth Arden. Pat laughed off that idea, emphasizing that she only patronized American designers and stating that she bought many of her clothes off the rack.[19] Moreover, as she told another reporter, comparing fashion views could be "fun," but clothing styles were not a serious issue in the race. Although she did not think the time was right for women to debate issues, she recognized that the public seemed to expect more information about her than they had with previous first ladies.[20]

Still, Pat had to be careful because not everyone was a fan of hers. Some people found the stories about her "superwoman" abilities irritating and condescending. One constituent wrote Pat to inform her that she did not find the press reports about her frugality and housekeeping abilities believable. In fact, she found Pat's apparent attempt to "impress the little, little man's wife" so insulting that she intended to vote for Kennedy although she was originally a Nixon supporter.[21] An article in *Newsweek* noted that some people "simply don't want the personification of the middle-class housewife in the White House." The same article mentioned that other Americans found it "improper for a Presidential candidate's wife to participate, or be used, in a campaign."[22] One supporter even cautioned Pat not to draw too much attention to herself by "putting on a great act of graciousness." "Heaven forbid," he wrote, "we get another Eleanor Roosevelt."[23]

The most consistent criticism, however, concerned Pat's personality and perhaps contributed to the "plastic Pat" image that would haunt her during her husband's administrations. The general consensus seemed to be that Pat appeared unnaturally perky and artificially perfect. The aforementioned *Newsweek* author agreed that many people thought that "she does too much, and always too efficiently. She is too bland."[24] A supporter, in fact, advised her to "loosen up, fluff up a little more."[25] In a cover story on Pat, *Time* reporters summed up the image perfectly: "Pat Nixon is too serene, too tightly controlled; . . . she smothers her personality with a fixed smile and a mask of dignity." Although almost everyone who met her in person found her gracious, warm, and kind, her public persona suffered from her determination to remain calm no matter what the circumstances. She told the *Time* reporter that her stoicism was a part of who she was.[26] The stresses of the campaign no doubt exacerbated her tendency toward rigid self-control. Because she had little control over Dick's political campaign, maintaining her reserve was probably an important coping mechanism.

The public's perception of the Nixon marriage also contributed to the plastic Pat image. Three aspects of their relationship combined to help create this image. First, even as newlyweds, the couple did not indulge in public displays of affection. Neither Pat nor Dick had been raised to believe that such behavior was appropriate. Although there is evidence that the couple still enjoyed being together, Dick rarely took

Pat's hand to help her up a step, nor did he put his arm around her in public.[27] Second, his intense focus on the 1960 campaign revealed his lack of social skills. He did not like to make small talk (except about sports) and often seemed uncomfortable in informal settings. He concentrated on politics and political issues and assumed that everyone around him understood how he felt about them. Therefore, there was no reason to discuss his feelings or prove that they existed. If he ignored Pat at an appearance, it was because, he assumed, she knew that winning the election was vitally important.

Then there was Pat's own pride in her stoicism and self-control. She told more than one reporter that she never allowed herself to lose her temper and that the couple never fought.[28] Members of the press saw for themselves how she reacted when Dick snubbed her in public. They interpreted her smiling acceptance of these small humiliations as the reaction of a victim or automaton. The reality, however, was that Pat had a temper that she did not display in public. She could, and did, on occasion unleash it on her husband in the form of a biting remark or by giving him the silent treatment. On more than one occasion, Dick enlisted his mother to help convince Pat to speak to him again.[29] Like many women of her generation, she displayed a classic passive-aggressive personality. Numerous people overheard her make remarks to Dick about his mistakes in speeches or appearances. The public, however, saw only his rude treatment of her and not her biting remarks to him.

In 1960, Pat needed all the internal resources she could muster to endure the strain of a presidential campaign that far exceeded anything she had previously experienced in politics. The requests for information, souvenirs, or appearances, which she had learned to deal with during the vice presidential years, increased exponentially even before Dick won the nomination. Ladies asked for recipes to add to cookbooks; clubwomen wanted cast-off dresses, ball gowns, or hats to raffle off; people inquired about her favorite prayer, poem, or color; they invited her to serve as sponsor, patroness, or chairwoman of their organization; everyone, it seemed wanted something of hers or from her.[30] Pat recognized that even the people who offered to give her something really wanted something in return, so she was cautious about what she accepted in the way of gifts. When the president of a cosmetics company sent her a "preview package" of products, she told

Bessie Newton (the secretary from Dick's office who handled her correspondence) that she did not "want to thank him this time (his reputation is not good) [as] this may discourage further gifts."[31] Her natural instinct was not to accept many of the items offered, but she always deferred to her husband and his staff for advice. As a result, she sometimes wore campaign dresses made by constituents and even had her hair done by a representative of a national organization because Dick thought it was "a good idea."[32]

Pat worked hardest to retain control over the way the campaign affected her daughters. Even before the campaigning actually began, Pat lamented to a friend that it was "the children who really suffer" from demands of a life in politics. Realizing what the year would bring, she tried to provide the girls with some extra time and attention whenever she could. During their spring break, both Nixons took the girls to Florida for what was supposed to be a family vacation. Legislative business compelled Dick to leave after a few days, so, as Pat explained to Helene, they were "bachelor girls." In the end, the weather cooperated and they ended up with "three glorious days."[33] During their summer recess, the girls attended summer camp in California. They rejoined their parents in Chicago for the convention, where Dick thought they would have "a 'blast.'"[34] (Julie, in fact, did describe the thrill of riding in the parade and seeing all of the people clamoring after her father.[35]) After the convention, however, when the Nixons planned to take the girls to California for a few weeks of vacation before the intense campaigning of the fall, politics interfered again. Congress reconvened, Pat wrote Helene, "so that is out. Same old story?!"[36] Once the presidential race was in full swing, Pat "kept the girls' schedule" herself and limited their public appearances.[37]

She did not have as much control over her own schedule. By October, she and Dick were running a marathon, crisscrossing the country in their attempts to live up to his campaign promise to visit all fifty states. By his count, he had traveled over 65,000 miles and made 180 "scheduled speeches"; Pat accompanied him on most of those trips and listened to most of the speeches. The couple spent their days driving between appearances and their nights frequently flying to the next stop. They most often appeared together, but occasionally separated so as to increase their visibility.[38]

Election Day came after almost seventy-two sleepless hours of campaigning, traveling, making appearances, and smiling. The exhausted candidate and his wife and daughters flew from an election night eve speech in Chicago to California, where the adults would cast their ballots. After their early morning vote, the Nixons spent the day apart. Dick and his friend and aide Don Hughes drove to Tijuana for lunch while Pat went back to the hotel to catch up on correspondence, wash her hair, and wait.[39]

It turned out to be a long evening. Initial reports had Kennedy ahead by a landslide. As more results arrived, his lead in the popular vote dwindled. The candidates spent a long evening listening to results that kept Nixon's hopes alive long after the news stations predicted his opponent would win. By 11 o'clock, Nixon realized that he had to make some sort of statement. Despite the fact that allegations of fraud began to emerge from both Texas and Illinois, despite Pat's initial refusal to appear with him, despite the fact that Kennedy's victory was not yet guaranteed, Nixon thought it was in the best interest of his supporters to acknowledge that "if the present trend" continued, he would lose.[40] Still, he did not completely give up hope. In fact, Nixon finally went to bed with visions of a surprise upset in his mind.[41] His dreams did not come true. Although he came close, he lost the popular vote by a very slim margin; only 112,881 votes separated the two men. Of course, the all-important electoral vote told a different story. There Kennedy beat Nixon soundly, 303 to 219.[42] After fourteen years in public service, the Nixons were out of the spotlight.

For Pat, the situation was fraught with irony. Politics had never been her choice. In many ways, she hated the spotlight, the invasions of privacy, and the demands of the job. She told one friend that she had "given up everything" she ever loved because of her husband's career.[43] Even Dick realized on various occasions that she resented their political life. The loss in 1960 removed them from politics and gave her what she wanted; it should have made her happy. Instead, Pat was devastated. She refused at first to go with Dick as he conceded defeat. When she finally agreed to accompany him to the ballroom to thank their supporters, the look of grief on her face was overwhelming. Daughter Julie remembered that her mother "disliked intensely" those pictures because they "exposed too much pain."[44] Pat later wrote to Helene, describing her "state of numbness" during the days and weeks after the defeat. It was not just that their efforts had been for naught; her "faith

in the 'right' " had been "shaken to the point" that she "could not discuss the situation any more."[45] She had disliked parts of her job, but
she had believed that she and her husband were doing something important for the country. In the end, the country rejected them. Just as
with the slush fund crisis, Pat took the rejection personally. Years later,
Julie would write that the 1960 loss "disillusioned her [mother] beyond
redemption."[46]

But Pat was a survivor. In fact, both Nixons were. So they licked
their wounds and got on with the future. They needed to decide what
they were going to do, where they were going to live, and how they
were going to support themselves. Dick had plenty of offers to serve on
boards of directors, to join law firms, and to take up consulting work.
Recognizing that their daughters would be college bound in a few years
and that they had little savings and few assets other than their house,
the couple contemplated Dick joining Thomas E. Dewey's New York
law firm. They decided, however, to go back to California, where Dick
would join the law firm of Adams, Duque, and Hazeltine. Pat wanted
to move closer to family and friends. Dick perhaps also desired the
support of old acquaintances and family. In addition, California was a
logical place to begin rebuilding his career.[47]

With the decision made, it was just a matter of waiting out the
lame-duck period, getting through the inauguration, and saying good-
bye to old friends, none of which proved as easy as they hoped. They
took the girls to New York City before Christmas to enjoy the decorations and festivities and to get their minds off the coming transition.
They flew to the Bahamas the day after the inauguration, both to escape the New Frontier of Washington and to try to get some rest. Too
used to a frenetic pace, Dick could not handle the laid-back atmosphere of the islands, causing the family to cut their trip in half and fly
home. Back in D.C., they resumed a more normal routine. They attended and gave a series of good-bye dinners. Longtime Senate colleagues such as Everett Dirksen of Illinois and Styles Bridges of New
Hampshire invited them for evenings of reminiscing and recalling the
glory days of the past.[48] For their part, the Nixons entertained old
friends as well as some of the " 'angels' in the campaign." The parties
might have been business on some level, but Pat had a "gay" time. Still,
it was work. Pat wrote Helene that "the last rush of entertaining" had
their schedule looking "like campaign days."[49] Pat also took the time to

write thank-you notes to those, such as Jo Haldeman, wife of aide H. R. Haldeman, who had played "important, although unsung" roles in the campaign, as well as to all those people who wrote to offer their continuing support for the Nixon team.[50]

Her new status as wife of a private citizen allowed her the luxury of doing something she had been wishing she could do for years: turn down invitations. In fact, her correspondence reveals that she declined almost every invitation that arrived for her at home or her husband's office, whether it was for an event in Washington or California. She must have taken great satisfaction from being able to write on one invitation: "At the present time I do not plan to include speaking activities in my schedule."[51] Some people saw Pat's decision to forego the usual round of teas, lunches, and dinners required of politicians' wives as a "virtual disappearance act." They feared, reporter Ruth Montgomery noted, that she had "locked herself" into an "isolation booth" because of her disappointment over the election results.[52] Julie believes that her mother declined all invitations because her father was already in California.[53] Considering her opinion of many such events before the 1960 campaign, as well as her innate love of privacy, Pat's decision to avoid another round of political gatherings hardly seems surprising. Instead, she attended a few events with old friends.

Pat had to contend with social invitations because Dick moved to California in early 1961 while she and the girls remained back east. She explained to Helene that they "decided to let the girls finish school" in Washington. Nor did she want to make a hasty decision about where they would live in California. She had become "spoiled" by her short commute to "the center of any activity" in Washington and feared the "long driving choices" and the smog of southern California.[54] In the end, they could find nothing that suited their needs and had a house built. In the interim, they moved into a home rented from producer Walter Lang in June of that year. Years later, Pat told Julie that she regretted the decision to delay the move because it forced them to spend "seven months in limbo" before they could move on with their lives.[55]

As he had in 1946, Dick moved ahead of Pat, leaving her to do the organizing and packing. She also had to take care of hundreds of small details, from getting a California driver's license to finding tennis and piano teachers for the girls.[56] This time, however, besides packing up all of their belongings (which had greatly increased since their original move to Washington), she also had to help two teenagers adjust to leaving the only home they had ever known. In addition to calming the girls' fears and addressing their concerns, she had to oversee construction of the new house.[57] There was little time to consider the invitations that continued to arrive. Pat gladly used her busy to-do list to excuse herself from many of the gatherings.[58]

Free to control her own schedule for the first time in many years, Pat spent a happy summer, decorating the most luxurious house she had ever lived in and spending time with her daughters. This pleasant interlude began on a high note, with Pat receiving an honorary degree from her alma mater, the University of Southern California. Citing her service to the country and to "the cause of world peace and understanding," the USC regents stated that "in honoring her we honor all those women who express the same high qualities of womanhood in our colleges and in the comparative anonymity of private and public life."[59] Enjoying her newfound private life, Pat busied herself with gardening, picking out furniture, and entertaining a steady stream of her daughters' friends.[60] Writer Earl Mazo, who had known the family for years, reported that he had never seen Pat so happy.[61]

Her husband, of course, responded very differently to his new status as a private citizen. Nixon seemed torn between lamenting his situation and plotting his return to office. On the one hand, he spent much of the early part of the year alone in California, trying to work up enthusiasm for his new job but finding that everything about his life "seemed unexciting and unimportant."[62] He also had to contend with the honeymoon period of the Kennedy administration as the press and public fawned over the new president, his family, and his Cabinet and policy choices. On the other hand, he found ways to keep himself connected to the national political scene. Even as he and his remaining staff had packed up his office and written hundreds of thank-you and good-bye notes, he had known, he later wrote in his memoirs, that "someday" he would be back.[63] With that in mind, as he prepared to move west, he held a series of meetings in Arizona with a select group of friends and advisors. He maintained his contacts with key party leaders and made a couple of trips back east to give speeches and put in appearances.[64] Moreover, his title with his new law firm was "of counsel" rather than partner so that he could continue his political activities.[65]

Nixon also worked on a book about his experiences while in public office. A number of people, ranging from Adela Rogers St. John, one of his favorite journalists, to President Kennedy and Mamie Eisenhower, encouraged him to undertake the task. Although he was busy with speaking tours, GOP fund raising, and writing a syndicated newspaper column, he finally agreed to the project. He spent much of the summer and fall of 1961 writing the book, which he claimed was one of the hardest things he had ever done.[66] In fact, once again, Dick's work kept him so busy that he had little time for Pat and the girls. By the end of his first year as a private citizen, between writing, fund raising, and speechifying, he was, he admitted in his memoirs, exhausted, underweight, and short-tempered.[67]

He dedicated the book, *Six Crises*, to Pat. This made perfect sense, but the dedication's wording caused some controversy. Rather than writing a simple "To Pat" or expressing his love for her, which would have been completely out of character, he added the phrase "She also ran." For someone so consumed by politics, this might have seemed to him the highest compliment he could give his wife. It might have been his way of acknowledging her vital role in all of his crises. (This was, after all, a man who dictated letters to his daughters when they were away at camp rather than writing them himself.[68]) Some observers, however, found it odd. In combination with the lack of any loving references to her and his almost clinical descriptions of her treatment and actions in Caracas, the phrases seemed demeaning to some of Pat's admirers. It relegated her to little more than a campaign partner.[69]

Whether or not Dick intended the insult, circumstances soon increased the tension in the Nixon marriage. Enjoying her new life, her happy daughters, her decorating, and her time with old friends, Pat must have hoped that they were done with politics. But she knew her husband; would she really have believed that? Maybe she hoped the good times would last longer than a year. They did not.

Almost from the moment Dick moved to California, various Republicans started hinting that he should run for governor. The whisper campaign got louder as the year progressed. Old friends such as Whittaker Chambers, Republican advisors such as Leonard Hall, and national leaders such as Dwight Eisenhower and J. Edgar Hoover encouraged him to throw his hat into the California ring. Many of them argued that the governorship would provide him with a strong political base as the Republican front-runner and serve as a launching pad for a run against JFK in 1964 or 1968.[70] Additionally, Dick loved campaigning; he missed the thrill and energy of politics.

There were other voices, however, urging him not to run. Both former president Herbert Hoover and General Douglas MacArthur thought it was a bad idea. Dick also admitted to himself that he was not really interested in state affairs; he was drawn to national and international issues. If he won, he would have to limit himself to matters concerned with California politics. Moreover, the California GOP was a tangled, snarling mess of factions, wings, and blocs. As a national leader, Nixon had been able to stay above the internecine fighting; in the gubernatorial contest, he would have to jump into the fray.[71]

Amid all the other voices, Dick certainly heard the rumble that would be Pat's response to his decision to reenter politics.[72] Daughter Julie admitted that her uncle, Tom Ryan, told her that Pat had threatened to "take her shoe to" Dick if he thought about getting back into politics.[73] For Pat, it was not just about Dick thrusting them back into campaigning so soon after the trauma of the 1960 election. She also had friends in the California GOP. She knew that this race promised to be a tough, nasty fight. She realized that all of the things she despised about politics would be played out: the smears, the character attacks, the difficulties her children would face in a school they had only just started attending. She particularly worried about the girls. In a 1962 article in *Ladies' Home Journal*, she explained that in this campaign Tricia and Julie knew going in that "somebody is going to get *hurt.*" The 1960 campaign had been the first they were old enough to remember; that loss was still fresh in their minds.[74] Moreover, there was a real chance that he might not win. Pat could see no upside to this campaign.[75]

Dick's recognition of Pat's feelings about the California gubernatorial race shaped the way he told her about his decision. He waited until the last possible moment, the night before a promised press conference, to raise the issue with Pat and the girls. Most accounts state that Pat was opposed, that Julie just wanted everyone to get along, and that Tricia wanted him to run. Pat told Julie, however, that Tricia was also opposed.[76] According to her account, Dick accepted the vote of the majority of his family and went upstairs to write a statement saying that he was not running. Tricia then went to her mother because she felt badly about her father's sacrifice. She urged her mother to change her vote. Pat agreed and sent Tricia to tell him. This was not the version that appeared in Nixon's *Memoirs*. According to him, Pat told him that she thought it was a "mistake" to run, but that she would support him if he decided to declare his candidacy.[77]

Both versions epitomized the Nixon marriage at this stage. Dick had little to lose in asking Pat and the girls this way. If they said no and stuck to their guns, he had the perfect excuse not to run in a contest he had to know would be an uphill struggle. If, however, he presented his case and gave them time, the odds were in his favor that they would come around to the idea of his jumping in the race. Pat and Dick had been married long enough to know one another's patterns of behavior. He counted on Pat's loyalty to him, her belief in her marriage vows, and her history of going along with his wishes. She might detest politics, but she was duty bound to support her husband. As she told one friend at the beginning of the campaign, "I'm trapped. Which way can I go?" She did not and would not like it, but she would campaign.[78]

Going along as she had in the past did not mean that everything was as it had always been. Pat campaigned as she had promised, but most of her appearances were to community teas as part of the Action Package Program. She would go to a hostess's house and have tea with a group of women. She would chat with the women before leaving to attend another one. As she had in the past, she showed remarkable recall, "recognizing," one reporter noted, "a number of women who had helped her husband in his initial campaign." Shaking innumerable hands and drinking countless cups of coffee, Pat played her part as loyal political wife.[79] Unlike past battles, however, this time she spent most of the campaign on her own, participating in the meet and greets with women's groups rather than listening to her husband make the same speech all over the state. And although she agreed to "do what [aide] John Ehrlichman recommend[ed]" on occasion, Nixon's aides knew to tread lightly around her. They were careful about what they asked her to do.[80] Her absence from his appearances was so obvious that Nixon felt compelled to comment on it, telling audiences that Pat was spending time with the girls.[81]

As Nixon admitted to former aide Frank Gannon in an interview conducted in 1983, Pat was right about the race; it was a mess.[82] The difficulties began during the primary contest, where Nixon faced a strong challenge from the right. His opponent, Joseph Shell, had the backing of the John Birch Society, an organization based on the conspiracy theories and writings of candy manufacturer Robert Welch. Walking a tightrope so as not to alienate right wingers (and thus lose their donations) while also disavowing the theories of the Birchers, Nixon managed to win the Republican nomination in June. Still, it had been a rough fight, and he then had to face the popular sitting governor, Democrat Edmund "Pat" Brown. It would have been a tough battle for any Republican. After all, Brown not only had the advantage of being an incumbent, and one with no scandals or issues lingering about him, he also could call on powerful Democratic officials, including the president, to show their support. For his part, Nixon had just emerged from a brutal primary battle, was scrambling to get enough money to run his campaign, and had no firsthand experience with California issues. In fact, his first campaign strategies—promising to root out the communists in state government and to rid Sacramento of corruption—sounded more like the Nixon of 1960 than a candidate for California governor. They seemed to lend credence to Brown's persistent charge that Nixon was just using the governor's mansion as a stepping stone to the presidency. An election-eve gaffe drove the point home. During a four-hour telethon taped in the Nixon living room with Pat and the girls nearby, Nixon said, "When I become Pres...." His immediate correction did not help much. "When I become governor of the United States...."[83]

In the end, his future plans were less important than the popularity of Brown, the relative prosperity of Californians, and the actions of Nikita Khrushchev during the Cuban missile crisis. Kennedy's speech explaining the Cuban missile crisis to Americans aired during the last days of the campaign. In the national emergency, Nixon rallied around the president, knowing that it was killing any chance he had of defeating Brown. As he stated in his memoirs, they "had to play the dreary drama through to its conclusion."[84]

For Pat, the whole campaign had been a "dreary drama," reinforcing all of her opinions about politics. Once again, the girls suffered through their classmates' barbs about their father.[85] Once again, Pat had to deal with "smears" about her husband, their finances, and their lives. "The hardest part," she told one reporter, was "to hear things you know are not true.... Personal things."[86] From the old stories about Alger Hiss to the controversy about a loan Howard Hughes made to

Dick's brother, Donald, to recent questions about the price they paid for their new house, Pat fumed at the attacks on her husband and her family and gritted her teeth about the invasion of her privacy.[87] Worst of all, new rumors briefly circulated about Pat herself. One member of the Nixon team heard that Barbara Shell, wife of his Republican opponent, was spreading tales of "Pat Nixon's breakdown."[88] And once again, despite Pat's protestations to her husband, she campaigned while her daughters remained at home. Even worse, Dick encouraged the girls to participate actively in the campaign, to give up their time and their privacy to shake hands and smile and pose for pictures.[89]

By the end, they were exhausted, bitter, and angry—again. Nixon unleashed his frustration on the journalists waiting to hear his concession speech. After first refusing to appear before them, he then relented. He conceded defeat, congratulated his opponent, thanked his supporters, and then attacked the press for what he claimed was biased reporting. In his most surprising statement, he told astonished reporters that they would not "have Nixon to kick around anymore" because this was his "last press conference."[90] Although Nixon's display of temper shocked some of his advisors, he claimed in his memoirs that he never regretted the outburst.[91] Observers at the time and historians since have debated Nixon's state of mind. Some argued that he was drunk and out of control; others admitted that he had been drinking but that he was operating with a clear mind.

Pat reacted almost as emotionally as her husband to his losing the campaign. Just as she had in response to the slush fund crisis, the attempt to force Dick off the Eisenhower ticket in 1956, and Dick's 1960 defeat, Pat showed that she would not tolerate others attacking her husband. Julie recalled that Pat "shouted 'Bravo' at the conclusion" of the speech and fully supported his decision to lambaste the press. When he returned home after the concession speech, she and the girls embraced him. Pat was so spent by the loss that Julie claimed that she cried in front of the girls for the first time. In fact, both Nixons were so distraught that the Drowns took the girls to their home for a few days to give their parents time to deal with their emotions.[92]

Perhaps Pat was doubly upset because she recognized that something significant had changed in the Nixon marriage during this period. Certainly the emotional upheaval of committing to two major campaigns and losing them both had taken its toll. The brief period between the two gave them little time to recover either physically or mentally. This was especially difficult for Pat, who did not feed off the excitement of politics the way Dick did. She did not like the campaign trail, but she threw herself into it because she felt it was her duty. She had always been part of the team because she knew that Dick needed her.

More than that, however, she perhaps realized that she had become less important to the team. Obviously, Dick knew how she felt about politics and campaigning, and yet he had chosen to run in the gubernatorial race anyway. She must have finally realized that politics was too much a part of Dick's life for him to ever give it up. There would always be another campaign. Her life with him would always include some election, some connection to the political world—a world she told one acquaintance was filled with "the most vicious people in the world."[93] But Pat had to notice that the makeup of the campaign team had changed. Beginning with the 1956 campaign, Nixon had begun gathering newcomers around him. These young men, including H. R. "Bob" Haldeman, John Ehrlichman, and Ron Ziegler, had less political experience than older members of the team such as Leonard Hall and Robert Finch. They were less likely to stand up to Nixon, more fearful of telling him something was a bad idea, and more inclined to flatter him and follow his lead.[94] Nixon biographers have argued that these men fed Nixon's ambition and fueled some of his demons.[95]

Pat also made a decision around this time. Despite her husband's claim that he had given his "last press conference," she had to wonder whether that could possibly be true. To leave her husband would not have been in her nature, however. She endured; she did not give up. Instead, she may have increased the emotional distance between them. There are countless ways in which a wife can make life miserable for a husband. Yet Pat's decision to focus on her daughters and make the most of her situation was true to her nature. After all, that was what she had done her entire life.

The new phase of their life would begin in New York, not California, because the family agreed it was best they leave the Golden State. Although they loved their new house, they needed a fresh start. New York City offered something for everyone. For Dick, there was a major law firm offering him a six-figure salary and ample free time to continue his traveling and speaking engagements. He joined the newly christened firm of Nixon, Mudge, Rose, Guthrie, and Alexander. For the girls, the city offered the anonymity they longed for after years of being stared at and mocked because of their father. And for Pat, the city took her away from the memories of the 1962 race, put her in the heart of a busy city, and raised her hopes of being out of politics. Nixon's Republican rival, Nelson Rockefeller, was the governor of the state and controlled the party there. She thought she could count on being out of the political world for a time.[96]

The move to New York also gave Pat renewed opportunity to display her interior decorating skills. Pat and Dick flew to New York in March to look for a place to live. After rejecting the suburbs, they found a slightly run-down apartment in the same cooperative that housed Nelson Rockefeller. Dick gave Pat a free hand and an open wallet to do the decorating. She did just that, ordering new furniture and fixtures to complement the treasures they had acquired during their travels. The ironies of Pat's life were certainly apparent during her remodeling. She ordered a gold-plated trap for under the sink, yet still insisted on making the curtains for the girls' bedrooms by hand! She might have come a long way from her days on the truck farms in Artesia, but she was still the same make-do girl underneath.[97] She would continue to add improvements to the apartment over the years. In 1965, when fellow tenant Rockefeller upgraded the air-conditioning/heating unit in his apartment, Pat took advantage of the opportunity to install the same kind of system in the Nixon home.[98]

Before the family settled into their new digs, however, Dick made good on the promise he had first made to Pat back in 1947 during his very first congressional trip: he took the family on a European tour.[99] The Drowns and their daughter, Maureen, joined Pat, Dick, and the girls for a six-week trip that included stops in Rome, Berlin, Madrid, Paris, and Cairo. Being the former vice president of the United States opened many doors in world capitals, and the group visited world leaders as well as museums and palaces. The hectic pace set by three young people kept the adults on the go and opened Dick's eyes to the changes in his daughters. This six-week period was the longest span of unbroken time he had spent with his girls in years.[100] Dick wrote in his memoirs that the "trip was one of the happiest times" of his life in large part because of the time he got to spend with his family.[101]

Pat must have been in heaven. After all, she was traveling with all of

Mr. and Mrs. Nixon, Tricia, and Julie exit a plane in Berlin, Germany, July 1963.
Richard Nixon Presidential Library and Museum.

her family and her dearest friends, and there was no political campaign in sight. Maureen Drown Nunn, who was twenty years old at the time, remembered the trip as "just incredible." They saw "jaw-dropping" sights and enjoyed one another's company. Pat even saved the pope's life, according to Nunn. She explained that on their way to an audience with the pope, her father, Jack Drown, a large man at six foot four and 260 pounds, was walking with Pat when he tripped on a rug and stumbled forward. Pat caught him, prevented an international incident, and gave the party a good laugh.[102]

True to form, the trip was not all play for Dick; he worked almost the entire vacation. World leaders such as French president Charles de Gaulle and Egyptian premier Abdul Gamal Nasser invited him to private meetings. Even Spain's premier, Francisco Franco, with whom Nixon was not previously acquainted, took time out of his schedule to talk with Nixon about world affairs. Although he traveled as a private citizen, these meetings with foreign leaders allowed him to maintain important contacts and keep his name in the news while he built his knowledge base on world affairs.[103] At almost every stop along the way, Nixon held press conferences to discuss his meetings with the various leaders as well as to comment on policies of the Kennedy administration with which he found fault. In particular, he castigated JFK for being too soft on communism in Cuba and Southeast Asia. For Nixon, being a family man in Europe did not mean being out of touch with politics.[104]

The family returned from their trip and settled into a new life. The girls attended the exclusive Chapin School, and Tricia prepared for her debut. Pat continued with her decorating, and Dick began his law practice. Despite the media frenzy following "his last press conference" and the subsequent obituaries for his political career, Dick continued to get calls and letters from supporters urging him to run in 1964. He told everyone he had no plans to run.[105]

Pat either chose to believe him or decided to act as though she did, despite evidence to the contrary. She could not have helped but notice that although he was working very hard at his law practice, he was also spending a great deal of time flying around the country for speaking engagements. His critiques of Kennedy's actions both at home and abroad appeared frequently in the press.[106] She focused instead on getting the girls settled and exploring New York with them.

Kennedy's assassination in Dallas several months after their return from Europe stunned the Nixons. Nixon had been in Dallas himself that November day and witnessed the intensity of the anti-Kennedy feeling engulfing the city. Although he had been speaking out against some of the president's programs, the murder shocked Nixon. He worried that right-wing extremists had been responsible, and that the murder would discredit conservatism in general. His relief at finding out that assassin Lee Harvey Oswald was a communist was coupled with his sympathy for the Kennedy family. He and Pat flew to Washington for the funeral, and he wrote Mrs. Kennedy a sympathetic note.[107] Jackie sent him a nice note in return, urging him to be grateful for "what you already have—your life and your family."[108]

The assassination changed the political climate in the country.[109] Republicans found themselves facing not the incumbent president, but former vice president Lyndon Johnson, a skilled political operative. Utilizing the nation's grief to secure both his own position and his legislative agenda, Johnson acted quickly to win passage of the civil rights bill that had been stalled in committee. In addition, in his first State of the Union address, he declared War on Poverty.[110] Having watched Johnson operate during his long tenure in the Senate, Republicans knew that he would be a formidable opponent in 1964.

The Republican Party that confronted Johnson had other problems. Most importantly, it was divided into quarreling factions. New York governor Nelson Rockefeller and Arizona senator Barry Goldwater fought over the nomination. Rockefeller had the backing of the more liberal and moderate elements within the party, while conservatives built on Goldwater's grassroots network of supporters. Throughout the primary season, the opposing sides waged a vicious battle that left Goldwater a bruised and wounded candidate with only limited support from his party.[111]

For Nixon, the campaign was an exercise in frustration. He had repeatedly declared himself out of the race, but that did not mean that he was not considering all of his options.[112] Although he surveyed the possibility of joining the primary fight, he ultimately decided to hold himself ready to emerge as a compromise choice at a deadlocked convention. He watched in shocked dismay as Goldwater, having won the nomination, declared that "extremism in the defense of liberty is no vice."[113] Recognizing that the Arizona senator had little chance for victory against Johnson, Nixon nevertheless committed to a heavy campaign schedule of stumping for the Republican ticket. He traveled all over the country throughout October, speaking out in support of Goldwater and any other Republican candidate who wanted his help. In this way, he reestablished his credentials among the GOP faithful, earned the gratitude of conservatives across the country, and built a network of supporters for a possible run in 1968.[114]

In fact, as Americans spent the next four years fighting among themselves over Vietnam, civil rights, and a multitude of other issues, Nixon traveled the country voicing opposition to Johnson's policies and laying the foundation for his return to presidential politics.[115] He joined the increasingly large number of Americans concerned about the U.S. role in Southeast Asia.[116] He addressed the mounting frustration of African Americans with the slow nature of substantive change. He acknowledged the discussions taking place on college campuses over Vietnam and race relations.[117] Always advocating equal rights for all minorities and free speech for all viewpoints, Nixon captured the frustration and anger of older middle- and working-class Americans as he lamented the increasing lack of "law and order" in the United States.[118]

And Richard Nixon, who had been politically dead in 1962, mounted yet another resurrection. Without committing to a candidacy, he slowly, cautiously, almost surreptitiously began laying the foundation for his candidacy in 1968. He never said he was running. Instead he just gave speeches and talked to the press and traveled around the world, subtly reminding anyone who read the papers that he was an expert on foreign affairs and that he had a tremendous amount of national political experience. He wanted them to know just in case they should ever need him.[119]

While Dick was running around the country and the world, slowly building his political comeback, Pat was in New York, enjoying her time away from the public eye. She concentrated on her daughters, who were becoming young women. She took them to museums and shops and helped them with their homework. She encouraged them to bring their friends over and laughed with them over silly books and jokes. Tricia, who had gone to three different high schools, chose to attend Finch College in New York City, in part so she would not have to move again.[120] Julie, however, wanted to explore her options. Pat gladly set off on what she described to Helene Drown as a "college safari."[121] When Julie finally decided on Smith, her parents expressed some concern; they had thought a coed school would offer more chances for fun and socializing as well as educational opportunities.[122]

Julie's choice ended up providing her with a lifetime of socializing. During her freshman year, she became reacquainted with Dwight Eisenhower's grandson, David, who happened to be a freshman at nearby Amherst. Their friendship turned into romance.[123] Pat was thrilled with Julie's new beau. She wrote to his grandmother that David was "great in every respect—a refreshing exception in this day of the Beatnik rage." She did hope, however, that they would take their relationship slowly. In the same letter to Mamie Eisenhower, Pat called the youngsters' relationship a "wholesome uncomplicated friendship."[124] Perhaps that was a mother's wishful thinking. By the end of the year, the couple told their families that they planned to get married the following year.

With the girls more and more occupied with their own lives, Pat found other outlets for her energy. She enjoyed visits from her friend Helene but regretted that they were not more frequent. When together, she and Helene shopped, went to plays, laughed, and acted like girls again.[125] They continued to correspond and sometimes talk on the phone about their lives, their kids, and their mutual friends and interests. Helene occasionally offered suggestions for "diversion, relaxation or what-not."[126] Although Pat developed some new friendships in New York, none reached the level of intimacy she shared with Helene. She had never really cared for the social whirl, and, after a brief foray during her first years in the Big Apple, she gave it up. When her friend Carol Finch, wife of Nixon friend and advisor Robert Finch, visited her in New York, Pat admitted her reluctance to act as a typical lawyer's wife. "After you've been in political life," she explained, "at first you try your hand at charity work, but it's not the commitment of politics. You know, I do get restless."[127]

Pat was much more comfortable at work than at play. As a result, she took to helping out at Dick's office, occupying a desk next to Rose Mary Woods, where she would answer the phone as "Miss Ryan," maintaining her anonymity.[128] During the 1964 election, she was "slaving 14 hours a day," answering phones and typing letters. Even in the off year of 1965, the office was "bedlam." She was used to hard work, and, she explained to Helene, it broke "the monotony" and helped "the months and years fly."[129]

Her work in Dick's office raises some interesting questions about her relationship with her husband and his devotion to politics. The story that has been told is that Pat hated politics and everything connected to it and that the couple was estranged by this time. Certainly, Dick made an effort to shield her from some political talk. Kathleen Stans, wife of Nixon aide Maurice Stans, who became a friend of Pat's after the New York move, told Julie that she had received a call "from someone in the Nixon office" asking her not to bring up politics with Pat during one of their first get-togethers.[130] Dick could have been trying to hide his intentions from her, or he could have been trying to protect her from something he knew she disliked. The couple definitely spent a great deal of time apart. In October 1964, he went on a five-week campaign tour for Goldwater and other Republican candidates. He was home for a week and then left for Japan. Even after the election, in February 1965, Pat told Helene that Dick would be home for only two days during the remainder of the month. By the end of the year, Dick was "traveling constantly."[131] Most of the time, Pat stayed home. These facts would seem to confirm the accepted view.

The reality, as always, was more complicated. Pat did take pleasure in some of the perks of her husband's prominence. She evidently enjoyed meeting people such as General Douglas MacArthur and his wife and listening to the general "expound on the candidates, political strategy, revising the defense establishment, etc."[132] She obviously delighted in the opportunity to travel. Pat did choose to engage in politics at times. After all, her good friends the Drowns were "Goldwaterites" who were doing their part "for 'the cause'" in California just as she was in New York.[133] Along with the rest of the Republican Party, she bemoaned Goldwater's defeat in 1964. She clearly understood that Dick was politicking as well as practicing law. She knew that all those "panic-stricken campaigners who want[ed] *help*" called Dick's office because they thought he could save them from impending doom.[134] During the succeeding years, she recognized that his travels were as much for politics as for work.[135] She herself was playing around the edges of the political world. Perhaps without the invasions of her privacy and the infringement on her time with her daughters and the continual attacks on her husband's character, playing at politics around the edges did not seem so bad.

If her attitude toward politics was complicated, her relationship with her husband was truly convoluted. The ardent lover who had wooed Pat with romantic notes and the husband who wrote letters proclaiming how much he missed her when he was away aged into someone much less outwardly demonstrative. But he could still on occasion surprise her with a thoughtful gesture. While he was in California and she was in D.C., he sent flowers and candy for Mother's Day, a common enough present. Pat preferred to think that he had "remembered that she was the big consumer" of candy in the family and had carefully chosen her favorite variety.[136] Dick also occasionally brought her gifts from his travels during these years—for example, pearls from Japan.[137] The couple still conferred about their daughters' educations and boyfriends. In traditional fashion, Pat served as go-between when father and daughter had a misunderstanding.[138]

But there were clearly limits to the relationship. They did, after all, spend weeks at a time away from one another. Interestingly, Pat either chose not to go or was not invited on her husband's many travels. That Dick recognized Pat's withdrawal was apparent during a talk he had with Julie about Pat in January 1966. They agreed, Julie wrote in her biography of her mother, that Pat "needed something to do." Julie recorded in her diary that her father told her "that we all have to contribute and try if we want to be happy." Perhaps a bit of his frustration with his wife's reluctance to participate in his recent political activities seeped through as he told Julie that "you must learn to accept things as they are and forge ahead." When he and Pat disagreed and she froze him out earlier in their marriage, he had relied on his mother to smooth things out. Unfortunately, his mother had a stroke in 1965 from which she never completely recovered. She spent her last two years in a nursing home.[139] Maybe he was hoping Julie could take over the role of mediator. In any case, Dick's conversation with Julie made two things clear: he did not know how to talk to his wife about their estrangement, and he wanted her to accept his decision to continue to be politically active.

Pat also struggled with the tensions in their relationship. She worried aloud to the girls in 1966 that she was "a failure" to Dick.[140] She did apparently make an effort to include him in her life. When Helene offered suggestions, Pat thanked her for the advice but explained that "Dick keeps scheduled up to the ears so there is no possibility of 'involvement' for such frivolous activities."[141] As it became increasingly apparent that Dick was going to run again in 1968, Pat turned to her friend for advice and support. During a three-week stay with the Drowns in California in August 1967, Pat and Helene discussed her situation. Pat complained that she preferred to remain a private citizen, to live like everyone else. Helene, with the advantage of long years of friendship, pointed out that Pat had always sought something more than a quiet life in Whittier. When Julie questioned Helene years later about her willingness to push her friend into campaigning again, Helene explained that she thought "that Pat still had a deep belief in your father's unique talent."[142] The Drowns had always been supporters of Dick and hoped that this time he would win the prize.

Although Dick had been laying the foundation for a presidential run for almost four years, his family still had to make a formal decision to participate. Following the normal pattern, Dick decided at the last minute, Christmas 1967, that he would not be a candidate. He called the girls in and told them his "decision." They, of course, responded that he had to "meet the challenge." Pat, according to Julie, "could not bring herself to urge him to run," but agreed to support him if he "felt he had to make the race." With their backing, he went off by himself for awhile. When he returned in January, he announced that he had concluded that he should run. Julie wrote in her diary that her mother was "still opposed" but had become "reconciled" to the inevitable.[143]

When Nixon announced his candidacy at the end of January, Pat resumed her role as consummate candidate's wife, smiling, silent, and supportive. As she had in 1960, she spent most of the campaign by her husband's side, smilingly listening to the same speech again and again. She worked as hard as ever despite her initial reluctance and the fact that she was eight years older than she had been in 1960.[144] According to some accounts, however, Pat insisted that Dick not work quite as hard as he had in 1960. She forced him to take some time off each week. He went along with her demand in hopes of avoiding some of the mistakes of the 1960 campaign when the strain of continual campaigning had taken a toll on his health, appearance, and temperament.[145]

Once again, Pat proved a valuable asset to Dick on the campaign trail. She showed her usual incredible stamina, lasting all day, one reporter noted, on two cups of coffee and a soft drink. Another reporter claimed that she learned Pat had eaten nothing the day before "but a sandwich at 2 P.M."[146] She shook thousands of hands and accepted hundreds of bouquets of flowers. She stayed away from giving political speeches, instead telling stories from her childhood that reminded voters that her struggles epitomized the American dream. She returned to her mantra of her self-control.[147]

Her image, however, played a more important role in his success than her endurance. Just as she had in 1960, Pat epitomized the loving, loyal wife. She accompanied her husband all over the country, from small towns to big cities. She sat on stages and platforms listening to him give virtually the same speech again and again, nodding appreciatively and laughing at all the appropriate spots. And she would tell reporters with a straight face that "Dick never gives the same speech twice" because he always added something new.[148] In 1968, however, some journalists discovered a "new" Pat Nixon who embodied all the old qualities, but with the added bonus of years of experience. *Washington Post* writer Marie Smith found "a new sophistication . . . a confident sparkle in her . . . eyes" and a "more self-assured poise and composure" than she exhibited during earlier campaigns. Even constituents noted that "her manner [was] more lighthearted" than it had been eight years earlier.[149] This new relaxed appearance helped her carry out her main role in the campaign: softening the image of her husband and transforming him from, as one reporter put it, "a hard-driving husband" into a "warm, human family man."[150] In order to accomplish that feat, Nixon needed her to be by his side, showing her belief in him.

That kind of old-fashioned wifely devotion drove her critics crazy and her supporters wild. Just as they had in 1960, some reporters found her self-control maddening. *Washington Post* writer Mary Wiegers, who followed Pat throughout the campaign, marveled at her capacity to ignore distractions, whether they be hecklers or popping balloons, when she was on the platform with her husband. *New York Times* reporter Tom Wicker wrote of her ability to sit through speeches she had heard numerous times "with an only slightly glazed expression of awe and admiration." Others described her look as a "frozen expression."[151]

Mr. and Mrs. Nixon campaigning in Chicago, 1968. National Archives and Records Administration.

Although some commentators obviously characterized the happy home scenario as "calculated," the people who came out for the Nixon rallies ate it up.[152] They longed for that old-fashioned family unit with its authoritative father figure, with a devoted, loving wife by his side. Once more, Pat met beautifully the needs of Nixon's campaign.[153]

Although on the surface Pat's behavior mirrored her actions in the earlier presidential race, there were significant differences. First, Pat subtly distanced herself from the campaign. Whereas in 1960 she described herself as part of the team, in 1968, she described herself as a volunteer in the campaign.[154] In 1960, she had urged political couples to discuss their career choice together because they would both need to be involved in the effort.[155] By 1968, however, she was emphasizing that politics was Dick's career, not hers. She indicated that she had no role in his choice. In fact, she told a reporter for *Good Housekeeping* that she believed that "a man has a right to make his own decision about his career. A woman should support that decision."[156] Rather than an active participant, she seemed a reluctant passenger on the Nixon express.

Second, in contrast to Julie's assessment that her mother acted with even more reticence than usual, Pat occasionally allowed her personality to slip through her carefully erected public facade. When demonstrators (whom she called "SDS goons") confronted her during one campaign stop, Pat "bopped" one on the head with her bouquet. She did not intend, she told one of her companions, to "let him push me around."[157] Another time, she joked that she had been drinking "Romney's olive oil," a reference to Michigan governor George Romney's quip about why his hair was darker than it had been.[158] In one of her more telling remarks, she told a reporter that "in every game one person wins and one person loses. But the main thing is not to drop out." Although she was referring to her husband's political career, she could have been talking about her own life. She had certainly lost on more than one occasion, but she drew her strength from the fact that she did not drop out.[159]

Her most famous slip occurred during an interview with Gloria Steinem. Pat spent the first part of the session feeding Steinem her standard campaign answers. When the reporter persisted in asking more probing questions about her, Pat decided to give her a piece of her mind. In what Steinem recorded as a controlled but "resentful" tone, Pat chastised the "people who had it easy." She had never had the time to think about who she wanted to be or what she wanted to do; she had always had to work. She implied that she was still working while others were too busy asking foolish questions. Steinem came away from the interview with a new understanding of Pat and her relationship with her husband.[160]

Third, breaking with her usual pattern of never discussing campaign issues, Pat occasionally weighed in on some of the key topics of the day. Sometimes a small comment tacked on the end of a conventional statement would reveal something of her personality. In response to the riots at Columbia University, she spoke "with obvious feeling" about "these people [who] think the world owes them a living." As someone who had worked her way through college, Pat had little sympathy for what she perceived to be privileged students who did not appreciate what they had been given.[161] Pat's most consistently unscripted words exposed her support for what she called "woman power." Her desire to see a woman in the Cabinet and on the Supreme Court would be a persistent problem for her husband during his administration. He did not share her belief that a female judge would "pep up" the highest court in the land.[162]

The transformation of Pat's campaign habits perhaps reflected major changes that had occurred since the previous campaigns. Unlike during the earlier races, Tricia and Julie were old enough to be active participants in this one. They, along with Julie's fiancé, David Eisenhower, traveled all over the country, frequently meeting with groups of young people. Pat must have had mixed feelings about this development. On the one hand, she tremendously enjoyed her time with the girls. She told one reporter that it was "like a holiday" to be able to travel with her daughters and David.[163] On the other hand, she had always tried to protect the girls from the rigors of campaigning. It might have been hard to let go of that, even though the girls were twenty-one and nineteen.[164]

Key personnel changes in the campaign staff certainly affected Pat's behavior in 1968 and increased her desire to distance herself from the campaign. In June, H. R. "Bob" Haldeman joined the campaign staff on a full-time basis. Haldeman had worked for Nixon in both 1956 and 1960, serving as campaign manager in 1962. Haldeman's background in marketing brought a new philosophy to the campaign. He also, according to Julie, transformed the atmosphere at Nixon headquarters. A serious man who rigidly controlled all aspects of the campaign, Haldeman took the "fun" away for many of the old-timers. Julie also believed that he "underestimated" Pat's value to the campaign and implied that he escalated tensions between her parents.[165]

The divisions between the Nixons and within the Nixon staff mirrored the fissures erupting across America. People had worried in 1960 about the nation's perceived lack of direction; in 1968, people seemed to be moving in too many different directions, threatening national consensus. Nineteen sixty-eight was a year of almost continual upheaval as one crisis after another erupted. In January, the North Vietnamese mounted the Tet Offensive, which forced the Johnson administration to admit that the war in Vietnam was far from won. Just a little over a month later, in early March, Wisconsin senator Eugene McCarthy made a surprisingly strong showing in the Democratic primary, contributing to President Johnson's decision not to seek reelection. Five days later, James Earl Ray assassinated civil rights leader Martin Luther King Jr. in Memphis, Tennessee. Riots broke out all over the country and tanks surrounded the White House. In the meantime, throughout the spring semester, college campuses erupted with protests, with a major demonstration at Columbia University in New York shutting down the campus. After the California primary in early

June, Sirhan Sirhan gunned down Democratic candidate Robert Kennedy as he gave his victory speech.

Nixon won his party's nomination in July at a convention plagued by heat and last-minute concerns about challenges from the party's left (Nelson Rockefeller) and the party's right (Ronald Reagan). Hubert Humphrey won the Democratic nomination inside the convention center in Chicago, while outside, the police clubbed demonstrators in full view of the television cameras. Segregationist and former Alabama governor George Wallace's decision to throw his hat in the ring complicated the presidential race for both parties. By the time of the election in November, the American people were praying to make it to the end of the year in one piece.

Nixon spent the year promising to end the war in Vietnam honorably and to deal with the lawlessness at home harshly. Without giving any specifics as to his proposed method for dealing with the situation in Southeast Asia, Nixon continually pledged to "end the war and win the peace."[166] He stated unequivocally that his response to the "perpetrators of violence" in the cities and on college campuses would be "swift and sure." Echoing the fears of many Americans of all races and classes, Nixon spoke of the need to restore order to urban areas.[167] His appeal to what he would later characterize as the "silent majority" of Americans resonated, and the crowds attending his campaign stops grew accordingly.

His opponents did not give up without a fight. Wallace made a surprisingly strong showing in the late summer and early fall. He began to lose momentum, however, by fall as unions organized against him, and misstatements by some of his supporters undermined his viability. Meanwhile, Humphrey won the support of many on the left when he tried to distance himself from LBJ's policies on Vietnam. He also benefited from the president's last-minute announcement of peace talks. When South Vietnamese president Thieu refused to support the talks, based in part on Nixon's campaign statements, Humphrey's campaign suffered.[168]

In the end, however, Nixon's 1968 strategy worked. Following Haldeman's advice, he limited his campaign travel and carefully controlled his media appearances. In short, he packaged himself more effectively in 1968 than he had in 1960.[169] Still, the vote was closer than he would have liked. Once again, he spent a long night waiting for and watching the results.[170] Tellingly, Pat and the girls did not spend the evening with him. He waited out the returns with Haldeman and John Mitchell, his campaign manager and soon-to-be attorney general.[171]

Two presidential races, two different results. Ironically, the victory could not have been as sweet in 1968 as it would have been in 1960 for Pat. Then, she had been part of the team; the dream had been hers as well as his. That loss had taken something out of her. The experiences of the intervening years, as well as changes in her relationship with her husband and his career, meant that winning the presidential election was no longer her prize as well as Dick's. She might even have felt that she had been shut out. Pat was never one to give up without a fight, however. Just because she was not part of the big boys' team did not mean that she would not stand with her husband for what they believed in. She may not have chosen this life, but she intended to make the most of it.

CHAPTER 4

BECOMING FIRST LADY

Pat's years as first lady were hard. Issues she had struggled with throughout her husband's career intensified during her five and a half years in office. She had less privacy, a more hectic schedule, and more pressure to be "on" all the time. The American people, caught up in the whirlwind of socioeconomic and political changes of the previous years, looked to the presidential family for guidance in navigating the stormy seas or as symbols of the evils that still existed. Pat had learned about being first lady by watching Mamie Eisenhower, but that model seemed hopelessly outdated to many Americans. Pat had to find a way to please both those Americans who longed for the good old days as well as those who supported the emerging women's liberation movement. Additionally, she had to work constantly to maintain a relationship with her husband and to protect the integrity of the position of first lady.

As she had in the past, when confronted by a challenging situation, Pat Nixon tried to make the best of her years as first lady. She would not have sought out the job on her own, but she had vowed to support her husband in his quest for the presidency, so she accepted the consequences of that decision. Moreover, she had learned a thing or two over the years about politics and she was determined to use her role of first lady to accomplish some of her own goals. She continued her traveling; she found ways to showcase the little people as well as the big shots; and she was able to utilize her decorating abilities for a good cause. Her family, especially her daughters, continued to be her priority. Although they were growing up, they remained close to her. Their weddings were public affairs because they were the first daughters, but Pat found ways to make them personal and intimate. After years of fighting to get to the White House, the Nixons had made it.

Before they moved into the White House, however, the Nixons had some family business to take care of: Julie's wedding. Julie and David Eisenhower became engaged in November 1967 and originally planned to marry during the summer of 1968. Julie's father's presidential campaign changed the timing. A wedding, no matter how small, would seem too much like a publicity stunt.[1] So they agreed to postpone their plans until after November 1968.

Pat had mixed feelings about the nuptials. Although she thought the world of David, Pat wished that the couple would wait to get married. She worried that they were too young, that they were going to be the only married couple on their college campuses, and that they would be missing out on opportunities for fun and adventure.[2] But Pat trusted her daughter, swallowed her concerns, and dove headlong into wedding plans. Consequently, even as she flew across the country campaigning for her husband, she was working with Julie to plan the wedding.[3]

With Pat's encouragement, Julie and David made every effort to keep their wedding as intimate and personal as possible despite all the media attention and political pressures. They settled on 22 December as the wedding date but kept it secret until after the presidential race had been decided.[4] Proving that she could be just as stubborn as her parents, Julie refused to heed her father's suggestion that she delay the ceremony until after the inauguration so that she could be married in the White House. She insisted that she and David wanted to be married in a church, and she got her way.[5] They chose Dr. Norman Vincent Peale's Marble Collegiate Church in New York City, which the couple had attended on numerous occasions. They worked hard to prevent the guest list from turning into just a political who's who of Washington, inviting college chums, relatives, and longtime family friends as well as a select list of government officials. As a result, Uncle Don Nixon, Jack and Helene Drown and their children, and "Uncle" Bebe Rebozo joined former Nixon rival George Romney, vice president–

elect Spiro Agnew, and Thomas Dewey in the pews to listen as Dr. Peale united the couple in wedlock.[6] Two of the most famous guests were absent. David's grandparents, Dwight and Mamie Eisenhower, listened to the ceremony on a special closed-circuit monitor set up in their hospital rooms. Ike was too ill to leave the hospital, and Mamie did not want to leave his side.[7] The young couple did succeed in preventing the press from covering the ceremony itself, but could not keep the media from reporting numerous details about the nuptials.[8]

After the ceremony, during which Julie did not promise to obey David, the guests traveled by bus to a reception at the Plaza Hotel to continue the festivities. The church, the hotel, and even the city streets glittered with holiday decorations, adding to the merry tone of the day. The father of the bride, who reported in his memoirs that he teared up when Julie kissed him on the cheek as he gave her away, danced with the bride at the reception despite a slight case of the flu. It was a joyous day for the whole family.[9]

A month after the wedding, Dick took the oath of office on a cold, cloudy day as Pat held the same Milhous family Bibles she had held in 1953 and 1957. Along with the rest of America, she listened as Dick delivered his relatively short inaugural address. Acknowledging the divisions within the country and the unrest around the world, Dick called upon Americans to answer the "summons to greatness." He drew attention to the technological achievements in space even as he discussed the numerous hostilities around the world. He invited everyone to participate in the "high adventure" of trying to establish peace among the American peoples and across the nations.[10] Perhaps as Pat listened to the speech, she heard echoes of the man she had loved and supported throughout the years; perhaps it took her back to a time when they had worked to achieve such goals together. But she was not a member of the team now; she was a bystander, an observer, a supporting player with very specific responsibilities.

Those responsibilities did not include dealing with the challenging political problems facing her husband. From an unpopular war in Southeast Asia to the continuing chill of relations with the Soviet Union to an increasingly unstable Middle East, the man who prided himself on his knowledge of geopolitics confronted a world of problems. With the assistance of Henry Kissinger, former Harvard professor and advisor to Nelson Rockefeller, as his national security advisor,

Nixon ran foreign policy from the White House, frequently bypassing his secretary of state. The new president had implied at various times during the campaign that he had a plan to end the hostilities in Vietnam. Once in office, however, he struggled to find a way to extricate American troops without abandoning his South Vietnamese allies. The long-running conflict in Southeast Asia had also undermined trust in Americans' motives among developing countries around the world. Nixon had to contend with governments throughout Central and South America as well as in Africa that questioned American interference and threatened American business interests. The growing tensions between the Israelis and their Arab neighbors forced him to recognize the price of Americans' dependence on the oil-producing world. The cold war continued to color Nixon's worldview and permeate all foreign policy decisions.[11]

The situation within the country was no less volatile. African Americans, frustrated by the stalling of the civil rights movement as it moved into the North and the West, pushed for continued advances in economic and educational opportunities. Meanwhile, other minority groups followed the pattern set by the African American movement and began to demand social and economic equality. Women of all races and classes joined the struggle, challenging the very structure of family life. Long-haired young people seemed to be everywhere, protesting the war, demanding rights, ignoring social norms and parental authority. The economy, overheated by the military and social spending of the Johnson years as well as the consumer spending of the postwar decades, caused additional concerns. The resulting inflation undermined the earnings of many middle- and working-class Americans. In particular, white working-class men, feeling attacked by all sides, pushed back against the protest movements that threatened their worldview. It was this latter group that Nixon called the "silent majority" and upon whom he counted for support.[12]

While Dick confronted these foreign and domestic problems, he expected Pat to follow her normal pattern of traveling with him when he needed her to, acting as hostess at official functions, and carrying out her responsibilities as first lady. He and his staff felt free to call on Pat for photo opportunities or when a cause arose that needed a woman's touch. Dick expected that she would develop a first lady project, but one of his and his staff's choosing. The rest of the time, she should occupy herself with her normal duties of running the domestic side of his life.

As ever, one of Pat's first jobs was to move the family into their new home, now located at 1600 Pennsylvania Avenue. Because of her frequent visits to the White House as second lady, she had some idea of the facilities available in its family quarters. Not long after the election, she and Dick had met with President and Mrs. Johnson to begin the transition process. Lady Bird Johnson knew Pat from their years together in the Senate Ladies' Club and was "touched" by Pat's graciousness during their meeting.[13] Pat, sometimes accompanied by one of the girls, returned several times before the inauguration to check out spaces and to begin to make furniture selections. Like a number of other first couples, the Nixons required separate bedrooms. Pat told J. B. West, the head usher, that "*Nobody* could sleep with Dick" because he was too restless.[14] Because Pat had let Julie take some of the family's furniture to furnish her little apartment with David, Pat utilized the White House warehouse to fill in the gaps in the family living quarters. In addition to decorating the first couple's bedrooms, Pat had to furnish the rest of the rooms of the private areas. Dick also relied on Pat to help him outfit the Oval Office and a smaller hideaway office in the Executive Office Building.[15]

At the same time that Pat was making the White House hospitable for her family and a showplace for the public, she also had to decorate the newly christened La Casa Pacifica, which the Nixons purchased in San Clemente, California, as well as two small houses on Biscayne Bay in Florida. Furnishing the Spanish-style California home, which would become the western White House and the vacation houses in the Keys, added to Pat's already crowded schedule but also promised calm respites from the pressures of her new job and more privacy.[16]

As she set about settling her family into their new home, she discovered that even decorating decisions in the White House were political. The removal of the mantelpiece in her bedroom set off a small firestorm. The existing mantel had been placed there during the Truman renovations in 1951. The mantel featured a plaque stating that Abraham Lincoln had slept in the room. Before Jackie Kennedy moved out, she added another plaque inscribed, "In this room John Fitzgerald Kennedy lived with his wife Jacqueline during the two years, ten months, and two days he was President of the United States." In 1968,

the Committee for the Preservation of the White House and first lady
Lady Bird Johnson obtained a mantelpiece from a house designed by
Benjamin Latrobe, one of the architects of the White House. Believing
that this new piece was a better fit for the room, they ordered the old
one be removed to storage. The transfer did not take place until early
1969. Without knowing the backstory, some people jumped to the conclusion that Pat was attempting to remove all traces of the Kennedys.
According to Julie, at least one Washington paper accused Pat of trying
to erase history by removing traces of the Kennedys from the White
House.[17] Evidently, the ghosts of the Kennedys that Lady Bird noticed
during her years in the White House lingered into the Nixon years.[18]

In fact, although Pat had to deal with the legacies of all of her predecessors as first lady, the examples of Jackie and Lady Bird were most
prominent. Some earlier first ladies, such as Bess Truman and Mamie
Eisenhower, had just taken care of their husbands while serving as
hostesses and symbols of American motherhood. Their impact on the
political actions of their husbands and on the country happened behind the scenes, hidden from public view. Other first ladies had taken
on more public roles. Edith Wilson controlled access to her ailing husband, thus influencing decisions he made, and Eleanor Roosevelt
served as her husband's eyes and ears on various occasions. Pat's two
immediate predecessors, Jacqueline Kennedy and Lady Bird Johnson,
had each become identified with a particular cause: Kennedy began
one of the first modern restorations of the White House; Johnson lob-
bied for various environmental issues, concentrating on highway
beautification. Press speculation about Pat's project began before the
inauguration and continued in the months following 20 January.[19]

Pat's responses to questions about her project contained hints as to
her plan for dealing with the role in which she found herself. Ever the
professional politician's wife, she told reporters that she just wanted to
"assist" her husband in "what he wants to do." This was the kind of answer she had been giving for years, the kind of answer that had earned
her the "plastic Pat" label. Glimpses of a more independent, more determined Pat were evident, however, even in those early days. The same
reporter who recorded Pat's insistence that she merely wanted to "assist" her husband also noted that "there are those who see a gentle Pat
Nixon nudge behind the invitation to the Cabinet wives to sit in on the
first meeting of the Nixon Cabinet."[20] On her first day on the job, she

told a group of Republican campaign workers that they were all invited back. "We're going to have our friends here," she stated, "instead of all the bigshots!" Her first press secretary, Gerry Van der Heuvel, and the president both thought the remark inappropriate.[21] Obviously, she intended to do what was required of her, to play the role she had perfected of the dutiful, loyal, submissive wife. Dick and his staff would have a hand in making some decisions about how her time was spent. At the same time, however, she planned to use the skills she had learned and the tricks she had observed over the years to put forward an agenda that she thought was important. Rather than engage in grand gestures, she intended to use her time as first lady to serve and recognize ordinary people, particularly those who worked hard.

"Voluntarism," the catchall name for Pat's project, served several goals. It fit in well with the Nixon administration's courting of "middle America." It mirrored Nixon's centrist policies with its conservative emphasis on individual, rather than government, initiative and its liberal recognition of the needs of the elderly, young, or disadvantaged.[22] Additionally, it was a noncontroversial way to appeal to women because volunteering was a traditionally feminine way of going beyond housework without challenging the existing power structure.

For the administration, the first lady's visits to volunteer facilities provided the added bonus of wonderful photo opportunities for the press. For an administration that seemed constantly at war with the media, Pat's trips to schools for the blind, hospitals, and community gardens were a gold mine. In October 1969, John Ehrlichman congratulated Pat on the media reaction to a day care center visit: "The CBS lady reporter . . . nearly exhausted her vocabulary of laudatory words." Pat, noted Ehrlichman, won "the most favorable coverage of anyone associated with the Administration . . . in weeks."[23] As a result, Nixon and his aides sought more opportunities to send Pat out among volunteers throughout his presidency.[24] Over the years, even as the president's poll numbers fell, his staff noted that Pat's press clippings continued to be favorable.[25]

Volunteerism also worked for Pat. Despite the fact that it seemed straight out of the political wife handbook, such work flowed naturally from her background. Volunteering suited her belief, as she told one interviewer, that "a person is what he does."[26] Pat had worked hard since her childhood, and she had little patience for people who did not

understand the value of hard work. As second lady, she once told Helene Drown that she would rather work than go to all the teas, dinners,
and parties required of her. When she was a child, she had belonged to
the Campfire Girls and enjoyed assisting the elderly in her neighborhood; when her daughters were young, she helped out at their schools;
when the family lived in New York, she worked for Goldwater's election. During all her stints working on Dick's campaigns, she had never
been paid. Pat was not exaggerating when she told reporters that she
had been a volunteer all her life and "intended to continue."[27] Not surprisingly, then, she choose a first lady project that required and re-
warded individual effort. On her first solo tour, she told an audience
that she "really wanted to work." She did not "want to just lend [her]
name."[28] She intended to encourage people, and especially women, "to
become involved in programs designed to enrich the quality of life for
all." Pat pledged to do "all I can, with all I have, wherever I am."[29]

Showcasing volunteerism also allowed Pat to escape the big shots in
Washington and draw attention to the everyday people across the nation. She told her staff to make certain that her first tour was a working
trip, not a political one. She did not want to be greeted by local, state,
or federal officials with dozens of roses. Consequently, reporters commented with surprise that Nixon's staff had arranged that "no dignitaries [be] massed to greet" the first lady at the airports or hotels. She
grew impatient when local politicians or CEOs took up her time explaining their many successes. She wanted to see how the people were
being helped or visit with volunteers doing the actual work. Even skeptical reporters noted that Pat's plastic shell fell away when she inter-
acted with volunteers and the people they were serving.[30]

Pat's support for volunteerism manifested itself in numerous ways.
In addition to her tours of facilities, which drew national publicity to
various projects, Pat also hosted volunteers at the White House. On occasion, she volunteered her own services. In July 1969, for example, she
hosted a cruise on the Potomac for two dozen Washington schoolchildren as part of the Summer in the Parks program.[31] Her staff
worked diligently to find varied, interesting, and worthy causes for Pat
to visit and support from the multitude of groups soliciting her attention and support. Organizations such as the Institute of LifeTime
Learning or National Retired Teachers wrote to the first lady, hoping to

persuade her to visit their facilities, speak to their membership, or lend her name to their cause.[32]

Despite the politically noncontroversial nature of voluntarism, Pat did address politics, but in an upbeat way. For example, in March 1970, Pat visited college student volunteers in five states to celebrate what she called "protesting in a positive fashion." She met with young people from Michigan State University and the universities of Kentucky, Cincinnati, and Colorado at sites where they volunteered. After witnessing volunteers in action, Pat met with "selected leaders of the local volunteer movement" for informal " 'brainpicking' sessions" at the end of each day.[33]

On virtually all of her tours, Pat won over the public and most reporters with her sincerity and warmth. One young man, claiming that she reminded him of his mother, surprised her with a kiss on the cheek. Reporters noted that even young people wearing peace buttons seemed "to hit it off perfectly" with the first lady.[34] After meeting with her, many of those who were "skeptical" about her changed their opinions and acknowledged her sincerity.[35] Jim Tanck, who worked for the Office of Economic Opportunity, told Connie Stuart, Pat's press secretary, that many of the young volunteers that Pat met on tour "felt a genuine rapport with Mrs. Nixon. Many referred to her as 'relevant' or 'real.' "[36] Reporter Marie Smith, who recognized that the first lady's staff had carefully planned the trip to avoid "confrontations with militant student" protesters, nevertheless applauded Pat's efforts to communicate with the younger generation, and noted her growing ease with the press.[37]

Such remarks were high praise, especially considering the amount of hostility many young people felt for the establishment in general and the Nixon administration in particular. Growing out of the civil rights movement of the 1950s, fed by the boomer babies reaching college age during the 1960s, and galvanized by the Vietnam war, the student movement had been shocking the older generation for almost half a decade by the time Nixon took office. Politicized students protested against racism, paternalistic university regulations, and the limits of liberal reform. Their anger and frustration with the continuation of the war in Vietnam exploded regularly on major college and university campuses, sometimes forcing administrators to cancel classes. Their rejection of the older generation extended to social mores as well. Young people understood that blue jeans, long hair, rock and roll, and casual drug use upset their parents almost as much, if not more, than their views on the war. Nixon's failure to end the war quickly increased the tensions on college campuses.[38]

Why, then, did Pat make her college tours? The president, according to one aide, did not want her or the girls "to get involved with [the] student situation."[39] Moreover, although the tour was carefully orchestrated to protect her from demonstrations (she did not stop at any campus with the potential for negative student activism, only visiting the small, conservative School of the Ozarks), she still encountered a few protesters at several locations. In preparation for trouble, the administration sent along a large security contingent.[40]

There were plenty of other volunteer groups to visit; why did Pat enter the lion's den? Her close relationship with her daughters convinced her that she could communicate with young people more effectively than anyone else in the administration. She seemed less shocked by the new hair and clothing styles than others of her generation.[41] She had commented at the end of the tour that it was "refreshing" to be surrounded by so many young people. She certainly succeeded in relating well to the students she met. Gratified to know "that I'm not as old as I seem," she bragged that she had experienced no "generation gap."[42]

The president's staff may have recognized that Pat's college tours were a good way to gain some favorable publicity and ease tensions with student leaders. Because Dick did not want Pat exposed to protesters, perhaps a member of Pat's staff pushed the idea as a way to utilize her skills to help the administration. After Pat returned from the first trip, Connie Stuart contacted Haldeman about following up the tour in order "to capitalize on its success." She wanted the president to invite the kids to the White House for lunch.[43] That idea was rejected.

Pat apparently wanted to do the tour. It was a project made for her: meeting young people, working hard, trying to help others. These were causes she believed in strongly. That might explain why Pat told some of the students she met that she wanted them to visit her in the White House. Perhaps she related to their frustration. In a press conference in Denver, Pat reiterated the invitation, explaining that she had "no influence" at "the high level."[44]

Her commitment to the young volunteers did not withstand the tensions of the times. When her invitation to the students resurfaced in April 1970, Pat rejected the idea of bringing eleven of the students to D.C. because she thought it would "cost too much money." Even when Connie Stuart suggested having the Center for Voluntary Action cover the costs, she refused to go along with it. According to Connie, Pat said that she did not "feel the kids were worth the money."[45] Even taking into account Pat's frugality, the remark seems out of character. Pressure from the West Wing might explain the turnaround, or perhaps her trust in the young people's sincerity might have been shaken by the escalation of violence on college campuses across the country. Throughout the month of March and into April, student demonstrators turned up the pressure by bombing buildings to protest the continuation of the war.[46]

The violence culminated in tragedy at Kent State and Jackson State in early May 1970. Responding to Nixon's announcement of the U.S. invasion of Cambodia, student protests erupted on campuses across the country. In Kent, Ohio, national guardsmen shot at rioting students and killed four students. A sympathy demonstration in Jackson, Mississippi, ended in tragedy when law enforcement officers turned their guns on the protesters, resulting in two more deaths. The response of Americans of different ages and backgrounds to the student deaths revealed how divided the country was. While some reacted in horror to the government killing their own young people, others applauded the officials for finally taking action against the protesters.[47]

The fact that the killings at Jackson State University, a predominantly black college, garnered far less publicity than those at Kent State University, a predominantly white college, reinforced the belief of many African Americans that the civil rights movement did not go far enough. After the progress of the early 1960s with the passage of the Civil Rights and Voting Rights Acts, the movement had stalled. Destroying Jim Crow laws in the South had been easy compared to breaking down economic and educational barriers around the entire country. As African Americans struggled to find ways to overcome those obstacles, white Americans, especially working-class men and women facing hard economic times, resented what they perceived to be continual handouts to blacks.[48]

Nixon, determined to hold onto his Southern constituency, tried to appease the African American community without alienating his white constituents who wanted to slow desegregation. Ironically, although Nixon appointed judges sympathetic to white Southern sensibilities and developed a quota system of affirmative action that undermined black employment gains, his administration actually increased school desegregation.[49]

Pat's staff tried to connect her to this effort by encouraging her to lend support to the Postal Academy Program. Intended to educate high school dropouts from urban areas, the Postal Academy promised to help its graduates get jobs. Pat first visited one of the facilities in September 1970 and "expressed her interest in the Program." Less than six months later, however, her staff was scrambling to dissociate her from what some officials within the administration characterized as a troubled program plagued by internal dissension and rumors of radicalism among its student population.[50] Internal disagreement about the Postal Academy's successes and failures epitomized larger misunderstandings within American society about race. These "street academies" succeeded in teaching young African Americans from the ghettoes, many of whom were dropouts from the public school system, by using tactics that frightened members of the older generation. In more informal settings, black history books, street games, and "rap sessions" were used. Teachers did not recite the Pledge of Allegiance or sing "The Star-Spangled Banner." Such practices convinced some leaders within the Postal Service, which sponsored the academies, that they were "training ground for dissidents, malcontents, anti-white, anti-establishment types."[51] Caught between these voices, Pat's staff wondered what "their objective" was in participating. Their honest answer was to "win the black vote" as well as recognizing an "outstanding program."[52]

Most of Pat's projects focused on far less controversial issues. In addition to continuing to honor volunteers, Pat also lent her name and prestige to various efforts to clean up the environment. Working to steer clear of beautification, which had been Lady Bird's project, Pat's staff looked for projects that emphasized ordinary Americans' opportunities to clean up their surroundings. In late 1969, Pat observed that the river outside her home, the Potomac, needed attention. Her staff jumped on the chance to find ways to build on her "sincere interest" in environmental awareness.[53] As a result for the next few years, Pat participated in the Legacy of Parks program, which transferred public

Mrs. Nixon greets visitors to the White House, December 1969. Richard Nixon Presidential Library and Museum.

lands to communities to turn into recreational areas for local children. She also lent her prestige to commemoration of national historic sites.[54]

Pat also worked to make the White House more accessible to different kinds of people. Recognizing that many citizens who lived near the White House had never visited the president's house, Pat insisted on holding special hours every month for such tours. She also arranged special tours for the blind during which they were allowed to touch furniture and feel the wallpaper and the draperies. Similarly, she insisted on sign language interpreters for the deaf. Upset that the White House did not stand out in the evening skyline, she convinced the proper authorities to turn the lights on in the evening.[55]

Pat made a similar effort to make better use of the presidential yacht, the *Sequoia*. Discovering that it spent much of its time sitting in the harbor, she suggested "it would be fun to share the boat." Consequently, in 1969, she created a biweekly cruise for local children, hosted by a rotating group of Cabinet wives. She served as its first hostess, and according to reporters, she enjoyed the cruise "as much as the youngsters."[56]

Pat also left her mark on the interior of the White House. Jacqueline Kennedy had begun restoration of some of its rooms during her husband's tenure as president. Mrs. Kennedy led a nationally televised tour of the White House and explained the need to redecorate, restore, and refurbish many of its rooms. When Pat arrived eight years later, she was determined to continue and expand on her work. Millions of visitors walking through the White House had taken a toll on everything from wall coverings to furniture. By the middle of her second year as first lady, Pat was ready to address the need. She persuaded Clement Conger, deputy chief of protocol and curator for the State Department, to work with her and the Committee for the Preservation of the White House to restore many of the public rooms. Repainting, repairing, and restoring floors and furniture were scheduled, and the two began an intensive search for appropriate furnishings and artwork. An aggressive campaign to seek donors to fund these purchases was launched. Working together, Conger and Pat turned the White House into a first-class museum. Pat even succeeded in convincing the Pennsylvania Academy of Fine Arts to allow the White House to display the Gilbert Stuart portrait of Dolley Madison that had hung in the White House before the British burned it down in 1814.[57] Other portraits by Stuart as well as rare porcelain used by presidents Monroe and Madison and a Regency-period chandelier were displayed in newly refurbished rooms. Years later, when Jacqueline Kennedy Onassis returned to the White House for the first time since 1964 to see the portraits of herself and her husband, she commented on what a good job Pat had done.[58] Conger stated publicly that Pat had succeeded in transforming the White House into an "authentic showplace."[59]

Although Pat enjoyed putting her decorating skills to use, she had to fit her antique hunting into a packed schedule of responsibilities. Her hectic schedule must have reminded her of the craziest days of campaigning or her experience filling in for Mamie Eisenhower while also carrying out her own responsibilities as second lady. She went to breakfasts, lunches, teas, dinners, and dances. In between, she attended ceremonies for a wide variety of causes and received honorees of numerous awards at White House receptions. She was responsible for overseeing official dinners, and she made decisions about everything from food to table linens. She also played a role in determining the entertainment featured at these dinners. Once again, she, like Lady Bird, lived in the shadow of Jackie Kennedy, who remained better known for bringing art and culture to the White House. Despite the number of renowned musical artists the Nixons invited to perform at the White House, the public never associated them with high culture. This would prove to be a source of frustration for both wings of the White House.[60]

In the midst of all of her other activities, Pat continued to spend a significant amount of time on her correspondence. As she had during the vice presidential years, Pat closely followed the work of her correspondence staff, devoting, on average, five hours a day to composing, editing, and signing letters to the people who wrote to her. The correspondence staff opened the letters and composed drafts of standard replies. Pat looked over any newly composed responses and personally answered many of the letters.[61]

Examining Pat's correspondence from even a single year reveals the variety of mail she received. In addition to the standard requests for recipes, Gwen King, her correspondence secretary, fielded questions about the first lady's favorite songs, prayers, and colors as well as whom she thought should play her in a movie (Julie was the answer).[62] Sometimes letters informed the staff about rumors circulating in the public. For example, one man wrote in asking Pat to autograph a book she had supposedly written. He received a gracious letter explaining that the first lady had not written the book in question.[63] Children wrote to the first lady to tell her about their lives or to ask questions about hers.[64] Adults wrote to her asking her advice on a variety of subjects, some of them highly personal. One young man wondered whether she could help him assuage his fiancée's feelings about his desire for a career in politics. Gwen King responded that Mrs. Nixon faced the "challenges of being a political wife by becoming active herself."[65] During the election year of 1972, the staff spent a great deal of time explaining Pat's view of the issues, which usually involved restating the president's position. They also had to "clarify the misunderstanding" constituents had on everything from health care to money spent on Pat's travel to her secretaries' salaries.[66]

Pat's staff faced a new challenge in March 1971, when President Nixon announced first daughter Tricia's engagement to Edward Cox. Connie Stuart explained to a former colleague that the short time frame necessitated by the planned June nuptials was "consuming" all of their "time, thought and energies." Stuart and other members of the staff had to find a way to fit wedding planning into an already tightly packed schedule. Pat did not make Stuart's job any easier by refusing to cancel all of her other engagements. "Mrs. Nixon," Stuart explained, felt "so responsible to those groups who want to see her or want her to do something" that she would not let them clear her schedule.[67] Instead, Pat worked with her staff to ensure that existing obligations were met, necessary routines maintained, and important exceptions acknowledged and addressed even as she insisted on setting aside time to assist Tricia in designing, arranging, and planning for the wedding of her dreams.[68]

Tricia had managed to keep her on-again, off-again relationship with Ed Cox something of a secret from the press over the years. The couple first met in December 1963 at a Christmas dance during Tricia's senior year in high school and first year of living in New York. Over the years, Tricia visited frequently with Ed's family either in their New York City townhouse or the family home on Long Island. She did, however, date other young men, and reporters connected her with all sorts of eligible bachelors, including Barry Goldwater Jr. and Prince Charles. But she kept coming back to Ed.[69] Despite their attraction to one another, the young couple seemed to have very different political beliefs. Tricia occasionally expressed views that were to the right of her father, most notably when she sent a public letter of support to Georgia governor Lester Maddox during his fight against desegregation. Although she explained years later that her strict constructionist view of the Constitution sparked the letter, her action still clashed with Ed, who worked for Ralph Nader's Raiders and interned at the *New Republic*. He appeared to be more liberal than his bride. A closer examination of Ed's family tree, however, revealed a long history of Republicans who had been active in politics.[70] The similarities in their personalities and backgrounds evidently finally won out over surface disagreements, and the couple became engaged five months before the official announcement.

Although the public perceived Tricia as the more shy of the two Nixon girls, she planned a wedding that was much more of a public spectacle than her sister's. From the engagement announcement at the reception for the Irish prime minister through the debate about the wedding cake recipe, the American public shared in the excitement of the prenuptial hoopla.[71] (In fact, the public seemed more excited than the father of the bride. Like many men of his generation, Nixon did what he could to avoid the details of wedding planning.[72])

The ceremony took place in the Rose Garden of the White House on the afternoon of 5 June. Although rain threatened to force the event inside, Tricia, with her father's support, held out hope that the clouds would part long enough for her to be married under the specially designed pavilion. After the exchange of vows, the happy couple and their 400 or so guests moved into the East Room for dinner, dancing, and cake. A core group of reporters attended the wedding and reception and filmed the event for showing that evening as a television special. Tricia even refused to escape secretly from the reception, as many former White House brides had done. Instead, she left the party and the White House grounds wearing her wedding dress, in full view of reporters.[73]

Pat had a wonderful time at the wedding. Not only did her daughter have the wedding of her dreams, but Pat also danced with her husband, something usually reserved for inaugurations. Pat's behavior after the ceremony showed just how happy she was with the day. As the staff began cleaning up and restoring the White House for its more mundane functions, Pat went around and shook hands with all of the janitors and staff who had helped to make the day so special. She then sent the entire staff home, rounded up some leftovers, and took them up to the family quarters for a "picnic supper on the Truman balcony." Later, the group gathered around the television to watch the televised version of the day's events to relive the joy.[74]

Pat's thoughtfulness after the wedding typified her relationship with the domestic staff of the White House. Although overseeing household operations was part of her responsibility as first lady, Pat never treated the housekeepers, janitors, cooks, or drivers as if they were "help." One White House waiter told a reporter that Pat always went around and thanked the staff after parties.[75] She trusted them to do their jobs and respected their competence, but she was not above getting her hands dirty and taking care of something herself. Old habits died hard for someone like Pat, who was used to doing things for herself. Even in the White House, she occasionally ironed her own dresses and delighted in joining the staff to open boxes of Christmas decorations and climb ladders to trim the tree.[76]

Of all of Pat's responsibilities as first lady, however, the one she enjoyed the most was the opportunity to travel. She had been the most traveled second lady, and she continued to hold that record when she moved up to the top slot. During her five years as first lady, Pat visited thirty-two nations around the world, several more than once.[77] She accompanied her husband on his groundbreaking trip to China and set new precedents herself by traveling solo as an official representative of the United States to the inauguration of President William Tolbert of Liberia in 1972 and repeating the task in 1974 in Brazil by attending the swearing-in ceremony of Ernesto Geisel. Wherever she went, she espoused the same practice she had utilized during her travels in the 1950s: she strove to "make as many friends as possible" for herself and her country.[78]

Her husband, who excluded her from most important policy decisions, recognized her as an asset when it came to foreign policy. Years later, he told former aide Frank Gannon during a series of interviews that Pat always handled herself "very properly" even during sensitive diplomatic conversations she might inadvertently overhear. He explained that she "listen[ed] and she nod[ded]," but she never made "comments of her own." At the same time, however, he relied on her to notice things he did not because, as he put it, she was "very observant."[79] Giving Pat some responsibility in small diplomatic tasks also provided Nixon with cover from the increasingly vocal feminists who demanded more of a role in government policy. She was a woman he could trust to do only what he expected her to do.

Pat's foreign traveling did more than feed her desire for the adventure of visiting new places; it was a way of reconnecting with her husband and to the Pat and Dick team of old. She had never been more a part of his life and work than when they traveled together during the vice presidential years. Certainly the circumstances had changed: now they traveled with a huge entourage of aides, security personnel, and reporters, and feelings toward the United States had hardened over the years. But her husband's faith in her abilities, demonstrated by his willingness to send her off by herself, must have gratified her. She seized the opportunities to prove herself.

Pat's trip to Peru in 1970 epitomized her value as a foreign ambassador. On 31 May, an earthquake measuring 7.75 on the Richter scale devastated about half of Peru, killing at least 50,000 people and displacing hundreds of thousands of others. Mud slides followed the initial quake, causing further damage. Homeless, injured, and starving survivors rushed to the coastal areas in search of medical attention and news of loved ones. As news reports filtered back to the United States, President Nixon promised $10 million in aid as well as loaning army and navy helicopters for the search-and-rescue missions.[80] The American public, moved by the devastation, had begun donating supplies and money to be sent to the people of Peru. Similarly empathetic, Pat wanted to help. During a weekend at Camp David, the couple discussed the situation, and Dick raised the possibility of Pat delivering donations from the American people down to Peru personally.[81]

A week later, she flew to Peru and met Consuelo Gonzáles de Velasco, wife of the Peruvian president, in Lima to deliver the donations, visit the injured and homeless, and review the damage. She took with her over 18,000 pounds of "clothing, blankets and other goods" as well as cash donations.[82] During her brief stay, she accompanied Mrs. Velasco on a tour of the most devastated regions, flying on a small plane, sitting only on a repurposed kitchen chair with no seat belt. Walking amid the rubble, she hugged children and offered comfort to those who had lost everything.

Her genuine concern and sympathy did much to ease the tension that had existed between Peru and the United States since Velasco's ascension to power.[83] An editorial in *La Prensa*, the main newspaper in Lima, noted the "profound significance" of Pat's visit. "In her human warmth and identification with the suffering of the Peruvian people," the editorial continued, she had "gone beyond the norms of international courtesy." The people of Peru appreciated "the understanding and concern that she demonstrated in our sorrow."[84] Upon her departure, Velasco awarded her the Grand Cross of the Order of the Sun. Even the *Washington Post*, which rarely had much positive to say about the Nixon administration, admitted that she had "threaded her way among all . . . potential sources of trouble admirably and with skill." Epitomizing the "simple human response" required by the tragedy, the editorialist continued, she succeeded in communicating "to the Peruvians she met a genuine desire to help and to have done so with great tact, for all of which she deserves much credit."[85]

If the trip to Peru showed the potential for Pat to serve as a goodwill ambassador, her trip the following year to Africa displayed her determination to break through the restraints of her first lady role. In early January 1972, Pat set out on an eight-day, 10,000-mile trip to the African continent where she visited Liberia, Ghana, and the Ivory Coast. The primary mission of the trip was to participate in the inauguration of William Tolbert, the new president of Liberia. For the first time, the first lady would be the official representative of the United States. As such, Pat met privately with President Tolbert as well as Prime Minister Dr. Kofi A. Busia and President Edward Akufo-Addo of Ghana and President Felix Houphouet-Boigny of the Ivory Coast. Her official party of forty included the U.S. ambassador to Liberia, Samuel Z. Westerfield, as well as the Reverend Billy Graham (he and Tolbert were both ministers) and Mrs. John H. Johnson, wife of the president of Johnson Publishing Co., which published *Ebony* and *Jet*.[86] In addition to official meetings, press conferences, and speeches before political bodies, the Africans treated Pat and her entourage to a whirlwind of dinners, receptions, and presentations.

Pat took her responsibilities on the trip very seriously. Julie noted in her biography of her mother that Pat sneaked away from family activities on Christmas day to go over her briefing notes and organize her thoughts for the upcoming trip. Although the State Department and the staff of the West Wing prepared remarks for her, she went over them, making changes where she felt necessary and highlighting points she wanted to emphasize.[87] In Liberia, she pleased her hosts by noting how "impressed" she was by the "considerable development" that had occurred since her last visit in 1957. In Ghana, she traveled out into the hills of Aburi to pay her respects to eighty-three-year-old Chief Osac Djan, whom she had met during a vice presidential visit. He told her that she had forged a friendship between the American and Ghanian people that "not even a lion could break." Before she left Ghana, she spoke before the national assembly, delivering a rare public political speech.[88] In each of the three countries, Pat spoke with the leaders about her husband's upcoming trip to China, explaining that he did not intend to normalize relations but to open a dialogue. She also reiterated America's promise of financial assistance to aid in development and announced the creation of two graduate scholarships for women to travel to the United States to study.[89]

It was not her official pronouncements, however, that earned her the accolades either in the countries she visited or back home; it was

Mrs. Nixon dances with Ghanaian woman during her trip to Africa, January 1972. Richard Nixon Presidential Library and Museum.

her warmth, her enthusiasm, her genuine appreciation of and affection for the people she met. In Monrovia, Liberia, she gushed to reporters that she could not "wait to get around and meet some people." She certainly did that. She waded into crowds, shaking hands, giving hugs, and patting backs. At the inauguration ceremony, she gave President Tolbert a "warm cheek-to-cheek embrace."[90] He called her a woman of "courage, strength of character and fortitude of spirit."[91] When a group of women presented her with "traditional bright-blue lappa cloth," rather than politely accepting the gift and slipping it under her chair, she stood up and began to try to tie it around her waist. The women realized what she was trying to do and took over, dressing her in native fashion, complete with headdress. Pat's delight in the outfit and her willingness to model it in front of her audience and the cameras spoke volumes about her respect for the culture and the people she was visiting. The story was repeated everywhere Pat went. All of the news photos show Pat with a huge grin on her face, whether she is watching a traditional tribal dance, listening to a speech, or traveling in a motorcade.[92]

Pat returned home triumphantly, heralded by the press. *Time* magazine declared her "African Queen for a Week," and the *New York Times* marveled that "They loved her in Monrovia. . . . They loved her in Accra, too."[93]

Pat would make one more solo trip as first lady. In 1974, she attended the inauguration of President Ernest Geisel of Brazil and made a stop in Caracas, Venezuela. By this point, her credentials as a diplomatic asset had been well established. However, caught up in the midst of the Watergate scandal, the media paid little attention to the first lady's travel itinerary. Most of the attention was on her husband's political problems back in the United States.[94]

During her husband's groundbreaking trips to Peking and Moscow, Pat proved that she did not have to be flying solo to make a difference during an official trip. While Dick met with diplomatic leaders and negotiated wording on communiqués, Pat toured the countries, met with whatever citizens she was allowed to, and attended cultural events. Dick's meetings opened communications between countries, while Pat's efforts helped to forge good feelings among peoples of countries involved in international relations.

Dick Nixon, a determined anticommunist in the 1940s and 1950s, had been working on thawing the cold war between the United States and the People's Republic of China for years. In an article in *Foreign Affairs* in 1967, he argued that Americans could not "afford to leave China forever outside the family of nations." Rather, the long-term goal should be to "pull China back" into the world community.[95] During the first years of his presidency, he dropped hints, both to the American people and to the Chinese, of his desire to move toward greater openness between the two giants. He and his national security advisor, Henry Kissinger, explored different avenues of communication with Mao Tse-Tung and Chou En-Lai of China. By mid-1971, their efforts had paid off. China extended an invitation to the president to visit Peking. Not only would Nixon be the first U.S. president to visit the People's Republic of China, but, because of China's self-imposed isolation, one of a limited group of Westerners who had ever been there. As a result, there was tremendous worldwide interest in the trip. When China decided to allow the American press to tag along with the president and Mrs. Nixon, people around the world followed the February 1972 journey.[96]

Mrs. Nixon laughing with women at the Evergreen People's Commune, People's Republic of China, February 1972. Richard Nixon Presidential Library and Museum.

Because Dick remained sequestered with the Chinese leaders much of the time, Pat was the representative who introduced Americans to China and who represented the American people to the Chinese. If she had not already realized what a great responsibility she had on her shoulders, the briefing paper she got from the State Department made it explicitly clear. Emphasizing her role in the "unique opportunity" the trip created to "to reestablish communication between the women of China and America," the State Department reminded her that she would be "the first leading American woman the Chinese have met." The "intensive U.S. television coverage" provided her with the "unprecedented opportunity to influence the way in which Americans view the Chinese, Chinese women and the Chinese social order."[97] Pat responded to the pressure by intensifying the normal homework routine she followed before any trip: studying her State Department briefing papers carefully, reading *Quotations from Mao*, learning useful phrases of Chinese, and worrying about her schedule.[98]

On most of the trips she had taken both during the 1950s and so far as first lady, Pat had insisted on attending more than the usual ladies' teas and receptions. She had asked to visit hospitals, schools, and other facilities that helped women or the poor. This time, however, she had very little say in what she would do, where she would go, or whom she would meet. She need not have worried. Although she had the feeling that she was being isolated from the public, she won over the people she did meet and dealt diplomatically with those who tried to convert her.[99] Correspondent Helen Thomas recounted that when Pat's guides, invariably young women from the Revolutionary Committee, would try to engage her in a political discussion, "she would smile and say 'Oh, yes, I'm acquainted with his philosophy.'"[100] From the cooks in the kitchen of the Peking Hotel to the vice chairman of the Evergreen People's commune to Premier Chou En-Lai himself, the Chinese melted under Pat's warm smile and genuine enthusiasm for experiencing new cultures. During her visit to the kitchen, with its 115 cooks, she gladly sampled their creations, including a "fiery stuffed pickled squash."[101] Sitting next to Premier Chou En-Lai at a state dinner, Pat commented on the cute pandas drawn onto the cigarette holder. Chou offered to give her some. When Pat asked if he meant the cigarettes, he responded that he meant the pandas. Taken aback, Pat gladly accepted the gift.[102]

While Pat met with the Chinese people, her husband worked with Chinese officials, especially Chou En-Lai, to produce concrete results from the newly opened communications. The resulting joint statement, the Shanghai Communiqué, acknowledged that although there were "essential differences between China and the United States in their social systems and foreign policies," the two nations would work toward establishing "peaceful coexistence." On the stickiest issue, American support for Taiwan, the United States recognized that there was "one China" of which Taiwan was "a part" and stated that reconciliation of disagreements should be in Chinese hands alone. Both sides looked forward to opening channels of communication and trade.[103] Although the Shanghai Communiqué did not include specific proposals, Nixon thought the statement was important in that both the United States and the People's Republic of China agreed to impose "restraints on themselves." He believed, as he stated in his toast at the closing banquet, that his efforts to open talks with the Chinese had "changed the world."[104]

Nixon also realized that talking with the leaders of the People's Republic of China would worry the Soviets. Although willing to speak with communists, he had not foresworn his old animosity toward the Soviet Union or his determination to limit the Soviets' ability to threaten the United States. Nixon and Kissinger simply intended to do whatever was needed to protect American interests, even if that meant meeting with the enemy. Early in the administration, Nixon had re-opened strategic arms limitation talks that had begun under the Johnson administration. The Soviets, anxious to move the talks forward and concerned by Nixon's openness to the People's Republic of China, invited Nixon to Moscow to continue the talks.[105]

As a result, in late May and early June 1972, Pat, Dick and entourage traveled to Moscow, where Dick met with Soviet leaders while Pat followed her usual separate schedule. Accompanied at various times by either Mrs. Andrei Gromyko or Mrs. Leonid Brezhnev, Pat took a ride on the subway, watched a rehearsal at the Bolshoi Ballet School, visited with schoolchildren, and toured the GUM department store. She also attended the Russian circus, where a performing bear startled her—a sight so out of the ordinary that the press reported it in the American papers.[106]

As had become her pattern, Pat won over both the Russian people and the reporters who accompanied her. The Russians, as well as the Poles during the couple's visit there, appreciated the first lady's delight with the ballet and the circus, her obvious affection for the schoolchildren she met and hugged, and her easy manner with the wives of the Soviet leaders. (In fact, at one point, Mrs. Nixon grabbed the hand of Mrs. Brezhnev, who was unused to the throng of reporters and the crowds constantly surrounding the women.) Pat's determination to stop and talk with the people who had come out to meet or see her also earned her the affection of the populations. One incident exemplified her appeal to the ordinary peoples she encountered on her trip. During the Nixons' stopover in Warsaw, Pat attended a Chopin recital. When the crowd applauded as she rose to leave, she walked toward them, intending to shake hands and talk to the people. Her interpreter attempted to lead her back to the official party. She refused to join the group until she had waded into the crowd of men and women, who responded very warmly, with some men taking off their caps and others kissing her hand.[107]

For their part, reporters, "even the sometimes critical U.S. correspondents," were "extremely complimentary." The *Globe* described her as a "remarkable saleswoman," the *London Daily Mail* claimed she was the "best boost for womanhood since they invented lipstick," and the *Herald* reporter got a "warm feeling" at the sight of Mrs. Nixon and Mrs. Brezhnev holding hands.[108] Pat earned the respect and gratitude of some of the reporters by her behavior during her visit to the GUM department store. Throughout the trip, reporters had been forced to battle the Soviet police guarding Mrs. Nixon. The situation came to a head on the third day of the visit. As Pat walked through the store, hundreds of people crammed onto balconies or stood in adjacent aisles to wave and to catch a glimpse of her. Reporters trying to cover the event found their views blocked by the Soviet security detail. Pushing became shoving, which became fists flying through the air. Pat saved one reporter from being manhandled by a big Soviet officer by pulling the reporter to her and giving him a lick of her ice cream cone. Her obvious distress at the situation and her attempt to remedy it did much to win the "open admiration of reporters."[109]

In light of Pat's foreign triumphs, some members of the press reported the emergence of a "new Pat Nixon." Supposedly this new Pat exuded confidence, warmth, and charm where the old Pat had been stiff, formal, and diffident. No longer the plastic Pat of yesteryear, new Pat wowed people both at home and abroad with her diplomatic skills, fashion sense, and candor. "Something dramatic has happened," one paper stated, although the author of the piece could not explain exactly what that something was. Whether a new image had been created by her staffers in the East Wing, ordered by the president's men in the West Wing, or evolved naturally through her three years' experience with being first lady, many journalists agreed that the Pat Nixon they encountered in 1972 was very different from the woman who joined her husband in the White House in 1969.[110]

Even in the fashion arena, Pat won points for updating her style. Back in 1969, fashion watchers agreed that Pat had great legs and nice features, but dull taste in clothes. In an article in *Time* magazine, designer Bill Blass criticized her "ghastly red lipstick," while Geoffrey Beene called her clothing choices "overly cautious." Designer Donald Brooks thought she needed "overhauling."[111] The following year, *Time* printed another story about Pat's wardrobe. This article focused on Clara Treyz, Pat's personal shopper. Once again, designers complained that Pat's conservative and frugal style made her look like a "mother-in-law who never makes trouble." Her clothes, ignored designers suggested, were old-looking and "dull."[112] By 1972, however, she modeled the latest looks for a spread in *Ladies' Home Journal,* including clothing by the designers who had disparaged her years earlier. Perhaps most shockingly, several of the photographs showed her in pants, something she had said she would never wear because her husband did not like them. The "quiet style" transformed into something much more modern and bold.[113]

Although she had modified her wardrobe, both she and her staff denied that she was any different than she had been in the past. Press secretary Connie Stuart grew "tired of hearing" about the first lady's new image. She claimed that Pat was the "same woman she always has been." The "newness" came from those who had never known her before suddenly "discovering" her warmth and generosity.[114] Stuart knew firsthand how little Mrs. Nixon was willing to adjust to suit the changing times. When Stuart replaced Gerry Van der Heuvel as the first lady's press secretary, Pat informed her that she should have no illusions about making over the first lady's image. "I am who I am," Pat told Connie, "and I will continue to be."[115]

The periodic stories of a new Pat Nixon resulted from several different sources. First, the image of the first lady as plastic Pat who sat behind her husband with a blank expression on her face, or as the indefatigable campaigner who never commented on substantive issues, or the ultimate housekeeper and mother who could and did do everything herself, persisted well into the Nixon presidency. Because some segments of society, including members of the press, still accepted those images as real, whenever the media "discovered" Pat doing something that contradicted one of those stereotypes, they were shocked to find their older image was wrong. For example, in March 1970, *Time* asked "What ever happened to the matron in the Republican cloth coat, the silent partner in the Nixon marriage?" The article described an energetic, confident first lady on her college tour, standing up to protesters. But was this a different Pat than the one who stood up to demonstrators in Venezuela?

Misinformation and miscalculation contributed a second factor that helped to lead to the "new Pat" stories. Reporters trying to unearth the story behind the image frequently ran into a stone wall of friends and family who refused to say anything derogatory about Pat. Norman

Vincent Peale told Judith Viorst that he understood that she wanted "some warts on the portrait" of Pat to jazz up her story for the *New York Times Magazine,* but he could not give her any because there were none. Even Alice Roosevelt Longworth, who was "famous . . . for her acid tongue," could find nothing "unkind" to say about Pat. While Pat's friends were fiercely loyal, employees also hesitated to tell stories that might show their boss in a less than perfect light. Whether they feared the wrath of Pat or the displeasure of the president, they either said nice things or nothing at all.[116]

Pat herself contributed to the maintenance of her image. During her tenure as second lady, she granted numerous interviews in which she discussed her housekeeping skills. She told countless reporters, including Dick's cousin, Jessamyn West, that she never got tired, sick, or afraid. She said she could listen raptly to Dick give the same speech numerous times because he always changed it a little.[117] Her fierce sense of pride and inbred determination to keep private feelings private accounted for some of her reluctance to admit to any weakness or to share intimate details of her life. She might also have taken cues from her husband and his political advisors, who had encouraged the image of Pat as the ultimate housewife during the 1950s.

The last factor that explained the periodic appearance of "new Pat" stories was the fact that Pat did evolve over her years as first lady. Being first lady provided what Muriel Humphrey called a "magic wand."[118] For Pat, that meant having opportunities to accomplish something on her own for the first time since Dick came back from overseas after World War II. It took her a few years to figure out that she was free to take on projects she was interested in, to test the waters to see what she could do, and to fight with the president's staff to protect her goals. Her reactions to her efforts to redo the White House in 1970 and her reluctance to claim credit for her work certainly seemed like more of the old Pat. Her willingness and enthusiasm, as well as the confidence in her abilities evident in her manner following her trips to Peru and Africa, however, did show that Pat was coming into her own.

By the summer of 1972, Pat Nixon was beginning to enjoy being first lady. She loved the traveling she had done that year. She hoped that Dick recognized the value of her efforts in Africa; she was the darling of the media. Even the liberal papers, which tended to view her husband in a negative light, had good things to say about her efforts. Her daughters were happily married and living their own lives, but still close enough for visits and talks. Living in the public eye was not something she would ever relish, but at least she had a job, something useful to do. All of those years as a politician's wife, she had spent too much time performing mindless tasks. As first lady, she could see that she was accomplishing something. She was just starting to figure out what being first lady meant in the summer of 1972. But that is when everything fell apart.

CHAPTER 5

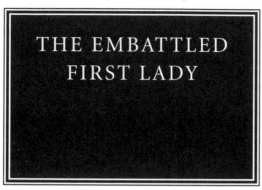

THE EMBATTLED
FIRST LADY

Along with the fulfillment she found through her overseas duties and
her work on the White House, Pat Nixon spent her years as first lady
fighting an ongoing battle to retain control over her responsibilities
and to maintain some sort of relationship with her husband. Even as
Pat remained the good soldier, going where she was told to go for campaigning duty, making the standard polite comments, and smiling her
best candidate's wife smile, she found herself engaged in almost constant warfare with her husband and some of his advisors. In their attempt to manage all aspects of the administration, they assumed that
they would be able to control the first lady as well. But Pat had had
years of experience of dealing with her husband, and she refused to
give up without a fight. Her constant efforts to protect her schedule,
her staff, and her projects from interference from the West Wing, and
the ongoing friction that this created between Dick and herself, made it
increasingly difficult for Pat to maintain her usual pose as the perfect
politician's wife. Her frustration mounted as her husband faced the
greatest challenge of his career. Yet she exhibited her traditional loyalty
even when he ignored her advice. In the end, Pat finally escaped the
world of politics, but at a high cost to herself and her family.

Tensions within the country mirrored the discord in the White
House. The seemingly never-ending conflict in Vietnam continued to
polarize Americans, even as Nixon implemented his plans to end the

war. The political victories of the African American civil rights movement inspired numerous other minority groups to fight for the elimination of political, social, and cultural barriers to equality. The efforts of Chicanos, Asian Americans, and American Indians to draw attention to the discrimination they experienced daily succeeded in making white Americans aware of the problems existing in their country and resulted in a few political victories. Perhaps the most shocking and divisive of these movements was the women's liberation movement, which affected Americans of all ethnicities, races, and socioeconomic classes.[1]

Of all the foreign policy problems that Nixon confronted, the Vietnam war was perhaps the most difficult. When he took office in 1969, there were over 500,000 American troops engaged in what appeared to be a "quagmire." Despite billions of dollars and almost 40,000 American casualties, the conflict seemed no closer to resolution in 1969 than it had in 1965, when Johnson escalated American troop engagement.[2] Once in office, Nixon followed a multipronged strategy to try to extricate the United States without appearing to lose the war. First, he instituted a Vietnamization policy of training South Vietnamese troops so that they could take over the fighting from the Americans. That way, Nixon could begin to bring American boys home. Second, he intended to undermine North Vietnam diplomatically by isolating the Vietnamese communists from their allies in Peking and Moscow. Third, in 1970, he ordered the invasion of Cambodia in an attempt to cut off what U.S. military leaders believed was the main supply link between North and South Vietnam. Last, while carrying out peace negotiations, he increased the military pressure by dropping thousands of pounds of bombs on Cambodia, Laos, and North Vietnam as well as mining Haiphong Harbor. The North Vietnamese, however, remained resolute in their determination to force the Americans out and to win control of their country.[3]

At home, the antiwar movement maintained its pressure on the administration to end the fighting immediately despite overt and covert administration efforts to curtail its impact on Americans. The antiwar movement, no longer composed of just students, expanded to include housewives, clergy members, and the working class. Demonstrations moved beyond the coasts and into small-town America. Frustrated, Nixon applauded Vice President Spiro Agnew, who characterized the leadership of the protests as an "effete corps of impudent snobs" and allowed the FBI to increase its monitoring and infiltration efforts. Divisiveness increased, anger mounted, and neighbors and family members argued with one another about the war, its meaning for America's future, and how it should be ended. The president characterized the fighting as a "positive polarization." He believed that it would ultimately work to his advantage by building support among the white middle and working classes, who worried about the impact of social upheaval on their everyday lives.[4]

Pat experienced political conflicts over the war in concrete ways. The constant threat of antiwar demonstrations limited her travel from her earliest days as first lady. Responding to an edict from the president, Pat's staff organized her March 1970 college tour to circumvent possible demonstrations. Even though they avoided college campuses in their planning, the first lady still faced protesters on her trip. She concentrated on the upbeat young volunteers she met and refused to "take off on shouters" because, she explained, "they have a right to shout if they want to."[5] A month later, however, her cancelation of a planned student visit to the White House exposed her frustration with the students. As demonstrations continued through the years, Pat's schedule was frequently adjusted because the president did not want his wife or daughters to encounter protesters. Pat was particularly upset when campus unrest forced the family to forgo Julie and David's college graduations in May 1970. With many universities and colleges closed in response to massive protests after the Kent State shootings, the Secret Service advised the young Eisenhowers that it would not be safe for their families to attend the ceremonies. Instead, the Nixons held a mock commencement at Camp David. According to Julie, Pat was "quieter than usual" at the party. She told her daughter that she found it "difficult to accept that the mood of the country had changed so little" since 1968.[6]

Giving up her daughter's graduation was not the last time demonstrations affected Pat's life. In April 1971, the president's staff informed East Wingers that because they expected "demonstrations and peace marches from the 19th of April through the 8th of May . . . it would be unwise to schedule Mrs. Nixon to do something outside of the house."[7] For Pat, who occasionally felt claustrophobic in the White House, such restrictions must have weighed heavily.

In January 1972, one protester let the Nixons know that they were not protected even in the White House. During a dinner honoring Medal of Freedom winners DeWitt and Lila Wallace, a young woman performing with the Ray Conniff Singers stepped forward, pulled a cloth protest sign out of her dress, and chastised the president for "bombing human beings, animals, and vegetation." The president "looked a little shocked," according to the singer, Carol Feraci, "but he was obviously trying to keep his smile."[8] H. R. Haldeman noted in his diary that Nixon dismissed the event as not doing any "harm," but the first lady "was pretty disturbed about it."[9] Because Pat never gave any indication that she disagreed with her husband's handling of the war, her discomfort probably resulted from the audacity of this young woman attacking her husband in such a public forum and to his face. Despite the ambivalence of her own feelings toward her husband, she was almost always protective of him when someone else attacked him. Moreover, because Pat had long merged her political identity with his, she might have also taken this young woman's protest as a personal insult.

While antiwar protesters disrupted Pat's schedule, the women's movement complicated her public image. Throughout most of her political career, she had represented the ideal American housewife and mother. The Republican Party had encouraged this, and her husband used it to his benefit in his various campaigns. Despite negative feedback from some members of the press and a segment of the American public who found her superefficiency irritating and artificial, Pat's natural inclination to be self-sufficient and to take care of her family allowed her husband to portray her as the typical wife and mother. Her early efforts as first lady reinforced this image. She told reporters that she just wanted to help her husband accomplish his goals. As she ventured out on her initial solo trip as first lady in June 1969, she explained that there was "no more exciting role in life for a woman than to be a help to her husband." That did not mean, she went on, that women did not have "other responsibilities . . . to make a contribution . . . to become involved in programs designed to enrich the quality of life for all."[10] Her volunteer projects and her work on restoring the White House both fit in nicely with the image she and the Republican Party had crafted for her. The many women who happily wore "Pat for First Lady" buttons in 1968 and who wrote to her asking for recipes obviously admired her and saw her as one of them.

The emergence of the woman's liberation movement challenged the underlying assumptions of the ideal housewife that Pat represented. As with most movements, the modern women's movement that gained recognition in the late 1960s and blossomed in the early 1970s resulted from the work of numerous groups of supporters with various agendas. The most radical of these groups originated within the ranks of the African American and student movements of the 1960s. In the process of working for the rights of African Americans and protesting the war in Vietnam, many young women recognized their own oppression. They found to their dismay that when they tried to bring their concerns about the sexism they encountered to their brethren within their movements, the men ignored or discounted the issues. Eventually, these women broke away to form their own organizations. Building on lessons they had learned from the broader protest movement and from community building, these young women staged demonstrations outside the Miss America pageant to focus attention on the objectification of women's bodies; they organized campaigns to strengthen rape laws; they created consciousness-raising groups to give women a place to share their stories and support one another. They demanded that the government protect a woman's right to control and make decisions regarding her own body.[11]

While younger women worked to change the existing political and economic structures, a group of professional and politically active women built on groundwork laid earlier in the century by women in the National Woman's Party to make the system more amenable to women's needs. Some had spent years working to build a presence for women in the Republican and Democratic parties. Others participated in organizations such as the Business and Professional Women's Clubs or the General Federation of Women's Clubs or various labor unions. In the early 1960s, they had gathered enough momentum to force President John Kennedy to form the President's Commission on the Status of Women and eventually to convince him to sign the Equal Pay Act of 1963. They rejoiced when Title VII of the Civil Rights Act of 1964 included prohibitions against gender discrimination. When passage of these two acts did little to undermine the rampant economic and political inequities women encountered, however, they decided to form their own group, the National Organization for Women. Their aim, like that of their more radical sisters, was to protect the rights of women over their money, their children, and their bodies. Unlike the younger women, however, the NOW women intended to work within existing political structures to try to secure the necessary changes.[12]

By the early 1970s, although the women's movement had succeeded in questioning traditional assumptions about women's lives, not everyone was happy with the result. The Equal Rights Amendment made it through Congress and seemed headed for ratification by the states. Additionally, Americans watched new television shows featuring liberated women such as Maude and Mary Richards, read in women's magazines such as *Ladies' Home Journal* about former housewives and mothers jumping into careers, and saw examples in their own neighborhoods of a new outlook. Although many women and men leaped at new opportunities, others felt rejected and insulted. Conservative Phyllis Schlafly responded to the quick ratification of the ERA in a number of states by creating a StopERA movement of her own. Schlafly and other conservative women connected the ERA to many of the other changes in society, particularly what they perceived to be the denigration of the roles of mother and wife. In attempting to expand the possibilities for women in terms of careers, female activists appeared to dismiss the work of housekeeping and seemed to imply that women who chose to stay at home were not acting properly. For women who had devoted their lives to caring for their families, this devaluation undermined everything they had ever accepted as truth.[13]

Pat, like many other publicly active women of her generation, was caught between the reality of her life and the transformation taking place around her. On the one hand, her views were limited by her experiences and the situation in which she found herself. As she pointed out in a magazine interview, during her time in the workforce, she had "competed against and worked with men without difficulty." Ignoring the fact that she was describing a special set of circumstances created by World War II, she insisted that she had "always done the things [she] wanted to do" and "never felt discriminated against." In her mind, she supported women's rights because she believed in "equal rights and equal pay for equal work." Feminists could not help but notice, however, that despite her statement to the contrary, she had not always done the things she wanted to do. After all, she had admitted on more than one occasion that politics was not the life she would have chosen. Moreover, her constant applauding of her husband's "special support" for women's rights rang hollow when placed beside his veto of legislation such as the Comprehensive Child Development Bill, which would have aided working women by providing funds for child care.[14]

On the other hand, Pat did appear to be launching her own personal women's movement right there in the White House. In the same magazine article in which she insisted that she did not "believe in parades and things like that" to achieve equality, she modeled pantsuits. For years, she had told people that Dick hated women in pants, yet there she was, wearing them. Additionally, she made no secret of the pressure she put on her husband both in public and in private about appointing a woman to the Supreme Court.[15] During the 1972 campaign, she voiced her support for the Equal Rights Amendment, although she did not actively campaign for it.[16] Her solo foreign trips as well as her historic meetings with Soviet and Chinese leaders also made her the most prominent American woman involved in diplomatic relations. They were small, in some ways symbolic, gestures, but they were important. For many women across America, the small victories were the most significant.

Pat's occasional public moments of independence hid the battle she waged in private for control over her position as first lady. Pat had always prided herself on running her own household. Even when her husband was vice president, she "got by" with an occasional cook/housekeeper. She still did most of the cooking, cleaning, and management of the Nixon home. When Manolo and Fina Sanchez, Cuban refugees, began working for the Nixons in 1962, Pat turned over some, but not all, housekeeping and cooking responsibilities to the couple. Naturally, then, when she became first lady, overseeing the household management duties should have been an easy adjustment for her to make. Decisions about menus for state dinners, seating arrangements, and entertainment issues usually fall to the first lady. For the first time in their marriage, however, her husband began interfering in her area. Despite his numerous responsibilities, Nixon took time out of his busy schedule to try to speed up dinner service at state dinners (at one point creating a "stopwatch" dinner served and eaten in fifty-eight minutes), made demands about what kind of entertainment should follow the meal (Dizzy Gillespie instead of the Strolling Strings Pat ordered), and even tried his hand at table arranging (Where to put the receiving line? Where to put the band?).[17] Because he thought poor performance in these areas reflected poorly on him, his administration, and the country as a whole, he felt compelled to work on them himself or turned to his staff, especially H. R. Haldeman, to resolve the problems.[18]

The changed character of his staff complicated this situation for Pat. Throughout his career, Dick had relied on a small group of loyal, devoted, and hard-working men and women to help him carry out his responsibilities and to take care of any number of tasks outside the realm of official business. Many of these people, most notably Rose Mary Woods, technically worked for or with Dick but also had relationships with Pat. This was not the case with his White House operatives. With the exception of Woods, the president's staff increasingly consisted of a new group of men with either no connection to Pat or an antagonistic one.

Although Nixon initially relied heavily on his Cabinet appointees, the president shifted tactics by the end of his first year in office and made more use of presidential assistants. He disliked the slow pace of legislative action created by the Cabinet model of government. Instead, he increasingly focused control within the White House, particularly in a small group of advisors who regulated his schedule, carried out his orders, and mirrored his vision for America.[19] National security advisor and later secretary of state Henry Kissinger served as Nixon's foreign policy sounding board and agent. They shared similar realist views of world power and needed one another to accomplish their goals. For domestic policy, Nixon turned first to Daniel Patrick Moynihan, who had previously worked in the Kennedy and Johnson administrations. Moynihan shared Nixon's hard-luck background as well as his more pragmatic than ideological view of society's ills. He also brought an impish spark to a rather somber staff. Nixon was sad to see him leave the administration at the end of 1969.[20] Nixon then increased the responsibility of John Ehrlichman, who went from assistant to the president for domestic affairs to head of the Domestic Affairs Council in early 1970. A Seattle lawyer who claimed in his memoirs that he first joined the Nixon team because he was bored with his successful, middle-class life, Ehrlichman quickly learned the political system. He became, along with his fellow UCLA alumnus, H. R. Haldeman, half of the most powerful team in America.[21] "Bob" Haldeman worked in marketing before he joined the Nixon team in a peripheral way in 1956. In his memoir, he said that he joined Nixon's team because he recognized that Nixon was "a fighter." He continued to work with Nixon through five campaigns. When Nixon won the presidency, he appointed Haldeman his chief of staff to act as "a funnel rather than a filter." Haldeman would be the "gatekeeper."[22]

Haldeman took these responsibilities seriously. In his efforts to keep out people who wanted to eat up the president's time with what he characterized as "long, time-wasting discussions of some minor departmental gripe," Haldeman built "a wall" around the Oval Office. Few got to see the president without going through him first. This exclusion included some people who should have had unconstrained access to the president: his doctor, his personal secretary, and, to a certain extent, his wife.[23] It might have been that Haldeman, in his quest for hyperefficiency, believed that these people either were not doing their jobs with enough speed or accuracy, or were consumed with issues that he thought were inconsequential. Having not been around as part of the inner circle as long as some others, Haldeman might not have understood the relationship Nixon had with these individuals. He may also have picked up cues from his boss, who preferred not to be bothered with personal details. Or perhaps Haldeman simply liked the power that went along with holding the keys to the president's office.[24]

Whatever his reasoning, Haldeman tried to keep Dr. Lungren, Rose, and Pat physically removed from the president. Haldeman assigned Dr. Lungren, Nixon's personal physician on campaign trips, to a separate plane and a distant hotel room, and he tried to move Rose Woods from her office right outside Nixon's to the Executive Office Building. When the Nixon administration bought a new plane to transport the president, Haldeman designed the layout so that the first lady's compartment was at the back of the plane. To see her husband, Pat had to walk through the staff offices. Haldeman's inability to maintain this barricade—Dr. Lungren reported him to the Secret Service; Rose retained her access to the president; Pat had the plane redesigned—only led him to find other ways to undermine those he saw as threats.[25]

The plane design was just one in a series of conflicts between Pat and Haldeman. The two had met during earlier campaigns, but had not really had much contact with each other. Their first real interactions came during the 1968 campaign. Because he had been such a peripheral player during the vice presidential years, the heyday of the Pat and Dick team, Haldeman never appreciated how vital Pat was to

Dick's success and treated her with a level of condescension that she found insulting. The bad blood between them intensified in the pressure cooker of the White House.[26] He accepted her influence on inconsequential issues: for example, he refused to "buck" her about her choice of decorator for the Oval Office, although he clearly disagreed with the decision. He resented, however, the way she "royally screwed up" his schedule for the president on occasion. For her part, Pat sensed his dislike of her and found his indifference to her successes infuriating.[27]

The tension between the two played out in their contest for control of East Wing functions. Consistent with her tendencies toward frugality and independence, Pat wanted as small a staff as she could get away with. She somewhat naively thought she could do things as she had when she was second lady. In fact, she at first handled her mail in her usual fashion, working with Bessie Newton as she had in the past. It soon became evident that the old ways did not meet the demands of her new responsibilities. Pat would have to have a real staff, but she wanted to keep it manageable. She started with a press secretary, Gerry van der Heuvel, who was chosen by Haldeman, and a social secretary, Lucy Winchester, who had been selected by Pat after prescreening by Ehrlichman. Although Pat eventually came to trust and confide in Winchester, she never warmed up to van der Heuvel, who accepted a diplomatic assignment to Rome in the fall of 1969. Haldeman then proposed bringing in Constance Stuart, whose husband worked in the president's office, as staff director.[28]

Much more dynamic than her subdued predecessor, Stuart led a small but loyal group of women in the East Wing. Stuart worked with Pat in making decisions about engagements, dinners, and the press. Stuart came to admire and respect her boss's experience and good sense, and Pat learned to trust Stuart. In fact, according to Stuart, they had a "very close" relationship, with each one "mother[ing]" the other. Although Connie tended to deal with Pat most directly, the other women working in the East Wing knew that they could approach Mrs. Nixon if they needed to, and she felt as comfortable talking to any of them.[29] Helen McCain Smith, Connie's assistant and Pat's press secretary after Connie's departure, found Pat "warm and outgoing, with an affectionate hug for anyone she knew." Smith described a relaxed atmosphere in the East Wing, one in which Mrs. Nixon treated the staff almost as girlfriends, giggling and gossiping as they got their work done.[30]

Stuart, who had been employed in public relations, also established better relations with the press and helped the first lady develop solid programs. Although she made a few mistakes as she learned her job, Stuart earned kudos from the women who covered the first lady by instituting regular press conferences and keeping them informed of Mrs. Nixon's schedule. Relations between the first lady and the media improved. The journalists in general responded favorably to Pat's sincerity even as they tended to characterize her as "a docile wife" who would do "what her husband and his aides want[ed] her to do."[31] The journalists and Pat recognized that her East Wing cohort worked hard to come up with various projects to utilize the first lady's willingness and desire to use her position to do good for the people.[32]

Still, Stuart and her crew's work was often an exercise in frustration. All proposals had to go to the West Wing for, as Stuart concluded one memo, "your thoughts, suggestions and support." Sometimes the approval was forthcoming; many times it was not. Often, the East Wingers had to settle for knowing that their ideas were "under consideration" and that they would be "called on" if they were "truly needed." Stuart advised the women to "trust in the intelligence and wisdom" of the men who worked directly with the president. Other times, the president and his aides made recommendations or suggested ideas that they had rejected earlier and now presented as their own. Lucy Winchester was a model of feminine decorum and restraint as she replied to a request for "social activities" by sending the West Wing a list that included several that had been "submitted before" and rejected. Obviously, she noted, "the timing" had not been "right." She hoped they would be useful now.[33] Penelope Adams, who coordinated the radio and television appearances of the first lady and her daughters, explained in her exit interview that the shifting of responsibility between the two wings frequently left the staff with little time to prepare adequately for various events.[34]

Thus, even with his choice in place to run the East Wing operations, Haldeman and his minions (all men) still distrusted the ability of the women working with the first lady to carry out their duties adequately. He recorded in his diary that he regretted having to intervene in East Wing affairs but thought Mrs. Nixon would need "better staff" to take care of the situation on her own. Evidently, hiring new people did not help because the West Wingers continued to be unhappy with their East Wing counterparts. In a 1971 memo, one staffer told the deputy assistant to the president, Dwight Chapin, that "The East Wing has so messed up the travels of the First Family that moves must be made immediately to correct them, i.e., take over."[35] That same month, Haldeman chastised Stuart after a *Washington Post* news story appeared about one of the entertainers who performed at the White House. Reporter Sally Quinn's humorous piece about Bill Schustick, a long-haired, bearded man who was supposed to perform sea chanties while Edward Villella danced, took no swipes at the Nixons. Quinn merely examined various responses of people to Schustick's laid-back dress and attitude. Haldeman did not find Quinn's piece amusing. Instead, he fired off a memo to Stuart to inform her that there was "a serious problem procedurally" in her handling of the entertainment at important dinners at the White House and demanded to know who was responsible for the situation.[36]

Connie Stuart's reply, sent ten days later, indicated that although the women of the East Wing understood exactly where they stood in the pecking order, they could give as good as they got. After indicating that Mrs. Nixon had selected the entertainers, Stuart assured Haldeman that their backgrounds were checked through the necessary departments, and reminded him that Sally Quinn "chews up everyone" in her stories. Stuart then put her head "slowly into the noose" by telling Haldeman what she really thought. Venting some of her frustration, she asked if he was "indicating that we shouldn't have longhairs in the White House just because they don't shave." Admitting that she found the article funny, she concluded proudly, "We do the very best we can, but the unknown looms menacingly when dealing with the entertainment profession. It's kind of like dealing with politicians."[37] Years of having proposals dismissed that would have allowed the first lady to address substantive issues had left Stuart with a reservoir of anger.

Of course, the real issue for both Haldeman and Stuart was that the first lady was determined not to let the president, his aides, or her staff tell her what to do. She was willing to listen to advice, but she wanted to make the ultimate decisions about how she acted on that advice. As a result, according to Lucy Winchester, "diplomacy" needed to be "exercised" when making requests of the first lady. Sometimes this meant

getting the president to recommend a course of action to her; sometimes "long time" associates might be called on "to sell Mrs. Nixon on
various projects" that Haldeman and company had "difficulty present-
ing to her." Even the president sometimes required backup in convincing his wife to sign off on a project. In 1972, concerned about Pat's reaction to a film about her scheduled to be shown at the convention,
Nixon conspired with Haldeman to get "Rose and Tricia to sit in with
her and rave about it" so that she would approve it for use.[38]

From Haldeman's point of view, Mrs. Nixon could be stubborn. On
more than one occasion, she "blasted" Haldeman for his interference
in her domain. Suggestions that she needed help often met with a polite "thanks, but no thanks." For example, in 1971, a West Wing staffer
commented that the man who handled the president's television appearances could help the first lady as well. Pat replied, through Connie
Stuart, that she would not be making "very many television appearances other than routine TV news coverage," so she saw no need for the
advice. By 1972, Haldeman was frustrated with "the same old stuff"
coming from Mrs. Nixon. Resentful of "anything [that] implied that
she has to have any help," she lashed out at the president and his chief
of staff.[39]

Faced with his inability to achieve the results he wanted, Haldeman
tried two other strategies in dealing with the first lady. Thinking that
Mrs. Nixon might resent him personally, he put someone else in charge
of working with her. John Ehrlichman, Dwight Chapin, and Alexander Butterfield took turns serving as liaison to the first lady. All ran into
similarly polite but resistant behavior. Ehrlichman believed that Pat
"did not adapt well to the White House." He found her "stubborn" and
difficult to deal with. Butterfield explained that he believed that she
"had come not to trust whoever was working with her from Nixon's
staff."[40]

Haldeman's other strategy of dealing with the first lady—operating
behind her back—validated Pat's mistrust of him. Obviously, because
of her position, Pat and the president's staffs would have to discuss
schedules, appearances, and strategies without her being present. She
had to rely on aides to provide background and set up travel plans.
There were times, however, when aides kept her so far out of the loop
that Pat ended up being surprised by obligations or commitments that
she did not know had been made for her.[41] More troubling for her,

however, was the realization that some of these meetings and communications were deliberately clandestine—that people were talking about her almost as if she were a commodity. Many of these confidential memos originated from campaign concerns. Couched in terms of "just developing some thoughts for the President to contemplate," Haldeman and his underlings would brainstorm strategies that would allow them to "effectively use Mrs. Nixon, Julie and Tricia to help candidates."[42] Again, Pat's objection was not to campaigning per se, but to the almost sneaky way in which her participation was being molded without her knowledge. She disliked being made to look like a puppet.

Her resentment did not free her from her husband's continued use of her for partisan purposes during his time as president. Obviously, she had been instrumental in helping him win office and would have a role to play when he ran for reelection in 1972. In between those efforts, however, Pat and her daughters would be required to politick for the Republican party as a whole and individual GOP candidates. As early as July 1969, staffers in the West Wing researched the most "effective" way to utilize the first family "in political and other public affairs." They wanted to know what the public thought were "Ideal First Family characteristics" and how the current residents of the White House fit those public expectations.[43] During the off-year elections, the Nixon staffers used the girls and Pat "to help candidates but not in a blatantly political way."[44] Rather than giving speeches at rallies, the Nixon women would be sent to state fairs and civic receptions. For example, senatorial candidate Lowell Weicker arranged for Tricia Nixon to visit the Danbury, Connecticut, state fair. Although he assured the press that her presence was "nonpolitical," Weicker and other Republican candidates worked to remain by her side as she signed autographs and chatted with the people who crowded her throughout the day.[45] The women's presence at events such as the Danbury state fair earned "Brownie points" for the administration and saved the president from wasting time visiting "good states" that were already safely Republican.[46] Nixon's people realized that Pat generated positive media coverage for her husband just by her presence. Thus, they wanted her to travel to "reasonably significant events that would not appear to be manufactured" in order to secure "regional news media coverage" as well as, they hoped, a "significant amount of national coverage."[47]

The need for positive media coverage intensified as the Nixon's reelection campaign got under way in early 1972. The groundbreaking trips to China and the Soviet Union created the image Nixon desired of a world leader and, he hoped, would lead to pressure on North Vietnam to end the fighting. Despite a new round of antiwar protests around the country and in Congress, Nixon succeeded in limiting their impact by focusing attention on continuing negotiations, withdrawing troops and thus lowering American casualties, and shifting media coverage to the excesses of the antiwar movement's actions rather than the message protesters advocated. Concentrating on the demonstrators jelled nicely with efforts by Nixon and his Committee for the Re-Election of the President (CREEP) to build support among working- and middle-class white ethnics who had become alienated by the perceived liberalism of the 1960s. Consequently, Nixon worried as much about the candidacy of former Alabama governor George Wallace as he did about the various Democratic Party candidates. Even after an assassination attempt left Wallace paralyzed, Nixon sent an aide to make certain that the governor would stay out of the race.[48]

Nixon and his CREEP aides took more aggressive action in dealing with his potential Democratic competitors in the presidential race. Having determined that George McGovern was the best choice from their perspective, the Nixon people did what they could to eliminate the other candidates. Well-placed photos of Ted Kennedy partying with young women resurrected memories of the Chappaquiddick incident that continued to haunt him. Numerous dirty tricks undermined the candidacy of Edmund Muskie until he bowed out of the race. Determined to get what information they could on the strategy of the Democrats, a group of men working with some members of CREEP broke into Democratic National Committee headquarters in the Watergate complex and attempted to bug the phones. Police caught them. The incident made the front page of the *Washington Post* but not the *New York Times*. In the days after the initial break-in, journalists kept the story alive by raising questions about connections between some of the burglars, the CIA, and the White House.[49] The Nixon team wrote it off as a "third-rate burglary" in public and worked to conceal their involvement in private.

For Pat and the girls, Watergate was just one of the issues they confronted during their campaign trips around the country. Although they were old hands at being on the road, this last race took a toll on them. As Tricia explained in a letter, "campaigning is just like oil in that it floats to the top and takes priority over everything else."[50] For the newlyweds Tricia and Ed Cox and Julie Eisenhower, who was without her active-duty husband, the constant travel, the need to smile and be polite, the food gulped down at countless receptions, and the lack of privacy proved draining. Moreover, the presidential race of 1972 created new issues for the girls. Not wanting to appear ignorant and yet determined not to say anything that might hurt their father's chances for reelection, they looked to him for advice in answering questions from reporters. He turned the question over to his aides but also responded personally. In July, Dick sent the girls a long memo giving them "anecdotes which would relate to some of the political events that have occurred over the years" as well as reminding them of "events"—such as his playing piano by ear—"that are not publicly known" but that are a "part of the Nixon story that is to you most heartwarming."[51]

By September, they were worn out. Having faced questions about the Watergate break-in, the continuation of the war in Vietnam, and the deteriorating economy for a couple of months, the girls asked to be scheduled out of the big cities and into the Southern border or mountain states, where the crowds would be friendlier and the "sharpies" nonexistent.[52] In fact, the new strategy in September was to ensure that the first family only did "easy States" and "easy events" from that point on. Happy to have Democratic opponent George McGovern as "the issue," the Nixon staffers wanted to keep the family "out of controversy or any kind of trouble."[53]

Although Pat did not like having to deal with the sharpies, her issues with campaigning differed from her daughters' concerns and problems. Whereas Julie did not mind giving television interviews and Tricia had been known to speak her mind, Pat disliked making public speeches and most of the time refused to do taped interviews. For her part, the first lady did not "tire out" the way the youngsters did. She amazed even her daughters with her ability to appear refreshed and ready to go at 7 A.M. and still look as pulled together after an eighteen-hour day. Pat seemed to draw energy from the hordes of people at her appearances, and she gladly dove into the crowds, shaking hands, hugging old people, and kissing babies.[54]

She even seemed more comfortable with her role as political activist during the 1972 campaign. During her trip to Africa, when a reporter asked if she would be campaigning for her husband during his next presidential race, she responded that she thought that was what she was already doing.[55] In September, she took the longest solo campaign trip of her long career of being, as one newspaper characterized her, a "political helpmate." Visiting seven states in six days, Pat did what she did best: she mingled with the people. She attended a program for newly sworn-in citizens in Chicago, sat in freezing rain listening to a speech about the National Park Service in Yellowstone, and visited with senior citizens in Riverside, California, in 102-degree heat. She was, she told reporters at the beginning of the trip, "taking the White House to the people." Although it was a campaign trip, she gave no speeches (only "remarks") and allowed no planned press conferences. She made one brief political statement about her husband's work on behalf of the elderly. Mostly she shook hands with grateful and adoring constituents, hugged children and old people, and smiled.[56]

The one rough spot in an otherwise overwhelmingly positive trip came at the beginning of the tour. In Chicago, a planned press coffee event turned into an impromptu press conference, during which reporters switched between normal softball questions about her appearance and tough queries about substantive issues. Thrown off guard, Pat stumbled her way through questions about the war, abortion, the Watergate break-in, and a recent incident involving Martha Mitchell, wife of former attorney general John Mitchell, and an FBI agent. She stated that she did not know anything about the Watergate or Mitchell situations except what she read in the papers. She strongly supported her husband's handling of the war in Vietnam, agreeing with her daughter Julie's stated willingness to die for the people of South Vietnam. Although she opposed "on-demand abortion," she did not want to prosecute women who had abortions because it was "a personal decision" to take that step.[57] She came through the experience with her dignity and reputation intact, but her husband decided that campaign staff should not allow any more press conference or question-and-answer sessions to occur. The questioners, he explained to Haldeman, were "too strident and rough . . . much rougher than" in the last election. Even though, the men admitted, Pat and the girls "handle it well," the resulting press did not "develop into a story" they wanted to read.[58]

Dick's response to the 1972 press conference epitomized the complicated nature of the White House version of the Pat and Dick team. He recognized her abilities and her usefulness to his political career; he even wanted to protect her from rough treatment by the press. But he did not convey these sentiments to her directly. In fact, he spoke to her on the phone for barely a minute that day.[59] Instead, in an effort to control the situation, he told Haldeman to cancel any future press conferences for the duration of the first lady's campaign tour. The intertwining of selfish political motivation with the effort to insulate his wife from the sharpies out in the field characterized Dick's behavior toward Pat.

As he had throughout his career, Dick appreciated Pat's people skills and understood that she would be an asset to him. When she traveled on her goodwill trip to Peru, he "pushed" Haldeman to gain "maximum follow-up" with the press. She was a vital part of his plan for his groundbreaking trip to China because she would provide "good people pictures." Nixon understood that the American people would respond much more positively to an image of the first family with a million Chinese than they would to a communiqué. Because he did not want to go sightseeing while he was in China, her presence was necessary to get the television coverage he thought crucial. The same would be true of his trip to the Soviet Union. Aide Charles Colson reported to Haldeman that after the SALT agreement and the "businesslike approach to the whole Summit," "Pat Nixon and her performance" proved effective with "the swing category type people."[60] Certainly during his last campaign in 1972, he understood that she and the girls provided him with good publicity. That was one reason he was so careful about keeping them away from hecklers, demonstrators, and hardnosed reporters. In the years after his resignation, Nixon spoke glowingly about his wife's contributions to his political career. In his memoirs, published in 1978, he acknowledged her years of service as wife, mother, and campaigner, all of which, he stated, she had done "magnificently." He was similarly complimentary during a series of interviews in 1983 with former aide Frank Gannon.[61]

Although Dick might have continued to see Pat's value to him personally and politically, during his presidential years, he left his underlings with a different impression of her. John Ehrlichman claimed in his memoirs that the staff took their cues from Nixon about how to treat his wife and daughters. Ehrlichman's sense was that Nixon "treated [Pat] as a respected, but limited partner . . . not a heavyweight."[62] Haldeman listened as the president repeatedly described his wife as a useful vehicle for garnering good publicity. At one point, Nixon referred to her, according to Haldeman, "as a prop."[63] Roger Ailes, who helped with Nixon's television appearances, wrote Haldeman that "the President should show a little more concern for Mrs. Nixon." Ailes suggested that Haldeman tell Nixon to "talk to her and smile at her." Perhaps knowing the fruitlessness of the recommendation, Haldeman wrote in the margin, "You tell him."[64] Because these were the men who controlled access to the president and conveyed his orders to others in the organization, their treatment of Pat set the tone for how everyone else would deal with her.

Nixon's reluctance to talk to his wife at times reinforced the impression that theirs was not an equal partnership. Early in his presidency, he wrote her a series of memos requesting help with decorating his office and bedroom and with adjusting the kind of music they listened to during meals.[65] Whatever the reason he wrote to her instead of asking her in person, especially when he saw her for dinner that day, the staff members who handled the memo had to have wondered about the nature of their relationship. Alexander Butterfield claimed that Nixon ate dinner in his office "most nights," although the presidential daily diary shows him eating with the first lady most evenings.[66] Some Secret Service agents also found it odd that the Nixons could spend hours together on helicopter rides from the White House to Camp David or walking around the grounds without carrying on a conversation.[67] The silence took on a different meaning if the first couple had an argument. Then, aides, frequently Haldeman or Butterfield, would find themselves playing messenger between the couple. This continued the pattern the Nixons had established early in their relationship. They had never been able to fight with one another face to face. Instead, they used intermediaries. In the early years, Hannah Nixon helped to smooth out differences; in later years, the girls served the same purpose. During the presidential years, Dick turned to his staff to negotiate with his wife.[68]

The absence of obvious displays of physical affection between the couple similarly strengthened negative perceptions about the Nixon marriage. Both Dick and Pat had been raised in households that discouraged public demonstrations of affection. Additionally, although Pat could be demonstrative, especially with children, Dick had always been emotionally awkward.[69] He could be kind, but he had a hard time being affectionate or relaxed. His efforts at showing his feelings usually came off looking forced and unnatural. Because the public expected a certain amount of physical closeness, the Nixons would "put on a show" of holding hands or linking arms when they needed to for pictures. They almost always moved apart as soon as the cameras disappeared. Ehrlichman said that the family "assembled and disassembled" itself daily during the campaign.[70] Again, this had been true throughout their marriage, but it became obvious to more people once they were in the White House.

One dramatic example of this disconnect between the couple occurred during a birthday celebration for Pat at the Grand Ole Opry in Nashville in March 1974. Dick played "Happy Birthday" on the piano to Pat while the audience and host Roy Acuff sang. As a very moved Pat rose from her seat on the stage and started toward her husband with open arms to hug him, he turned away and began playing with a yo-yo that he had brought for the host. An embarrassed Pat returned to her chair. Although news accounts of the appearance failed to mention the incident, the rebuff appalled members of Pat's staff. They knew that this had not been an isolated incident, resulting from stress due to tension over his Watergate problems. In fact, there had been a number of other similar public embarrassments when the president treated his wife in a callous and inconsiderate manner.[71]

Missing from all of these discussions was Pat's role in the relationship. The assumption, even on the part of her loyal staff, was that she was the victim in the marriage, the passive receptacle of her husband's boorishness who meekly did as she was told. Even Lester David, who wrote the first biography of Pat, devoted a chapter to Dick's poor treatment of her and analyzed the relationship almost exclusively from Dick's perspective.[72] Such a scenario, meant to be sympathetic to Pat, in fact demeaned her by depriving her of all control over her own life. Did Dick treat her badly? Certainly at times he did. He could be rude, inconsiderate, and self-absorbed. But she was a partner in the relationship even if her part was invisible to the public. Much of Dick's problematic behavior reflected the basic pattern of a relationship that had endured thirty years. The key difference was that their private habits were now displayed before the public.

A reporter's expressed dismay that the Nixons would be staying in separate locations during the 1972 Republican National Convention was a typical reaction to the Nixons' willingness to spend time apart. From the beginning of their marriage, however, Dick and Pat had spent considerable time away from one another. First the war, then his responsibilities as congressman, senator, and vice president, had necessitated periods of separation ranging from days to weeks to months. This pattern continued even during the "wilderness years," when Dick was technically out of politics. During that time, he still traveled to speaking engagements and campaigned extensively for Republican candidates. Pat traveled as well, going to California to visit Helene Drown or other old friends, taking vacations with the girls. During the vice presidential years, she complained periodically to Helene about she and her daughters being "bachelor girls," but she did not allow Dick's absence to prevent her from keeping active. Moreover, during the presidential years, despite his busy schedule, he did find time to spend with his wife and daughters. They had dinner, watched movies, went swimming at Camp David, and bowled at the White House.[73]

Similarly, the lack of public intimacy that disturbed some people was a carryover from Dick and Pat's backgrounds and continued throughout their marriage. As Dick told Frank Gannon in his 1983 interview, that was just the way he was, and she was that way too. He further explained that he thought love was much "greater when you don't make a big point of showing it off and talking about it."[74] Both he and Pat had been raised in families that did not believe in public displays of affection.

Although Pat prided herself on her stoicism and ability to hide her emotions, she was obviously more comfortable with physical affection than her husband. She was known for hugging children who came to visit the White House or whom she met on her many travels. On rare special occasions, she also hugged and kissed her husband publically. When he won the vice presidential nomination in 1952, she spontaneously kissed him (and then did it again for the photographers). After her trip to Africa in 1972, he met her plane and she ignored his outstretched hand to hug and kiss him.[75] Because in those instances he did not pull away from her, there were probably more times during their over thirty years in the public eye when she could have acted similarly. The fact that she did not could indicate that she shared his feelings about such public displays, or that she respected his reluctance to

President and Mrs. Nixon walk on the beach at San Clemente, California,
January 1971. Richard Nixon Presidential Library and Museum.

demonstrate emotion or that her feelings toward him had changed.
Because he was so awkward in expressing his emotions, he seemed to
rely on her to guide him. Interestingly, in his description of Tricia's
wedding reception, at which he and Pat danced, Dick wrote in his
memoirs that Pat was "an excellent dancer and the guests broke into
delighted applause as she steered me around the floor." He did not have
any dancing experience, so naturally she was leading. The remark
might also have been true for their emotional life as well.[76]

This emotional distance in addition to their willingness to tolerate
long periods of silence between them led many to believe that Pat had
no influence on Dick at all, that she was a cipher in the power structure
of their marriage. She did not discuss political strategies, government
policies, or presidential decisions with him. She repeatedly told reporters that she knew nothing more about certain subjects than what
she read in the papers. She had never seen herself in the role of advisor.
That did not mean, however, that Dick did not respect her opinion.
During a phone conversation with the secretary of state, William
Rogers, Nixon remarked that Rogers had followed Nixon's example of

marrying a wife smarter than he was. He told Frank Gannon that Pat had "enormously good intuition" and that he trusted her sense of people. He wanted her to go with him to China because he knew from past experience that she would charm the Chinese as she had done people throughout the world.[77] They had developed the habit during their foreign trips in the 1950s of meeting up in the evening to compare notes on what they had experienced during the day. That continued as they revisited some of the same places during the presidential years. Dick also listened to Pat's opinion on matters involving public opinion. What she thought of the vice president's performance on a televised interview could affect the way he perceived it.[78]

Although there were definite limitations, she could also prompt him to do some things she thought important. Haldeman included in his diary a number of instances of both Nixon's and his frustrations with Pat's ability to get her way. Whether she was causing scheduling problems or "trap[ping]" her husband into standing in a receiving line or pressuring him into social events such as attending the wedding of reporter Helen Thomas and her fiancé, Doug Cornell, Pat could compel Dick to act in a way she thought appropriate.[79] Interestingly, many of her victories involved the very area of social interaction in which Nixon recognized that he was weak. He had obviously decided over the years to follow Pat's lead in these matters.

Pat also let Nixon and his aides know when she was unhappy with their performance or with their treatment of her. Ehrlichman dismissed Pat's notion of herself as "an experienced campaigner" and explained that her "suggestions and complaints were tolerated without being much heeded by Haldeman and the rest" of the staff.[80] Their attitude toward her did not stop her from continuing to stand up for herself. In fact, in those early days in the White House, when everyone was learning how everything worked, Nixon and his aides decided that Pat's "complaining" and "whining" had no basis in reality. Ignoring the possibility that Pat might have legitimate gripes, they decided that it was Helene Drown's fault that the first lady could be so disagreeable at times. Helene had been spending time with Pat, helping her settle into her role as first lady and serving as a sounding board. As a good friend, Helene would sometimes take action on behalf of Pat and tell Dick or one of his aides what she thought of their treatment of the first lady. But that was not the way Ehrlichman saw it. In his memoir, he reduced the decades-long friendship between the two women into something sick, with Helene as the "waspish woman" turning "Pat's low-key requests and suggestions into mean-spirited demands." According to him, the president demanded that Ehrlichman tell Jack Drown to keep his wife away from Pat because she was causing too much trouble. Reluctantly, Ehrlichman explained, he did his duty, but was only successful temporarily.[81]

Helene's disappearance and then reappearance was an example of one way Pat coped with her husband and the men who surrounded him. As she had throughout their marriage, Pat tended to act in passive-aggressive ways. Ehrlichman faced an example of that behavior early on when he tried to force Pat to change the way she was handling her correspondence. He talked to her about it, offered her justifications for why her way would not work in the long run, provided alternatives, and waited for her response. He had anticipated tears or perhaps a tantrum; instead, she simply listened to him and then ignored what he said. She treated other aides, including Henry Kissinger, in a similar manner. If she disagreed, she politely went about doing what she thought best.[82] She acted the same way with her husband. If she did not want to go to Camp David for the weekend, she would not go. Sometimes this meant he would not go either; other times, he went by himself.

But Pat was not always passive. She could also be bitterly angry. Haldeman felt her wrath on more than one occasion as she fought him for control over the East Wing operations. Her husband obviously did not want to experience her anger—hence his efforts to push the task of disagreeing with her off on his aides. Sometimes, however, he could not escape the consequences of his actions. Pat "really hit him" when he reneged on a commitment she thought she had from him about appointing a woman to the Supreme Court.[83] Sometimes rather than blasting away at an opponent, particularly when that opponent was her husband, her anger emerged in snide remarks to or about him. Henry Kissinger was fond of telling his staff about the first time he met Pat. As he complimented her husband, she wondered aloud if Kissinger "hadn't seen through him yet?"[84] Outsiders who heard Pat's occasional bitter outbursts tended to see them as proof of Nixon's mistreatment of her rather than indicative of her own personality.

Despite her obvious anger on occasion, Pat continued to do her job, and to do it well. In fact, she seemed to get better at it and enjoy it more. By 1972, she was the toast of the media, going off on a diplomatic mission by herself, traveling to China and the Soviet Union. Even the election season of 1972 proved easier than in the past. She willingly went off on her own campaign tour, performing as the professional politician's wife that she was. Her tour schedule was light compared to past years, with no eighteen-hour days required. She seemed to have a new understanding of the world in which she lived. When a reporter asked her if she was "helping" her husband "politically" with the tour, she stated that she did not visit "places like this for political reasons." Confused, the reporter pushed further, asking if she did not regard her tour as a "political trip." Acknowledging her reality, Pat explained that "anything you do this time of year is political."[85] The convoluted statements revealed perhaps more than Pat realized. She did not sit in the freezing rain, as she did in Billings, Montana, because she was politically motivated; she did it because she knew it was important to the people who had come to see her, because it was her job, and because she believed in her husband. Pat had been around the political scene long enough to recognize, however, that everyone else looking at the situation would politicize her actions.

Pat survived all of the pressures she felt as first lady with help from a solid support network. Most importantly, she had her daughters. Despite their marriages, Tricia and Julie remained close to both of their parents. The girls were particularly attached to their mother and she to them. When Tricia had measles, Pat dropped everything and went to stay with her in Florida. When Julie had to have emergency surgery, Pat was on a plane winging her way across the country within an hour of getting the notification. The reverse was also true. Pat was lucky to have the girls close by throughout much of the presidency. Tricia lived with them until her marriage and remained in the D.C. area until spring 1973, when she and her husband moved to New York. The Coxes remained frequent visitors to the White House, Camp David, and the houses on Key Biscayne. Julie lived with her parents off and on as David went through his naval duty. When he was discharged, they also stayed in the D.C. area.[86] Julie, anxious to do something to help her parents, volunteered to work in the East Wing. Because this was around the time that Connie Stuart left to pursue other interests, Julie's presence proved invaluable to her mother.[87]

Pat also enjoyed the support of her loyal staff in the East Wing. Their efforts on her behalf certainly validated her legitimacy and her importance. They looked out for her in countless ways. In addition to fighting on her behalf with Haldeman's crew, they also made certain that her husband and his band of merry men remembered important dates. For example, in June 1970, Connie Stuart sent Haldeman a memo tinged with just a bit of sarcasm as she reminded him that 21 June was not only Father's Day, but also the Nixon's thirtieth wedding anniversary. She concluded with, "Pearls are the traditional gift for thirty years of wedded bliss."[88]

Pat's friendship with Helene Drown remained important throughout the years. Now, instead of letters, the women relied on the telephone. They also increasingly found excuses to visit one another. Because Pat could not fly out to California without some effort, Helene regularly flew to D.C. The two would chat and laugh and talk about their kids, old times, and the silly things that old girlfriends find funny.[89] Although it was sometimes difficult, Pat felt it was extremely important to keep up with her old friends. She made a considerable effort to maintain a personal touch, even going so far as to wrap her own Christmas presents for people with her own wrapping paper, rather than White House wrapping paper.[90]

Pat would need all the friends she could get as the Nixons began their second term in office. Even as they celebrated victory in November 1972, nagging questions about the Watergate break-in persisted.[91] The triumphs of January 1973, which included the pageantry of inauguration, signing the treaty ending American involvement in Vietnam, and celebrating the return of the American prisoners of war competed with the trial and conviction of the Watergate burglars and new inquiries about their ties to the White House. As the spring progressed, attention shifted from the break-in itself to the possibility of a presidential cover-up. By April, H. R. Haldeman, John Ehrlichman, and Attorney General Richard Kleindienst had resigned because of their participation in the affair. President Nixon fired his counsel, John Dean, for spilling administration secrets. Still the probes continued. In addition to journalistic inquiries, the Senate opened an investigation, and the new attorney general, Elliot Richardson, appointed a special prosecutor, Archibald Cox, to examine the evidence in the case. Throughout the summer, the American public watched various White House and

CREEP officials testify before the Senate committee in televised hearings. They saw John Dean admit to engineering a cover-up and Alexander Butterfield casually mention the existence of an Oval Office recording system. After that admission, the battle became about the tape recordings of conversations between the president and his aides. Everyone wanted to listen to the tapes because they believed that they would provide the definitive answers to the questions of "what the president knew" and "when did he know it." When Nixon claimed executive privilege and refused to hand over the tapes, the special prosecutor and the Senate committee submitted their requests to the Supreme Court. The court ruled that Nixon had to hand over the tapes.

The situation worsened in the fall. Even as Nixon delayed complying with the court order and sought a compromise, his vice president, Spiro Agnew, experienced his own political scandal. In early October, he pleaded no contest to charges of tax evasion and resigned his office. Nixon nominated Republican minority leader Gerald R. Ford to take his place. In the meantime, the special prosecutor rejected Nixon's compromise. When Nixon ordered the attorney general to fire Cox, Richardson refused, and Nixon fired Richardson. The scenario repeated itself with the deputy attorney general, William Ruckelshaus. Finally, the solicitor general, Robert Bork, fired Cox. This so-called Saturday Night Massacre intensified public pressure on Nixon, who finally agreed to release some of the desired tapes. Unfortunately, there was a long gap on one of the tapes.

The new year brought new revelations that would eventually lead to Nixon's resignation. In early February, the House began considering impeachment proceedings against the president. Demands for more tapes led to Nixon's release of edited transcripts. The public read in dismay the conversations the president had with his aides using language that included many "expletive deleteds." In May, the House Judiciary Committee began impeachment hearings, adopting three articles of impeachment by the end of July. When he lost another legal battle in early August, Nixon released the recording of his conversation with Haldeman on 23 June 1972, six days after the break-in. Known as the "smoking gun" tape, it revealed that Nixon knew days after the break-in that CREEP officials had been involved and, most significantly, he had ordered the CIA to obstruct the FBI's investigation of the break-in.

The Nixon family clung to one another for support the night before President Nixon resigned, August 1974. Richard Nixon Presidential Library and Museum.

With the release of this conversation, Republican leadership visited Nixon and told him that he did not have the votes to beat the impeachment articles. Nixon, realizing that he had no options, announced his resignation in a televised address the evening of 8 August. The morning of 9 August, he and Pat said farewell to their staffs and flew to California.

Throughout this entire period, Nixon denied his involvement and his guilt. He told the American public that he "was not a crook." When Haldeman and Ehrlichman resigned, he "regretted" losing "two of the finest public servants" he had ever worked with. He emphasized that he had no knowledge of the break-in before its occurrence, said that it was his responsibility as the man at the top to oversee the actions of his underlings, and promised that he would use all the power of his office to get to the bottom of the situation. One year later, with pressure mounting on all sides, he again insisted that the tapes would vindicate

him and show that everything he said in the past year about his innocence was the truth. Even after the release of the smoking gun tape, as
he was announcing his resignation, he did not admit to any wrongdoing. Instead, he said that he was resigning because he lacked the support in Congress to complete his term as president.[92]

For the girls, those last two years in office must have been like living
in a slowly tightening vise from which they could not escape. Wherever
they went, whatever they were doing, people asked them questions
about Watergate. Because they believed in their father's innocence,
they not only had to endure the unrelenting questions but also worry
about the impact of the charges on his well-being. They hurt for him.
Julie's response was to fight. She traveled the country to support her father and to show that the Nixons had nothing to be ashamed of. Tricia
tended to withdraw. She and Ed had moved to New York when he finished his military duty and joined a law firm. She visited the White
House and, according to her father, would come and sit with him in the
evenings.[93]

For Pat, the situation created the most difficult crisis of her political
career. During the summer and fall of 1972, it would have been easy to
see the rumors about White House connections to the burglary as one
more liberal media attack on her husband. On the campaign trail,
questions about it irritated her, and she tended to assure people that
the incident had been "blown completely out of proportion." She admitted to persistent reporters that she only knew what she "read in the
paper" and had not discussed it with her husband.[94] Considering that
the president had begun to isolate himself from his family, her statements rang true. By the spring of 1973, with new information available,
Pat and the girls readily believed that the president's closest aides had
betrayed him. These men, particularly Haldeman and Ehrlichman,
had treated the Nixon women as outsiders and junior partners in the
administration. The girls took the opportunity to encourage their father to get rid of them.[95]

Her husband's political problems took a more personal turn for Pat
beginning in the spring of 1973 as journalists began to investigate the
Nixons' finances. Once again, as during the slush fund crisis, Pat endured a public discussion of her family's financial holdings and activities. For someone as private and proud as Pat, this was humiliating.

The 1973 inquiries focused on the Nixons' income taxes. Large deductions for donations of Dick's prepresidential papers, most of which had been donated after a deadline imposed by a new law, enabled the Nixons to pay little in federal taxes despite their significant increase in income.[96] Pat, who had to sign the form authorizing an audit of their back tax forms, probably knew little about the convoluted deductions. Still, she too had to submit to a public audit of their accounts.

Then, in 1974, *Washington Post* columnist Maxine Cheshire published a story accusing Pat of keeping and wearing jewelry that had been given to her by foreign dignitaries. Acknowledging that there was "no precedent for judging the propriety" of Pat's actions, Cheshire reported that a number of the gifts had not been registered with the appropriate gifts unit in the White House. Cheshire ended the piece by repeating a Drew Pearson story from the early 1960s accusing the Nixons of keeping gifts given them during the vice presidency. The clear implication was that they were doing it again. Insulted, Pat turned all of the gems she had been holding to prevent theft over to the appropriate personnel. She labeled accusations that she had planned to keep the jewels as "for the birds." Clearly angry, however, she "began her rebuttal by cutting short" a reporter who tried to ask questions about the Cheshire article. In the end, she refused to discuss it at all.[97] Pat understood and accepted the inevitability of her husband's political battles, but she tended to take personally questions about her own actions and the family's finances.

Despite her growing internal frustration and embarrassment, Pat refused to let the public see how the revelations or attacks affected her. She did her best to carry on with her normal, if somewhat modified, schedule. She attended conferences, hosted dinners, and traveled around the country receiving awards. The day after Dick's speech announcing the resignation of Haldeman and Ehrlichman, she gave a luncheon for wives of Cabinet members and senators. While the televised hearings went on, she attended a luncheon with the Senate wives in the Senate dining room.[98] She continually assured reporters, and through them the American public, that she was fine, the president was fine, and everything was going to be okay. In August 1973, after Dick's second national address on Watergate, she praised his speech and through her press secretary "conveyed the feeling that Watergate" was "behind us now." Amid rumors in January 1974 that the president was beginning to crack under the pressure, Pat assured everyone that he was in "great health."[99]

By continuing to carry out her duties as first lady, Pat did more than just fulfill her obligations. Pictures of Pat laughing at a luncheon or congratulating the teacher of the year or smiling at the groundbreaking for a new park shifted attention away, if only briefly, from all of the negative publicity about the administration.[100] Additionally, these outings gave her an opportunity to meet with people who, if they did not support her husband, were certainly sympathetic to her situation. At a time when her life seemed a constant stream of new crises, these handshaking sessions could provide some needed distraction and were perhaps a reminder of happier days. As she explained to reporters, "We get this kind of assurance from all over the country every day about how people feel. . . . It gives the President a great lift." It probably lifted his wife's spirits as well.[101]

The same could be said about Pat's foreign travels during these troubled times. In early 1974, Nixon announced that Pat would be attending the inauguration of the new presidents of Venezuela and Brazil. This was her first trip to Venezuela since the disastrous 1958 visit with Dick. The mostly ceremonial visit served several purposes beyond the obvious diplomatic one. Nixon and his advisors realized that sending Pat promised even more favorable publicity than her domestic excursions generated. In fact, the president informed her that "press coverage of her arrival in Venezuela had been 'beautiful.'" The trip might have provided Pat some relief from the stresses of life in the world of Watergate, except the questions followed her there. To protect her from the press, security forces kept her away from the people of the country. Except for a couple of side trips to meet with schoolchildren, she spent most of her time fulfilling ceremonial functions. Although she stated that she enjoyed ritual and ceremony, Pat's preference had always been to get out among the masses of regular people.[102]

The ending of the Venezuela trip seemed to sum up the state of Pat's life at that point. Returning home with the flu, she felt feverish and tired. Rather than being able to rest or enjoy the feeling of a job well done, she faced more questioning on the plane ride home. The pressure got to her and loosened her usual tight control over her emotions. When a reporter asked her about "the strain of the past year," she "shot back angrily: 'No, I really don't wish to speak of it.' " Returning to her usual method of dealing with political problems, she explained that she had "faith in the judgment of the American people and the press people." "The truth" sustained her because she had "great faith in her husband." Moreover, she told the reporters that "this [issue]" was only being "covered in the metropolitan newspapers—even out in the country in the U.S.A. it isn't." Perhaps Pat's way of coping was to tell herself that only Eastern establishment press people knew or cared about the story. "The people" understood the truth.[103]

For all her outward show of bravado, the never-ending questions occasionally got to an increasingly tense Pat. Reporters noted her clenched fists and her willingness to cut them short, admonish them, or to become "visibly annoyed" with them—things she had done only rarely in the past.[104] Just as she had after the loss in 1960, Pat occasionally isolated herself. Despite her later statements of praise for her husband's speech and her support for the decision to get rid of Haldeman and Ehrlichman, Pat went into seclusion in the days after Dick's announcement of their resignations. She refused to answer her phone or speak with her press secretary in the immediate aftermath of Nixon's speech and declined to speak with reporters for days afterward.[105] More and more as she attended her luncheons and teas, she entered and exited surrounded by groups of Secret Service or her aides to protect her from the throng of reporters waiting to ask her about Watergate. Later that year, she briefly escaped the press and the claustrophobic walls of the White House. Donning dark glasses, a scarf to cover her hair, and a thick coat, she went out and walked the streets of D.C., window shopping. The bad weather caused everyone to watch their feet and so she was able to move about undetected.[106]

The Watergate crisis also took a toll on Pat physically. She got thinner, and her face appeared more puffy and lined. Her smoking, which she tried to hide from the public, increased. In fact, on several occasions, she even smoked in public.[107] There were rumors that she was drinking more than she normally did.[108] If she did indulge in liquor more than she had before, it did not affect her performance as first lady.

Pat received emotional support from her friends and the family's loyal constituents. Helene spent days and weeks at the White House serving as a "tonic" for Pat, distracting her, making her laugh, and boosting her up. Mamie Eisenhower, no stranger to the pressures of living in a fishbowl, sent her a note, offering a hideaway weekend, strictly on the "QT" and promising no reporters or questions.[109] Pat also took heart from letters from constituents who wrote offering their support and from the women who voiced their belief in her husband, either through separate speeches or at her events.[110] In fact, her correspondence, always a source of comfort and pride for her, became even more time-consuming as people wrote looking for answers. They wanted to believe the president, but they found the information flooding the media confusing. Pat received so many thousands of letters that she broke her own rule and sent out thank-you autograph cards rather than writing more personalized notes, as was her usual practice.[111]

Despite the strain of those months, and in the face of ongoing accusations, Pat continued publicly to profess support for her husband. In fact, as she had throughout their marriage, she encouraged Dick to continue to fight for his reputation and his presidency. Her position as Dick Nixon's wife had clearly colored her thinking. From the couple's vantage point, the press and the Democrats in Congress were on a witch hunt and looking for every opportunity to get rid of them. Pat could never sit still for that kind of attack. When the Supreme Court ruled that the tapes had to be released, she argued against it. She told Helene that she equated the tapes to "private love letters" that were not intended for everyone's eyes.[112] Even after she lost that battle with her husband and some Republicans mentioned resignation, she refused to give up. She told the press in May 1974 that her husband had "never considered resignation" and was not about to start. Even after she read the transcripts of the tapes, she argued with reporters about their treatment of her husband.[113]

Pat may have taken heart from knowing that Dick needed her as he had not for years. With fewer and fewer people around him whom he could trust, Nixon isolated himself from the press and the public, even sometimes from his family. At other times, he seemed to need them around. Snippets of evidence indicated that he recognized the important role his wife played in his life. Julie sent her mother a telegram while Pat was in South America, reporting that her father seemed "a little bit lonely and lost" without her. Anxious to avoid thinking about political problems, Dick and Pat often visited Julie and David's house in Bethesda, Maryland, for dinner and an evening of relaxing and reminiscing.[114]

Reporter Helen Thomas told a different sort of story in her memoir. She remembered the time that she and another reporter discovered that the Nixons planned to eat out at a restaurant for Valentine's Day. Hoping to catch an exclusive interview with an increasingly reclusive Nixon, the two reporters went to the restaurant and secured a table near the Nixons and their friend, Bebe Rebozo. After the meal, however, Thomas and her associate discovered a horde of reporters waiting outside. As Dick fended off questions and cameras, Pat sneaked over to Thomas. Rather than being angry at the intrusion, Pat told Thomas how touched she was that Dick took her out to dinner. With "all the troubles Dick has had, all the pressures" he was under, she was amazed that "he would do this" for her.[115]

Pat's belief in her husband continued right up to the end. According to Julie, the family did not want Dick to resign even after the smoking gun tape was released. Recognizing that he had lost the support he needed to continue as president, however, Dick prepared for the end by spending time with the people who had supported him the longest. For their part, they clung to one another. Pat kept her emotions under tight control for the sake of her daughters and her husband. She focused on practical matters: packing, organizing, saying good-bye to her staff.[116] She made it through the formal farewell speeches with tears glimmering in her eyes, but without the look of despair she displayed during the 1960 loss. If she was insulted by her husband's failure to mention her in his last remarks, she did not show it. Perhaps she recognized that his debt to her was too big for words. And then it was over and they took their last ride on *Air Force One,* returning home to California and away from politics forever. For Pat, knowing that this trip spelled the end of her and Dick's long political partnership must have made it a bittersweet journey.

CHAPTER 6

PEACE, AT LAST

In August 1974, Pat Nixon left Washington, D.C., and became a private
citizen again. She never had to give press interviews; she did not have to
make mandated public appearances; she did not have to sit and smile
through speeches she had heard numerous times and stand in receiving lines for hours shaking hands. Instead, she spent her days gardening, walking, reading, and eventually playing with her grandchildren.
She visited only with people she wanted to see. For the rest of her life,
and perhaps for the first time since her husband embarked on his career in government, Pat Nixon controlled her time and schedule. She
finally found the privacy she had desired for so long. She could just be
Pat Nixon, wife, mother, and grandmother.

Gaining her privacy did not end her difficulties, however. The fallout from Watergate followed them to California and complicated their
lives. Legal, financial, and health problems meant that Pat had to wait
years to enjoy her status as private citizen. Drawing on her last reserves
of strength, she nursed her husband back to health only to face her
own physical challenges. She fought hard to regain her health so that
she could finally take pleasure in her family as she had always dreamed.
In their later years, Dick and Pat reinvented their marriage even as
Dick, once again, fought to claim a place as elder statesman.

In August 1974, however, facing the immediate aftermath of the resignation and Watergate, Pat realized that she had not left her troubles

behind in D.C. Although she made every effort to disassociate herself from the political life, she did not cut herself off from the world. She read the newspapers. She knew that even after the resignation, the press continued to discuss the Nixons and their new lives. She knew that, especially in the days right after they left the White House, reporters camped out in San Clemente hoping for a picture or an interview.[1] In addition to worrying about the press, she confronted the huge task of unpacking and turning La Casa Pacifica into their permanent home by herself. Tricia and Ed stayed as long as they could, but Ed had to return to work. Julie and David were three thousand miles away. Pat, with the help of Manolo and Fina Sanchez, transferred their hastily packed possessions from the White House to their new places in California.[2] Her first order of business was carefully to position in his California bedroom the items she had taken from her husband's White House bedroom that morning.[3]

As she completed her lonely task, Pat must have been mulling over all that she had been through in the last year. Even for someone as controlled as Pat, the constant stress of her last days in the White House must have been overwhelming. The anger that she had barely restrained during her last months as first lady must have exploded once the pressure cooker of the White House was gone. She had been furious at the press for demanding "the last ounce of flesh" from her husband, at the public for attacking him, and at Republicans for their failure to support him in his hour of need.[4] Underlying everything must have been anger at her husband for putting her in that position. How could she not be angry at him, although whether or not she admitted that to herself is impossible to know. She never understood why he had not destroyed the tapes, why he had not listened to her advice. Her rage must have been mixed with disappointment and humiliation. Whether or not she believed he had committed any crimes, she acted as she had in the past when her husband was attacked: as though she had been the one accused. She still saw them as the Pat and Dick team. Consequently, his disgrace was hers too. For the proud woman who had resented having to air their family finances during the slush fund crisis, the long walk out of the White House and into the waiting helicopter on that last day must have been torture.

As she had in recovering from earlier crises, however, she retreated into herself, preferring to deal with her emotions in private. News ac-

Pat Nixon and Helene Drown in Tijuana, Mexico, June 1975. Richard Nixon Presidential Library and Museum.

counts in the days right after their arrival in California noted Dick's outing with his friends Robert Abplanalp and Bebe Rebozo as well as a beach picnic with Tricia and Ed. Pat attended neither. She did accompany him to Walter Annenberg's estate for a weekend gathering, but she was isolated from the public on the well-guarded estate.[5] When she met with friends, she worked hard to be cheerful and keep the mood light. She did not want to rehash the traumas of their last days in Washington.[6] Mostly, the couple kept to themselves and did not venture outside the estate grounds.[7]

They could not long escape the tentacles of Watergate, however. In early September, President Gerald Ford granted "a full, free and absolute pardon unto Richard Nixon for all offenses against the United States which he . . . has committed or may have committed or taken part in during the period" of his presidency. Nixon "accepted" the pardon, but admitted only that he had been "wrong in not acting more decisively and more forthrightly in dealing with Watergate."[8] Pat told Julie it was the "saddest day."[9] His acceptance of the pardon, while legally an admission of guilt, did little to assuage those clamoring for a more public mea culpa. Once again, the press and the public discussed Nixon's guilt and possible repercussions. Although the pardon eliminated the potential of prison for Nixon (a fate that awaited most of his former aides), he suffered more private punishments. Disbarred and facing hefty legal bills and subpoenas to appear at the trials of several former aides, a disgraced Nixon was without power for the first time in five and a half years. After having been president, it was hard to imagine doing anything else.[10]

The pressures took a toll on Nixon's health. Although accounts differed as to the state of his mental health, almost all agreed that he suffered from depression. His friends and family denied reports that he was suicidal but acknowledged that he had "his ups and downs."[11] More seriously, however, Nixon's phlebitis flared up. Nixon first experienced the disease's painful vein inflammation during the early 1960s and dealt with flare-ups during the later years of his presidency. In early September 1974, his personal physician, Dr. John Lungren, treated Nixon for a serious recurrence of the condition. Concerned when his first prescriptions did not take care of the problem, Lungren urged Nixon to go to the hospital. The former president refused. Pat took matters into her own hands and called Dr. Walter Tkach, who had been Dick's physician during the presidency.[12] Tkach examined Nixon and found him "suffering from severe physical strain and physical fatigue." The doctor urged him to follow Lungren's advice and go to the hospital. Tkach told reporters that the former president rejected hospitalization, saying that if he went to the hospital, he would "never come out alive." Recognizing that he could do nothing else for his patient, Tkach returned to Washington, where he told reporter Helen Thomas that Nixon was headed for a heart attack.[13]

Tkach was mistaken about the heart attack, but had been correct about the danger of the phlebitis attack. Within a few weeks of Tkach's visit, Lungren hospitalized Nixon for the condition. During his stay, Nixon received anticoagulant drugs, which seemed to help. Lungren sent him home, convinced that the immediate danger had passed.[14] He was wrong. A month later, Nixon was back in the hospital and undergoing surgery. After the surgery, Nixon went into shock as a result of some postoperative bleeding. He almost died. He spent the next six days drifting in and out of consciousness. In all, he spent twenty-three days in the hospital and returned home weak, underweight, and still suffering the effects of his surgery, his near brush with death, and his condition.[15]

Pat went into crisis mode during Dick's illness. She insisted on calling in Dr. Tkach. When Dick finally agreed to go to the hospital, she was a constant visitor. According to Julie, she brought him McDonald's hamburgers and they ate them while they watched *Bonanza* reruns every evening of his stay. During his second hospitalization, she was at his side in the recovery room to feed him ice chips. When he went into cardiac arrest, Pat was in a waiting room with Rose Mary Woods. She went immediately to his room and witnessed the doctors and nurses struggling to stabilize his condition. The sight was almost enough to break her legendary composure. Despite her fears, she remained strong for the girls and for Dick.[16] In fact, her husband credited her with saving his life. When he told her that he did not think he could make it through this crisis, she refused to let him "talk that way." She insisted that he could not "give up." Her determination and belief in him reminded him of her support during the fund crisis.[17] He later told a reporter for *McCall's* that he "might not have survived" without her. "Her immense capacity to comfort and encourage . . . pulled" him through the crisis, he explained. Referring perhaps subconsciously to their entire relationship, he stated that "her faith in me as a human being and as her husband led me out of the depths."[18]

Pat's vigilance continued when he eventually went home from the hospital. Pat watched his diet like a hawk. Reportedly sending him little notes on his dinner tray, she encouraged him to eat healthily and rebuild his strength. Jack Drown witnessed this behavior firsthand during a visit to La Casa Pacifica. Pat brought their lunches out on trays, with a note for her husband explaining that his meal met his doctor's guidelines—and one for Drown stating that his meal was designed to help him lose weight![19] In addition to her role as dietician, she encouraged friends who visited to limit their stay so as not to overtire Dick. She wanted him to recover in body and spirit.

That spirit had been lying beneath the surface during much of the first six months after the resignation. But Dick's usual response to defeat was not to crawl into a hole; it was to plot his resurrection. As he had so many other times, Dick did not assume that defeat meant permanent separation from political power and influence. Consequently, he set to work to salvage what he could of his reputation and to begin shaping his legacy. One of his first actions after arriving at San Clemente was to wage a campaign for his presidential papers. Those legal battles continued for years and ignited debates among political officials, reporters, and the public as to the ownership of all public records.[20]

He also set to work trying to sell his story to help pay his legal fees, provide him and Pat with a future income, and to tell his side of the Watergate story. A year after the resignation, he negotiated a deal with television show host David Frost for a series of interviews, during which they would discuss domestic and foreign affairs as well as Watergate.[21] Even as he recovered from his surgery, he had been working on his memoirs. He used what papers he had access to as well as calling on the memories of former aides and old friends. His small staff scoured the country interviewing people and copying papers to try to produce as accurate a version of his presidential years as possible.[22]

In addition to sharing his take on the past, he worked to secure his place in the present. As his health permitted, and increasingly in 1975, Dick met with a wide variety of people. He liked hearing the political gossip and offering his perspective on world and national events. Anxious to travel again (1975 was the first year in over a decade when he had not been abroad at least once), the former president sent out feelers to test his welcome in world capitals. He was particularly interested in visiting China again. Through various sources, the Chinese had let it be known that they would welcome Nixon. Waiting only for President Ford to make his first trip to Peking, Nixon allowed the Chinese to announce the news that he would be meeting with Mao in February 1976. Ford and his political aides, especially Kissinger, worried about his motives for going, his intentions while there, and his timing (the trip would steal headlines from Ford during primary season). Ignoring all of that, private citizens Dick and Pat flew off to a sort of déjà vu trip to Peking. Like last time, Dick met with Chinese leaders, including an elderly Mao; unlike last time, Dick had to do a lot more sightseeing. When they returned, Kissinger, appearing to forget his earlier anger, called to debrief Nixon about what he had learned. Dick was on his way to rehabilitating his image.[23]

But then the Watergate scandals resurfaced. In the spring of 1976, Woodward and Bernstein, who led the journalistic inquiry into the Watergate break-in, struck again. In April, the movie adaptation of their first book, *All the President's Men,* appeared on screens across America. Then in May, the pair published their monograph recounting the collapse of the Nixon administration. Entitled *The Final Days,* the book covered Nixon's last hundred days in office. The authors claimed in their foreword that they based their work on extensive interviews with participants in the actual events. Because the interviews were done as "background," however, none of the interviewees' names appeared in the book and there were no citations to sources. Instead, the authors wrote in a narrative style, with conversations recreated verbatim and the feelings and thoughts of participants included. Indicative of the public's appetite for all things Nixon (as well as juicy gossip about well-known figures), the book broke sales records.[24]

The book outraged the Nixon family and their supporters. In their monograph, the authors described Nixon as a danger to himself and the country, talking to portraits and drinking heavily. They painted Pat as a recluse, hiding in her bedroom, reading inspirational literature, sneaking alcohol from the pantry, and avoiding her duties as first lady.[25] Outraged by the characterization of her mother as a "nonperson," Julie responded publicly in a *Newsweek* guest editorial which defended her mother's character and record.[26] Pat's former press secretary, Helen Smith, wrote an article in *Good Housekeeping* detailing her version of Pat's final days in the White House. In the process, she countered many of the assertions in the Woodward and Bernstein book. She scoffed at the idea of Pat drinking secretly and heavily and asserted that "as the pressure mounted, she became even more conscientious" about keeping her "back-breaking schedule."[27] Conservative journalist Victor Lasky wrote what he entitled "The Woodstein Report," cataloging the inaccuracies in details and the denials of some of the characters in the book. Even Deidre Carmody in the *New York Times* questioned the technique of "reproduc[ing] verbatim quotations from conversations they had not heard."[28]

Despite the efforts of her family and friends, the image of Pat as a drunk became almost as embedded in the public consciousness as her earlier reputation as "plastic Pat." In fact, the two images melded together easily: the superficial facade hid the secret lush. Popular representations of her accepted the Woodward and Bernstein version of her life in the White House. From the *Saturday Night Live* skits of the late 1970s to the Oliver Stone movie, *Nixon*, in the mid-1990s, Pat's portrayers reinforced the impression that she survived the Watergate scandal by drinking heavily. Whether or not she was an alcoholic did not seem to be a matter of concern.

The fact that Pat had been a drinker complicated the situation for her defenders. Although she told countless reporters that she did not drink or smoke, she did both. Alcohol had been part of their family parties and social gatherings.[29] Pat and Helene joked in their letters about enjoying their drinks. This pattern of drinking and smoking on the sly did not stop once she became first lady; it was just harder to maintain the fiction that she abstained from tobacco and alcohol. As the wife of the president, Pat was surrounded continually by Secret Service agents, assistants, maids, and reporters. Her habit of having a drink, preferably Jack Daniels, became common knowledge to a larger group of people. The escalating tension during the Watergate crisis caused her to drink more and more openly than she normally did. This increased consumption did not affect her ability to carry out her duties as first lady. Considering the number of reporters following her every move as the crisis unfolded, any aberration in her behavior would have been exposed and examined. Her drinking habits only came to light after Nixon's resignation as the public looked for any bit of dirt on the former president.

The blows kept coming. In June, Nixon learned that the New York bar association had convicted him of ethical violations and revoked his license to practice law. He had already resigned from the California bar and the U.S. Supreme Court, but the New York bar refused to allow him to resign.[30]

Then in July, Pat had a stroke. Julie and David had flown to California for the Fourth of July holiday weekend, and the family had attended a bicentennial party organized by longtime supporters. Pat stayed late at the party and seemed fine. A couple of days after the party, she complained of being tired and went to bed early. The next morning, Dick noticed that she was having trouble with the simple task of making coffee. He woke Julie, and together they convinced Pat to allow them to call the doctor and phone for an ambulance. Ever the trooper, she walked to the ambulance on her own. At the hospital, doctors diagnosed her with a hemorrhage in her right cerebral cortex that paralyzed her left side and caused her speech to slur. She remained in the hospital for two weeks, undergoing drug and physical therapy. When she returned home, she continued the physical therapy.[31]

Although she was determined to regain her strength, she did feel, as Maureen Drown Nunn put it, that "the wind was blown out of her sails" by the stroke. She uncharacteristically admitted to one of the nurses in the hospital that she was "beat" and told Tricia that a procedure really had hurt.[32] Her body had never betrayed her before. No matter how many hours she stood in receiving lines or sat in the freezing rain or blazing heat, no matter how little sleep she got because she had flown through too many time zones, she had never worried about whether she could handle it physically. It must have been difficult to accept her own limitations. Her frustration with this weakness and her resentment at having to relearn basic skills occasionally surfaced. Years afterward, when Clare Boothe Luce commented that she could see no signs of the stroke, Pat forcefully reminded her that only through willpower was she able to move beyond being a "baby" again and regain full use of her arm and hand.[33]

Because she had always been the strong one, Pat's family, friends, and the press looked for reasons for her stroke. They pointed to the fact that she had been reading *The Final Days* or that Dick told her that his disbarment had been made public and would be all over the news. Dr. Joyce Brothers conjectured that the stress of inactivity after her forced retirement from Washington compounded the build-up of pressures from her years as first lady to aggravate her hypertension.[34] Far easier to find someone or something to blame than to recognize that Pat was a sixty-four-year-old woman who had not had a physical in over a year, who smoked, and who had been under an extraordinary amount of stress.

In the months and years after the stroke, Pat's family and friends made a concerted effort to reduce her stress, and she devoted herself to restoring her health and her image of strength. Her circle of visitors tightened even further. Even those who did get to see Pat understood that they would have to limit their time together so as not to tire the former first lady. When she met with friends, however, she strove to be her old self. Friends who had not seen her for awhile marveled at how well she looked. At one event, she delighted guests by telling jokes that had everyone "howling." The shopkeepers and restaurateurs in San Clemente did their part to keep her occasional trips to their businesses secret, but she went to town.[35] Proving that the stroke had not broken her iron will, she occasionally ignored her weakened left side and acted as if nothing were wrong. Biographer David Lester wrote of the time she determinedly walked without a limp past a reporter she happened upon in an elevator.[36] She might still spend most of her time within the protective walls of San Clemente, but she would not let the world see how she suffered.

In the meantime, there were happy changes. In 1977, Julie and David decided to move to the West Coast. They were both working on biographies of famous relatives: he was writing a book about his grandfather, and she was working on one about her mother. Pat's joy increased even more in 1978 when Julie announced that she was pregnant.[37] Jennie Eisenhower's birth in August 1978 was followed by the arrival of Christopher Cox, Tricia and Ed's son, in March 1979. Two more grandchildren, Alex and Melanie Eisenhower, added to Pat's joy. Children had always delighted her, and she thrilled to hear the sound of little voices ringing throughout the house.[38]

As time went by, Pat and Dick also felt that they needed to make other changes. In early 1980, they moved back to New York City. Julie and David had decided to move to Pennsylvania, leaving Pat grandchildless on the West Coast. Additionally, La Casa Pacifica did not seem to serve the couple's needs as it had earlier. It was too big and, with the retirements of the Sanchezes, too unmanageable. Pat could not keep up with the gardens as she had in the past. New York offered a variety of activities for both Pat and Dick as well as the anonymity of city life. They bought a townhouse that included a small garden for Pat and a library for Dick.[39] Their pleasure in the Big Apple lasted about a year and a half. By that time, they discovered that their faces were too well known to blend in, even in New York City. Dick also had some concerns about Pat and the stairs in their townhome. They sold the Manhattan digs and moved to a suburb in New Jersey. There they could enjoy their grandchildren away from the prying eyes of the media. In 1983, Pat suffered another mild stroke. She had to rest more frequently but continued her visits with her grandchildren.[40]

Pat also seemed to enjoy a closer relationship with her husband. Perhaps the double blow of the resignation and his close brush with death made him realize how important she was to him. Perhaps her stroke helped her to recognize her own limitations and to let go of some of her anger. Perhaps they were just two people who had been married a long time who were finally alone together enough to get comfortable with one another. Although they often spent their days apart—he working on his books, speeches, and political analysis and

*President and Mrs. Nixon posed with President and Mrs. Gerald Ford, President
and Mrs. Ronald Reagan, and President and Mrs. George Bush at the dedication
of the Richard Nixon Library, July 1990. Richard Nixon Presidential Library and
Museum.*

she reading or working in her gardens—they usually had dinner together. He appeared to be more solicitous of her needs and desires. He
watched her carefully to make certain that she did not get overtired. In
addition to the second stroke, she fought off several bouts of pneumo-
nia and bronchitis.[41] By the early 1990s, the years of heavy smoking
caught up with her; she suffered from emphysema and eventually lung
cancer. She died in June 1993 with her husband and daughters by her
side. Less than a year later, Dick suffered a major stroke; he died within
the week. The Dick and Pat team was no more.

Even in her last years, Pat had remained something of an intriguing
mystery to the press and the people. Articles about her appeared occasionally in women's magazines, and her name remained on the list of
Most Admired Women in America. In fact, for almost 20 years, *Good
Housekeeping* readers chose Pat as "one of the 10 most admired women
in the world."[42] The variety of her obituaries continued the pattern of
speculation about the former first lady. Some writers painted her as a
kind of secular saint, while others described her as the hapless victim
of her manipulative husband.[43] Although most emphasized her do-

mesticity, at least one journalist discovered that Pat had been a "stealth feminist" who preceded first lady Hillary Clinton in taking an official position in her husband's administration.[44]

The variety of Pat's obituaries reveals three essential characteristics of her life. First, Pat's life was hard from beginning to end. She accepted the hardship, faced it, fought against it when she could, and then moved on. She never let it define or limit her. In fact, she was proud that she rarely got sick or tired or complained. Second, she was "of the people," and they recognized that. Pat might have dined with kings and queens on occasion, but she never forgot where she came from or who she was. Her obsession with her correspondence was less about the political benefit it provided her husband and more about the effect on the recipient's life. For many women, Pat exemplified the struggles of their generation. They had been raised to stand by their husbands and endure in their marriages. If there were times they were unhappy, then they dealt with it.[45]

Third, the obituaries recognized the importance of Pat's relationship with Dick. Almost all of the articles mentioned her dislike of politics and her almost "Tammy Wynette–ish" willingness to "stand by her man." In describing her this way, the authors turned her into a caricature of herself. Even without necessarily meaning to, they resurrected the image of plastic Pat. They turned Pat's life into Dick's life. They gave him all the decision-making power and assumed she just went, albeit unhappily, along for the ride. Their relationship became less of a marriage and more of an employer–employee situation.

Such a version of reality ignored the fact that Pat made her choices. She might not have always liked it, but she chose to live the life she did. She recognized that the thrill of traveling all over the world, the satisfaction of helping people in trouble as she did in Peru, and the pride of representing the United States in Africa came at the price of the frustrations of living in the public eye. She might not have been happy with certain aspects of her life in politics, but it was a life she chose to lead, and it was one that brought her immense satisfaction at various times. The little girl from Artesia learned at an early age that life was not fair, but if you worked hard, you might get part of what you wanted.

In the process of working hard, Pat helped to transform the first lady's role. Although observers at the time often criticized her for failing to focus on a specific cause, the way Lady Bird Johnson did, or for appearing to mirror Mamie Eisenhower, Pat succeeded in pushing some of the limits of acceptable first lady responsibilities and behaviors. She traveled more than any first lady up to her time and accompanied her husband on his groundbreaking trip to the People's Republic of China. Press reports of her interactions with the Chinese as she toured the country offered Americans a glimpse into the formerly closed society. Building on her experiences as the second lady, Pat refused to limit her official first lady itineraries to ladies' teas and receptions. She wanted to visit hospitals and schools. Her determination to meet with wounded American soldiers during a visit to South Vietnam meant that she became the first first lady to travel to a combat zone. Pat showed that the first lady was not just a ceremonial prop.

Pat also traveled successfully on her own. Her journey to Peru after the earthquake brought humanitarian relief to the wounded and needy citizens of Lima and helped to forge a new relationship between the two countries. When she attended the inauguration of the new president of Liberia, she became the first wife of a sitting president to serve as an official United States representative to a foreign country. Pat's enthusiastic response to the peoples she met in South America and Africa served a diplomatic purpose for her husband and secured an opening for future first ladies to explore. In fact, Pat's initial success with handling diplomacy on her own led to her taking additional solo trips during her husband's terms in office.

Like almost everything else connected to Richard Nixon, Pat's expansion of the role of first lady was overshadowed by Watergate. Rather than celebrating her accomplishments, Pat spent her last months in the White House avoiding reporters and urging her husband to fight. Instead of the press inquiring about her next trip or commenting on her appearing in a pantsuit in a women's magazine (another first), the focus was on the growing scandal. Even Pat's obituaries twenty years after the resignation concentrated more on Watergate than on her activities as first lady.

In focusing on the end, however, reporters and the public missed the extraordinary story of the transformation of Thelma Catherine Ryan into Pat Nixon. They lost the adventurous woman who drove herself across the country and later flew into the mountains of Peru buckled onto a folding chair in a small airplane. They forgot the teacher who could make her students and later people she met around the world feel special. They ignored the young woman with laughing eyes who brought joy to the African women she met when she joined their dance. Pat Nixon never lost sight of Thelma Ryan.

NOTES

CHAPTER 1: LESSONS LEARNED

1. Lester David, *The Lonely Lady of San Clemente* (New York: Thomas Y. Crowell, 1978), 21–23; Julie Nixon Eisenhower, *Pat Nixon: The Untold Story* (New York: Simon & Schuster, 1986), 17–18; http://www.piochenevada.com/history.htm, accessed 8 March 2010; and http://www.nevadaweb.com/cnt/pe/ely/, accessed 8 March 2010.

2. Eisenhower, *Pat Nixon*, 19. Interestingly, the 1910 census lists Matthew Bender living both with his mother and stepfather in Nevada and his grandparents in Los Angeles. See 1910 Census, Los Angeles Assembly District 73, Los Angeles, California; roll T624_83; page 5A; Enumeration District 192; image 398; 1910 Census; Pioche, Nevada; Roll T624_858; page 2B; Enumeration District 44; image 561.

3. Years later, when Pat first filled out her application to teach, she listed her birthdate as 17 March 1913. She did the same thing on her Social Security application. Although this might have been a deliberate attempt to make herself one year younger, it might also have been a mistake. Her parents usually celebrated her birthday on St. Patrick's Day. Her childhood friends thought she was born in 1913. That would seem to indicate that the mistaken date originated early in her life. She corrected the information in her Social Security file in 1975. Thelma Patricia Ryan, Social Security application, Social Security Administration.

4. Eisenhower, *Pat Nixon*, 17, 19. For purposes of continuity, I will refer to her as Pat even though she did not call herself that until college.

5. Eisenhower, *Pat Nixon*, 18, 24.

6. Ibid., 19; Louise Raine Gwinn, 3 June 1970, OH 870, Oral History Program, California State University, Fullerton, 3–4 (hereafter COPH); Carmen De Remer Griffin, OH 869, COPH, 3; Myrtle Raine Borden, 21 April 1970, OH 813, COPH, 12.

7. Eisenhower, *Pat Nixon*, 19–20; Borden interview, 2.

8. Borden interview, 1–4; Gwinn interview, 1–2, 4–5.

9. Borden interview, 3–4.

10. Eisenhower, *Pat Nixon*, 21. The evidence surrounding Will's drinking is inconclusive. None of the oral histories gathered for the various Nixon projects mentions his drinking, nor does Lester David's biography. In fact, scholars would not

know anything about it except for Julie Eisenhower's brief discussion in her book about her mother.

11. For a discussion of Eleanor Roosevelt's relationship with her father, see Blanche Wiesen Cook, *Eleanor Roosevelt* (New York: Viking Press, 1992), 1:56–79; for Betty Ford, see John Robert Greene, *Betty Ford: Candor and Courage in the White House* (Lawrence: University Press of Kansas, 2004), 2–3.

12. Eisenhower, *Pat Nixon,* 21, 26.

13. Jessamyn West, "The Unknown Pat Nixon," *Good Housekeeping,* February 1971, 127.

14. Eisenhower, *Pat Nixon,* 27.

15. Ibid., 28; Borden interview, 3; Gwinn interview, 4.

16. Gwinn interview, 6; Borden interview, 11.

17. Virginia Burbee Stouffer Endicott, oral history, *Collection of Sixty Interviews for Pat Ryan Nixon,* compiled by Alice Martin Rosenberger, 1978, Whittier Public Library, Artesia, California.

18. "'Rise of Silas Lapham' Shows Remarkable Progress," *Excelsior Life,* 6 March 1929, "PN Misc. Photos and Original Clippings," envelope, box 1, Pre-Presidential Series 265, Patricia Ryan Nixon Collection (hereafter PRNC), Nixon Presidential Library, Yorba Linda, California; "'Rise of Silas Lapham' Draws Enormous Attendance," clipping, no paper, n.d., "H.S.," box 1, PPS 265, PRNC.

19. Ralph Farnum, note in *Green and White,* Excelsior Union High School, 1929, box 1, PPS 265, PRNC.

20. Griffin interview, 9.

21. Ira C. Holmes, COPH 880, 3–4.

22. David, *Lonely Lady,* 19.

23. Eisenhower, *Pat Nixon,* 31–33.

24. Ibid., 32–35; "Looking into the Future," Excelsior Union High School, 1929, negative, "H.S.," box 1, PPS 265, PRNC.

25. Ibid., 34.

26. "Cast of 'Broken Dishes' Has Had Experience in Drama," [Fullerton Junior College] *Weekly Torch,* 27 April 1932, "PN Misc. Photos and Original Clippings," envelope, box 1, PPS 265, PRNC.

27. Eisenhower, *Pat Nixon,* 35–37, 39; West, "The Unknown Pat Nixon," 127; Pat Ryan to Bill Ryan, [October 1933], "PN Early—Brothers," box 2, PPS 265, PRNC.

28. Eisenhower, *Pat Nixon,* 37–39, 41. Perhaps this is where the rumors of a first marriage originate.

29. Ibid., 441–442; Commencement Program, University of Southern California, 1937, "PN Early—USC," box 2, PPS 265, PRNC.

30. Eisenhower, *Pat Nixon*, 42–43; letters of recommendation, application to Bureau of Teacher Placement, University of Southern California, [April–May 1937], "PN Early—USC," box 2, PPS 265, PRNC.

31. Eisenhower, *Pat Nixon*, 40.

32. Ibid., 45–47.

33. Ibid., 47–49.

34. R. E. Slaughter, 28 April 1937, and W. G. Campbell, 3 May 1937, attached to Bureau of Teacher Placement application.

35. Virginia Burbee Stouffer Endicott and Mildred Eason Stouffer, oral histories, both in Rosenberger, comp., *Collection of Sixty Interviews for Pat Ryan Nixon*.

36. See various oral histories in Rosenberger, comp., *Collection of Sixty Interviews for Pat Ryan Nixon,* including those by Mildred Eason Stouffer, Frances King, Fay Kerl Caldwell, Phyllis McCandless Andrews, Margaret Kroener Huntsberger, and Robert O. Blake. The story of the young men visiting Nixon came from Edward M. Benson.

37. J. Robert Cauffman, Lois Beatty Mills, and Edward M. Benson, oral histories, all in Rosenberger, comp., *Collection of Sixty Interviews for Pat Ryan Nixon*.

38. IEisenhower, *Pat Nixon: The Untold Story*, 52.

39. Ibid., 52–53; Margaret Langstaff Kaping and Sherril Neece, oral histories, in Rosenberger, comp., *Collection of Sixty Interviews for Pat Ryan Nixon*.

40. Eisenhower, *Pat Nixon*, 54–55.

41. Elizabeth A. Cloes, California Oral History Project, 2–3. Elizabeth was in the car with Dick and Pat for these early encounters. She explained in an oral interview that he proposed on the third encounter. Nixon claimed that he asked her to marry him the first night they met. For Nixon's version, see Richard M. Nixon, *RN: The Memoirs of Richard Nixon* (New York: Grosset & Dunlap, 1978), 23. For Pat's version, see Eisenhower, *Pat Nixon*, 56–58.

42. Nixon, *Memoirs,* 4–6.

43. Ibid., 9–12.

44. Ibid., 9.

45. Eisenhower, *Pat Nixon*, 60.

46. Richard Nixon to Patricia Ryan, 11 January 1939, "Early Marriage—WWII," box 2, PPS 265, PRNC.

47. Eisenhower, *Pat Nixon*, 59–61.

48. Helene Drown, speech, attached to Jack Drown to Richard Nixon, 28 April 1986, "Drown," box 2A, Helene and Jack Drown Collection, Nixon Presidential Library and Museum; "A Tribute to Jack Drown," memorial program, 28 September 1999, "1990s," box 4, Drown Collection; Eisenhower, *Pat Nixon*, 71.

49. Eisenhower, *Pat Nixon,* 71–73; Nixon, *Memoirs,* 25–26.

50. Pat Nixon to Helene Drown, postcard, postmarked 10 January 1942, "Correspondence: 1942–1951," box 1, Drown Collection.

51. Richard Polenberg, *War and Society: The United States, 1941–1945* (Philadelphia: Lippincott, 1972), 30–34; David M. Kennedy, *Freedom from Fear: The American People in Depression and War, 1929–1945* (New York: Oxford University Press, 1999), 478, 620–621.

52. Nixon, *Memoirs,* 26–27.

53. Ibid., 28–29.

54. Eisenhower, *Pat Nixon,* 83.

55. Ibid., 58.

56. Ibid., 85.

57. David, *Lonely Lady,* 64; Earl Mazo, *Richard Nixon: A Political and Personal Portrait* (New York: Harper, 1959), 43.

58. David, *Lonely Lady,* 64.

59. Nixon, *Memoirs,* 35–37.

60. Hortense Behrens, oral history, in Rosenberger, comp., *Collection of Sixty Interviews for Pat Ryan Nixon.*

61. Donald Fantz, oral history, in Rosenberger, comp., *Collection of Sixty Interviews for Pat Ryan Nixon.*

62. Eisenhower, *Pat Nixon,* 87.

63. Nixon, *Memoirs,* 36.

64. For a discussion of women's participation in the political process, see, among others, Mary C. Brennan, *Wives, Mothers, and the Red Menace: Conservative Women and the Crusade against Communism* (Boulder: University Press of Colorado, 2008); Catherine Rymph, *Republican Women: Feminism and Conservatism from Suffrage through the Rise of the New Right* (Chapel Hill: University of North Carolina Press, 2006); Lisa McGirr, *Suburban Warriors: The Origins of the New Right* (Princeton, N.J.: Princeton University Press, 2001). For the traditional view see, Betty Friedan, *The Feminine Mystique* (New York: Norton, 1963).

65. Eisenhower, *Pat Nixon,* 88–89.

66. Irwin F. Gellman, *The Contender, Richard Nixon: The Congress Years, 1946–1952* (New York: Free Press, 1999), 61–88; Nixon, *Memoirs,* 37–41. The legend of Tricky Dick would actually develop during later campaigns, especially the 1952 vice presidential campaign. Purveyors of the label would use the campaign against Voorhis as an example of Dick's trickiness even though the term was not used at the time. See Gellman, *Contender,* 289.

67. Nixon, *Memoirs,* 36.

68. Ibid., 40.

69. David, *Lonely Lady,* 65–66.

70. Stephen E. Ambrose, *Nixon* (New York: Simon & Schuster, 1987–1991), 122.

71. Eisenhower, *Pat Nixon,* 92.

72. Nixon, *Memoirs,* 42–43.

73. Ibid., 48–52; quotation on 50.

74. Ibid., 44–45, quotation on 44; Herbert S. Parmet, *Richard Nixon and His America* (Boston: Little, Brown, 1990), 140–141.

75. Robert Griffith, *The Politics of Fear* (Rochelle Park, N.J.: Hayden, 1970); M. J. Heale, *American Anticommunism: Combating the Enemy Within, 1830–1970* (Baltimore, Md.: Johns Hopkins University Press, 1990), 145–146, 161, 165–166.

76. For the best, though controversial, scholarly account, see Allen Weinstein, *Perjury: The Hiss-Chambers Case* (New York: Random House, 1978).

77. Nixon, *Memoirs,* 71–74.

78. Ibid., 75–78.

79. Ambrose, *Nixon,* 136.

80. Pat Nixon to Helene Drown, various letters, February through November 1951, "Correspondence: 1942–1951," box 1, Drown Collection.

81. Pat Nixon and Joe Alex Morris, "I Say He's a Wonderful Guy," *Saturday Evening Post,* 6 September 1952, 93; quotation in "Pat Nixon Has Same Problems as Other Young Wives Who Watch Budget," 9 October 1950, [unknown paper], "1950—Apr.–Dec.," PPS 266, box 1, PRNC; Pat Nixon to Helene Drown, [12 March 1951] and [3 November 1951], "Correspondence: 1942–1951," Drown Collection.

82. Pat Nixon to Helene Drown, [3 November 1951], "Correspondence: 1942–1951," box 1, Drown Collection.

83. Nixon and Morris, "Wonderful Guy," 93.

84. Helen Daniels, oral history, in Rosenberger, comp., *Collection of Sixty Interviews for Pat Ryan Nixon.*

85. Pat Nixon to Helene Drown, [4 September 1951], "Correspondence: 1942–1951," box 1, Drown Collection.

86. See letters, Richard Nixon to Pat Nixon, September 1947, "1947—Correspondence," box 1, PRNC.

87. Pat Nixon to Helene Drown, [February 1951], "Correspondence: 1942–1951," box 1, Drown Collection.

88. Eisenhower, *Pat Nixon,* 101; Nixon, *Memoirs,* 67.

89. See, for example, Pat Nixon to Helene Drown, [4 September 1951], "Correspondence: 1942–1951," or Pat Nixon to Helene Drown, [8 January 1952], "Correspondence: 1952," both in box 1, Drown Collection.

90. Pat Nixon to Helene Drown, [3 November 1951], "Correspondence: 1942–1951," box 1, Drown Collection.

91. Pat Nixon to Helene Drown, [4 September 1951] and [February 1951], "Correspondence: 1942–1951," box 1, Drown Collection.

92. Pat Nixon to Helene Drown, [November 1951?], "Correspondence: 1942–1951," box 1, Drown Collection.

93. Pat Nixon to Helene Drown, [3 November 1951], "Correspondence: 1942–1951," box 1, Drown Collection.

94. Pat Nixon to Helene Drown, [February 1951], "Correspondence: 1942–1951," box 1, Drown Collection.

95. See various letters, Richard Nixon to Pat Nixon, September 1947, "1947—Correspondence," box 1, PRNC.

96. Eisenhower, *Pat Nixon*, 97–98.

97. Quotation in Pat Nixon to Helene Drown, [February 1951], "Correspondence: 1942–1951," box 1, Drown Collection. See also Pat Nixon to Helene Drown, [November 1951?], "Correspondence: 1942–1951," box 1, Drown Collection.

98. Pat Nixon to "Folks," [1947], "1947—Correspondence," box 1, PRNC.

99. See, for example, Catherine to Pat Nixon, n.d., "1948," box 1, PRNC; Pat Nixon to Helene Drown, [12 March 1951?], "Correspondence: 1942–1951," box 1, Drown Collection.

100. Pat Nixon to Helene Drown, [February 1951], "Correspondence: 1942–1951," box 1, Drown Collection.

101. Richard Nixon to Pat Nixon, 22 September 1947, "1947—Correspondence," box 1, PRNC.

102. Pat Nixon to Helene Drown, [12 March 1951?], "Correspondence: 1942–1951," box 1, Drown Collection.

103. Pat Nixon to Helene Drown, [February 1951], Correspondence: 1942–1951," box 1, Drown Collection.

104. See "1950 Campaign Itineraries April–Nov.," box 1, PRNC.

105. George Reade Jr. to Pat Nixon, 9 November 1950, "1950—Apr.–Dec.," box 1, PRNC.

106. Marjorie Sharpe, transcript of radio show, 1 November 1950, "1950—Apr.–Dec.," box 1, PRNC.

107. Nixon and Morris, "Wonderful Guy," 18.

108. Pat Nixon to Helene Drown, [February 1951] and [November 1951?], "Correspondence: 1942–1951," box 1, Drown Collection.

109. David, *Lonely Lady*, 79–83.

110. Nixon and Morris, "Wonderful Guy," 57.

111. Ambrose, *Nixon*, 16, 244.

112. Marjorie Sharpe, transcript of radio show.

CHAPTER 2: THE PAT AND DICK TEAM

1. Ruth Montgomery, "New Pat Nixon Is Enchanting," 21 August 1956, *New York Journal-American*, Center for American History, Austin, Texas.

2. For a general overview of American life during these years, see James T. Patterson, *Grand Expectations: The United States, 1945–1974* (New York: Oxford University Press, 1996), 311–374; Elaine Tyler May, *Homeward Bound: American Families in the Cold War Era* (New York: Basic Books, 1988), 284.

3. Patterson, *Grand Expectations*, 105–136, 207–242.

4. David McCullough, *Truman* (New York: Simon & Schuster, 1992), 857–903.

5. For changes in the Republican party, see Lewis L. Gould, *Grand Old Party: A History of the Republicans* (New York: Random House, 2003), 303–330. To better understand the conservative wing of the GOP, see George H. Nash, *The Conservative Intellectual Movement in America since 1945*, 30th anniversary edition (Wilmington, Delaware: ISI Books, 2006).

6. Herbert S. Parmet, *Eisenhower and the American Crusades* (New York: Macmillan, 1972), 45–60.

7. Richard M. Nixon, *RN: The Memoirs of Richard Nixon* (New York: Grosset & Dunlap, 1978), 83.

8. Ibid., 83–85.

9. Irwin F. Gellman, *The Contender, Richard Nixon: The Congress Years, 1946–1952* (New York: Free Press, 1999), 418–420. By law, Nixon could not change his vote for Warren once favorite son status had been applied.

10. Jack Drown to Richard Nixon, 9 June 1952, "Drown, Jack and Helene, 1956 and before, 1957, 2/2," Richard Nixon Vice Presidential Papers, box 225, Richard Nixon Library and Museum, Yorba Linda, California.

11. See, for example, Fawn McKay Brodie, *Richard Nixon: The Shaping of His Character* (New York: Norton, 1981), 255–256; Stephen E. Ambrose, *Nixon* (New York: Simon & Schuster, 1987–1991), 261–265.

12. For Richard Nixon's version of events, Nixon, *RN: The Memoirs of Richard Nixon*, 85–89. For Pat Nixon's perspective, see Lester David, *The Lonely Lady of San Clemente* (New York: Thomas Y. Crowell, 1978), 82–83, or Julie Nixon Eisenhower, *Pat Nixon: The Untold Story* (New York: Simon & Schuster, 1986), 114–116.

13. Eisenhower, *Pat Nixon*, 116.

14. Ibid., 116–117.

15. Ibid., 117.

16. Ed Harris to Pat Nixon, 30 August 1952, "1952—Aug. 1—Sept. 21," Pre-Presidential Series 266, Patricia Ryan Nixon Collection (hereafter PRNC), Nixon Presidential Library, Yorba Linda, California.

17. Pat Nixon and Joe Alex Morris, "I Say He's a Wonderful Guy," *Saturday Evening Post*, 6 September 1952, 18. For a discussion of the campaign strategy, see Ambrose, *Nixon*, 271–273.

18. Nixon and Morris, "Wonderful Guy," 93.

19. Ibid., 93–94.

20. Richard M. Nixon, *Six Crises* (Garden City, N.Y.: Doubleday, 1962), 78–79.

21. Dwight D. Eisenhower, *Mandate for Change, 1953–1956* (Garden City, N.Y.: Doubleday, 1963), 65–66.

22. Nixon, *Six Crises*, 73–129; Earl Mazo, *Richard Nixon: A Political and Personal Portrait* (New York: Harper, 1959), 100–137; and Nixon, *Memoirs*, 92–108.

23. Nixon, *Six Crises*, 87.

24. Nixon, *Memoirs*, 103.

25. H. H. Albert to Pat Nixon, 24 September 1952, "1952—Sept. 24 (A–L)," PPS 266, box 2, PRNC.

26. Mrs. W. R. (Roberta) Wiley to Pat Nixon, 23 September 1952, "1952—Sept. 23 (K–Z)," PPS 266, box 2, PRNC. There are four folders of letters in this box.

27. Garry Wills, *Nixon Agonistes: The Crisis of the Self-Made Man* (Boston: Houghton Mifflin, 1970), 91–114.

28. Marcia Elliott Wray, Oral History Program, California State College, Fullerton, 988, 16–17.

29. Eisenhower, *Pat Nixon*, 120–121.

30. Ibid., 123, 125.

31. Ibid., 126.

32. Nixon, *Six Crises*, 73–129; Ambrose, *Nixon*, 295.

33. Nixon, *Memoirs*, 111, 113.

34. Parmet, *Eisenhower and the American Crusades*, 150–160.

35. Patterson, *Grand Expectations*, 276–310.

36. Fred Greenstein, *The Hidden-Hand Presidency* (New York: Basic Books, 1982), 155–227.

37. Nash, *Conservative Intellectual Movement*, 395–398.

38. Eisenhower, *Pat Nixon*, 130–131, 168.

39. Pat Nixon to Helene Drown, [14 July 1953?], "Correspondence: 1953," box 1, Helene and Jack Drown Collection, Nixon Presidential Library and Museum.

40. Eisenhower, *Pat Nixon*, 170.

41. Her appointment books list Brownie and PTA meetings along with recep-

tions and state dinners. See, for example, Pat Nixon, appointment book, 1955, "Appointment Book," box 1, PPS 270, PRNC.

42. Pat Nixon to Helene Drown, 13 July 1955, "1955," box 1, Drown Collection.

43. Pat Nixon to Helene Drown, [1 April and 3 February 1953], "Correspondence: 1953," box 1, Drown Collection.

44. See various versions of these calendars in appropriately marked folders in box 1, PPS 273, PRNC.

45. Marilyn Irvin Holt, *Mamie Doud Eisenhower: The General's First Lady* (Lawrence: University Press of Kansas, 2007), 68–69. For invitations to the White House, see "Eisenhower File, Correspondence 1953–1960," Special File, PPS 268, box 1, PRNC. For evidence of their relationship, see correspondence between the two in "Nixon, Vice President and Mrs. (Pat and Dick)," box 14 and 32, Mamie Doud Eisenhower Papers, Dwight D. Eisenhower Library, Abilene, Kansas.

46. Ibid., 64–65, 79–82, 124–128.

47. Ibid., 60–69.

48. In 1955, Eisenhower suffered a heart attack; in 1956, doctors operated on him for a bout of ileitis; and in 1957, he suffered a stroke.

49. "Mrs. Richard Nixon's Busy Schedule Re-arranged for Increased Duties," Whittier, California, *News,* 26 October 1955, "1955, October," box 3, PRNC; Pat Nixon to Helene Drown, 1 October 1955, "1955," box 1, Drown Collection.

50. Pat Nixon to Helene Drown, n.d., "1958," box 2, Drown Collection; Isabella Taves, "Pat Nixon Problems of a 'Perfect Wife,'" *Redbook,* May 1956, 30, 31–33, 90, 92; Pat Nixon to Helene Drown, 13 December 1958, "1958," box 2, Drown Collection.

51. Rose Mary Woods and Don Murray, "Nixon's My Boss," *Saturday Evening Post,* 28 December 1957, 20–21, 77+.

52. See, for example, Pat Nixon, handwritten notes, on Lucille Armour to Pat Nixon, 22 February 1953, "1953 Jan. 20–Feb.," PPS 267, box 1, PRNC or P. J. Everts to Pat Nixon, n.d., "1955 March [1 of 2]," box 3, PPS 270, PRNC.

53. Marie C. Norrie to Pat Nixon, 25 April 1954, "Correspondence April [2 of 2]," PPS 269, box 1, PRNC; Helen Ruth Hillier, "Wife of Veep Proves 'Regular,'" *Flint News Adv.* [*sic*], 9 September 1955, "1955, September," box 3, PPS 270, PRNC; Ohittabibeh[?] Aga Khan to Pat Nixon, 24 January 1957, "PPS 268–270, 72, 75," PPS 272, box 1, PRNC.

54. Mrs. Joseph V. Quarles to Pat Nixon, 8 August 1960, attached to Pat Nixon to Mrs. Joseph V. Quarles, 7 October 1960, "23—Pat Nixon—General—1960—Q," box 13, PPS 275.

55. "Miles Traveled by Mrs. Nixon on Campaign Tours since July 1952," 8/59, PPS 273, box 1, PRNC.

56. Earl Mazo, "Mrs. Nixon Helps Out as Speaker," 26 September 1956, *New York Herald Tribune*, Center for American History.

57. Polly Cochran, "Second Lady of the Land Smiles for Everyone in Indiana," *Indianapolis Star*, 30 September 1958, brown envelope, PPS 273, box 3, PRNC.

58. See, for example, Don to Herb [Klein], 6 October 1959, "Pat Nixon—Granted—Interviews, Pictures, Appointments, Calls 1959," PPS 274, box 1, PRNC; Bob Wilson to Aylett Cotton, 12 September 1956, folder 12, box 47, White House Special File, Nixon Presidential Library.

59. Catherine E. Rymph, *Republican Women: Feminism and Conservatism from Suffrage through the Rise of the New Right* (Chapel Hill: University of North Carolina Press, 2006), 131–159; Mary C. Brennan, *Wives, Mothers, and the Red Menace: Conservative Women and the Crusade against Communism* (Boulder: University Press of Colorado, 2008), 31–57.

60. Nona B. Brown, "Women's Vote: The Bigger Half?," *New York Times*, 21 October 1956, 237.

61. Edith Evans Asbury, "Mrs. Nixon Busy but Not Anxious," *New York Times*, 21 August 1956, 15; Taves, "Perfect Wife" 30–33+; Ruth Montgomery, "Believes Mate Is 'Man of Destiny,'" 20 September 1959, *New York Herald Tribune*, envelope "Pre-1960," Center for American History.

62. Frances Lewine, "Mrs. Nixon Honored as 'Ideal Wife,'" [no newspaper title given], 26 February 1957, "Pat Nixon—Awards 1957," PPS 272, box 1, PRNC.

63. Mrs. Richard H. Kirchner to Pat Nixon, 26 June 1954, "Correspondence, June 1954," box 1, PPS 269, PRNC.

64. Inez Robb, "Reader Has Company in Holding Pat Nixon Should Drop Her Iron," n.d., *New York Herald Tribune*, envelope, "Pre-1960," Center for American History.

65. Taves, "Perfect Wife," 33; David, *Lonely Lady*, 81.

66. Pat Nixon to Helene Drown, [1 April 1953?], "Correspondence: 1953," box 1, Drown Collection; Pat Nixon to Helene Drown, [8 February 1956],"1956," box 2, Drown Collection; "The Nixon/Gannon Interviews," University of Georgia, Athens, 8 April 1983, day 3, tape 3, http://www.libs.uga.edu/media/collections/nixon/transcriptintro.html, accessed 20 May 2008. Herblock was the pen name of *Washington Post* cartoonist Herbert Block. Herblock cartoons frequently showed Nixon carrying out Eisenhower's dirty work. See for example, http://www.washingtonpost.com/wp-srv/politics/herblock/gallery/6.htm, accessed 21 May 2010.

67. Pat Nixon to Helene Drown, [14 July 1953?], "Correspondence: 1953," box 1, Drown Collection.

68. Taves, "Perfect Wife," 92.

69. Pat Nixon to Helene Drown, n.d., "1958," box 2, Drown Collection.

70. David, *Lonely Lady,* 97–98.

71. Pat Nixon, desk diary, "1953," PPS 267, box 1, PRNC; Pat Nixon to Helene Drown, [14 July 1953?], "Correspondence: 1953," box 1, Drown Collection; Pat Nixon to Helene Drown, 23 October 1954, "1954, June 16–December," box 1, Drown Collection; Pat Nixon to Helene Drown, 13 July 1955, "1955," box 1, Drown Collection; Pat Nixon to Helene Drown, n.d. [December 1956?], "1956," box 2, Drown Collection.

72. Eisenhower, *Pat Nixon,* 171; David, *Lonely Lady,* 97; Taves, "Perfect Wife," 91; Elizabeth Newton to Mary Jane McCaffree, 12 March 1958, "EN 1957/1958 Day Files Mc," box 1, series 432, PRNC.

73. Margaret Fuller to Julie Eisenhower, 8 July 1978, "1953: Sept.–Dec.," PPS 267, box 1, PRNC; Margaret Fuller to Wade H. Nichols, 3 May 1956, *Redbook* article, May 1956," box 1, PPS 271, PRNC; Taves, "Perfect Wife."

74. Eisenhower, *Pat Nixon,* 146.

75. There is extensive correspondence between the two women. For example, see Pat Nixon to Helene Drown, 16 August 1954, "1954, June 16–December," box 1; or Pat Nixon to Helene Drown, [11 December 1956], "1956," box 2, all in Drown Collection. Quotation from Helene Drown to Pat Nixon, n.d., "1958," box 2; or Pat Nixon to Helene Drown, n.d., "1959," box 2, all in Drown Collection.

76. Pat Nixon to Helene Drown, [9 June 1953?], "Correspondence: 1953," box 1, Drown Collection.

77. Pat Nixon to Helene Drown, [6 July 1953?], "Correspondence: 1953," box 1, Drown Collection.

78. Pat Nixon to Helene Drown, [6 July 1953?].

79. "Official Trip to the Far East and South East Asia, 1953. The Vice President and Mrs. Nixon and their Party," n.d., "1953: Far East Trip—Background Flight," PPS 267, box 2, PRNC; and schedule for flights for Asia trip "1953: Far East Trip—Background Flight," PPS 267, box 2, PRNC.

80. Taves, "Perfect Wife," 30–33, 90.

81. Nixon, *Memoirs,* 119.

82. Pat Nixon, travel diary, 5 October 1953, "1953: Diary October 5–17, 1953," PPS 267, box 4, PRNC.

83. Pat Nixon, travel diary, 8, 9, and 14 October 1953, "1953: Diary October 5–17, 1953," PPS 267, box 4, PRNC.

84. Pat Nixon, travel diary, 14 October 1953, "1953: Diary October 5–17, 1953," PPS 267, box 4, PRNC; Pat Nixon, shorthand notes, schedule for Madras, "1953: Nov. 29–Dec. 4 India," PPS 267, box 3, PRNC.

85. Handwritten note of Julie Nixon Eisenhower, n.d., "1953: Nov. 29–Dec. 4 India," PPS 267, box 3, PRNC.

86. Pat Nixon, travel diary, 16 October 1953, "1953: Diary October 5–17, 1953," PPS 267, box 4, PRNC.

87. "Nixon/Gannon Interviews," 13 May 1983, day 5, tape 1.

88. Pat Nixon to Helene Drown, n.d., "Correspondence: 1953," box 1, Drown Collection; schedule for Ceylon, "1953: Nov. 27–29 Ceylon," PPS 267, box 3, PRNC; itinerary for Mrs. Nixon, 22 November 1953, "1953: Nov. 20–24 Philippines," PPS 267, box 3, PRNC.

89. Participation in meetings and social events during the vice president's visit, 12–15 November 1953, "1953: Nov. 12–15 Korea," PPS 267, box 3, PRNC.

90. Pat Nixon, handwritten notes, program of visit to the government of the union of Burma, "1953: Nov. 24–27 Burma," PPS 267, box 3, PRNC; Pat Nixon, handwritten notes, itinerary for Teheran, "1953: Dec. 9–12 Iran," PPS 267, box 4, PRNC; Pok Hee Ching to Pat Nixon, 14 November 1953, "1953: Nov. 12–15 Korea," PPS 267, box 3, PRNC.

91. Pat Nixon, handwritten notes, 1953, "1953 Handwritten Notes," PPS 267, box 4, PRNC.

92. Ann Lockwood to Pat Nixon, 11 February 1954?, "1953: Nov. 24–27 Burma," PPS 267, box 3, PRNC; Eleanor Newton to Pat Nixon, 4 December 1953, "1953: Nov. 29–Dec. 4 India," PPS 267, box 3, PRNC; Nixon, *Memoirs,* 134.

93. William Theis, "Nixons a 'Team'" 17 January 1954, *Journal-American* (New York), Center for American History.

94. Pat Nixon to Helene Drown, 29 December 1955, "1955," box 1, Drown Collection; Pat Nixon to Helene Drown [8 February 1956], "1956," box 2, Drown Collection.

95. Pat Nixon to Helene Drown, [14 July 1956], "1956," box 2, Drown Collection.

96. Earl Mazo, "Mrs. Nixon as Ambassador," 12 April 1957, *New York Herald Tribune,* envelope, "Pre-1960," Center for American History.

97. Nixon, *Six Crises,* 183–184.

98. Ibid., 215. The Caracas riot is one of the six crises of the book. For other accounts of the situation, see Mazo, *Portrait,* 207–246; Nixon, *Memoirs,* 185–193; Ambrose, *Nixon,* 463–479, among others.

99. Eisenhower, *Pat Nixon,* 175.

100. Interestingly, Nixon reported that he went back to check on his wife;

Nixon, *Memoirs,* 191. Every other source, however, has Vernon Walters going back to the second car. See, for example, Eisenhower, *Pat Nixon,* 176; Ambrose, *Nixon,* 477.

101. Eisenhower, *Pat Nixon,* 176–177.

102. Paul Harvey, "Mrs. Nixon," released 22 May 1958, "1958," PPS 273, box 3, PRNC; J. Edgar Hoover to Pat Nixon, 26 May 1958, "1958," PPS 273, box 3, PRNC; Gwen Gibson, "Pat Tired but Unconquered Heroine," 16 May 1958, *New York Herald Tribune,* Center for American History; "Laud Courage of Mrs. Nixon" 14 May 1958, *New York Herald Tribune,* Center for American History, and Eisenhower, *Pat Nixon,* 177–178, 175.

103. Eisenhower, *Pat Nixon,* 176.

104. Elizabeth A. Cloes, Oral History Program, California State College, Fullerton, 3.

105. Pat Nixon to Helene Drown, n.d., and Helene Drown to Pat Nixon, n.d., "1958," box 2, Drown Collection. Quotation in "Mrs. Nixon Matches Wit with Ladies of Press," *Evening Star* (Washington, D.C.), 27 November 1958, A5, "London 11058, PPS 27," PPS 273, box 3, PRNC; "Britain Meets the Nixons—A Close Look, a New Size-up," *U.S. News & World Report,* 5 December 1958, 42; "Mrs. Pat—A British View," *Spectator,* as reprinted in *New Republic,* 22 December 1958, 5.

106. "Mrs. Nixon Will Take along Gum for Soviet Children," 21 July 1959, *New York Herald Tribune,* Center for American History; "Mrs. Nixon Hopes Wife Joins President on Trip," 7 August 1959, *New York Herald Tribune,* Center for American History.

107. Ruth Montgomery, "They Like Pat and Show It," 4 August 1959, *New York Herald Tribune,* Center for American History.

108. "Diplomat in High Heels," *New York Times,* 28 July 1959, 11.

109. "Mrs. Nixon Is Honored by Negro Press," 25 May 1957, *New York Herald Tribune,* Center for American History.

110. William Rogers to Pat Nixon, 3 January 1957, "1957," PPS 272, box 1, PRNC.

111. Pat Nixon to Helene Drown, [31 August 1953?], "Correspondence: 1953," box 1, Drown Collection.

112. Richard Nixon, handwritten notes, 19 February 1954, "Correspondence 1954, February," PPS 269, box 1, PRNC.

113. Maureen Drown Nunn, interview by author, 16 August 2008, Richard Nixon Library.

114. Helene and Jack Drown were both active members of the Republican party and often campaigned for various local candidates. See, for example, Helene Drown to Pat Nixon, n.d., "1958," box 2, Drown Collection.

115. See, for example, Pat Nixon to Helene Drown, [1 April 1953], "Correspondence: 1953"; Pat Nixon to Helene Drown, [21 January 1954?], "1954, January–June 15"; Pat Nixon to Helene Drown, 7 November 1955, "1955," all in box 1, Drown Collection; Pat Nixon to Helene Drown, 31 October 1957, "1957"; Helene Drown to Pat Nixon, n.d., "1958," both in box 2, Drown Collection.

116. See, for example, Pat Nixon to Helene Drown, [6 July 1953?], "Correspondence: 1953"; Pat Nixon to Helene Drown, [4 June 1954?], "1954, January–June 15," and Pat Nixon to Helene Drown, 23 October 1954, "1954, June 16–December," all in box 1, Drown Collection.

117. Helene Drown to Pat Nixon, n.d., "1958," box 2, Drown Collection.

118. Ambrose, *Nixon,* 529–530.

119. Pat Nixon to Helene Drown, 23 October 1954, "1954, June 16–December," box 1, Drown Collection. Quote from Pat Nixon to Helene Drown, [8 February 1956], "1956," box 2, Drown Collection. See also Pat Nixon to Helene Drown, [9 June 1953?], "Correspondence: 1953," box 1, and Pat Nixon to Helene Drown, n.d., "1959," box 2, Drown Collection.

120. See, for example, discussion of Betty Ford's choices during her years as a congressman's wife. John Robert Greene, *Betty Ford: Candor and Courage in the White House* (Lawrence: University Press of Kansas, 2004), 23.

121. This passive-aggressive technique is one she used on her daughters as well as her husband. See Eisenhower, *Pat Nixon,* 169.

CHAPTER 3: IN AND OUT OF POLITICS

1. Richard Nixon, handwritten notes, 19 February 1954, "Correspondence 1954, February," Pre-Presidential Series 269, box 1, Patricia Ryan Nixon Collection (hereafter PRNC), Nixon Presidential Library, Yorba Linda, California.

2. For a discussion of the "Dump Nixon" movement, see Richard M. Nixon, *RN: The Memoirs of Richard Nixon* (New York: Grosset & Dunlap, 1978), 169–179. Quote is by Richard Nixon as quoted in Earl Mazo, *Richard Nixon: A Political and Personal Portrait* (New York: Harper, 1959), 157. For Pat's view of the situation, see Julie Nixon Eisenhower, *Pat Nixon: The Untold Story* (New York: Simon and Schuster, 1986), 157–158.

3. Eisenhower, *Pat Nixon,* 171–172.

4. Isabella Taves, "Pat Nixon Problems of a 'Perfect Wife,'" *Redbook,* May, 1956, 30, 31–33, 90, 92; John Reilly, oral history, oral history, *Collection of Sixty Interviews for Pat Ryan Nixon,* compiled by Alice Martin Rosenberger, 1978, Whittier Public Library, Artesia, California.

5. Stephen E. Ambrose, *Nixon* (New York: Simon and Schuster, 1987–1991), 550–

553; Mary C. Brennan, *Turning Right in the Sixties: The Conservative Capture of the GOP* (Chapel Hill: University of North Carolina Press, 1995), 19–38; Laura Jane Gifford, *The Center Cannot Hold: The 1960 Presidential Election and the Rise of Modern Conservatism* (Dekalb: Northern Illinois University Press, 2009), 21–56.

6. There are numerous biographies of Kennedy. See, for example, Richard Reeves, *President Kennedy: Profile of Power* (New York: Simon & Schuster, 1993); Theodore Sorensen, *Kennedy* (New York: Harper & Row, Publishers, 1965). For a decidedly pro-Kennedy view of the presidential race, see Theodore H. White, *The Making of the President, 1960* (New York: Atheneum House, 1961).

7. Arthur M. Schlesinger Jr., *A Thousand Days* (Boston: Houghton Mifflin, 1965), 68; Theodore Sorenson, *Kennedy*, 95–223; Gary A. Donaldson, *The First Modern Campaign: Kennedy, Nixon, and the Election of 1960* (New York: Rowman & Littlefield, 2007), 109–126.

8. Richard M. Nixon, *Six Crises* (Garden City, N.Y.: Doubleday, 1962), 320–321.

9. Ibid., 336–342.

10. Copy of Detroit Telethon Interview, 8 November 1960, "Copy of Detroit Telethon Transcript November 8, 1960," PPS 275, box 1.

11. Her comment might also have been a subconscious warning to other wives, to prepare them for the reality of political life. Pat had never received such advice before they jumped into their careers.

12. Ruth Montgomery, "Nixon's Potent Weapon," 25 August 1960, "*Herald Tribune* 1960," Center for American History, Austin, Texas.

13. "Nixon Renews Bid for South's Vote," *New York Times*, 4 October 1960, 1. For more information on the Pat for First Lady campaign, see boxes of material in PRNC. For specifics see, among others, "Receptions," n.d. [1960], folder 7, box 40, White House Special File, Nixon Presidential Library; Elizabeth Newton to Pat Nixon, "FYI," 28 June 1960, "Republican National Convention—Chicago—July 25, 1960," box 3, PPS 275, PRNC.

14. Detroit Telethon Interview.

15. Pat Nixon, as told to Christine Hotchkiss, "What Keeps Me Going," *This Week*, 5 June 1960, 10ff, envelope "Pat Nixon 1960," Center for American History.

16. Maureen Drown Nunn, interview by author, 16 August 2008, RN Library; Olive H. Milgate to Pat Nixon, 5 January 1960, "23—Patricia Nixon—General—1960—M," box 12, PPS 275, PRNC; Mrs. Robert L. Earle to Pat Nixon, 22 April 1960, "18—Patricia Nixon—1960—Hat Requests," PPS 275, PRNC; Ed Koterba, "A Bouquet for 'the Other' Pat," *World Telegraph*, 1 November 1960, envelope "1960 Pat Nixon," Center for American History.

17. Montgomery, "Nixon's Potent Weapon"; Ruth Montgomery, "The Second

Lady Is Trying for First," *New York Journal-American,* 11 September 1960, envelope "1960 Pat Nixon," Center for American History.

18. Nixon as told to Hotchkiss, "What Keeps Me Going"; Emma Harrison, "Mrs. Nixon Limns a Homey Picture," 25 July 1960, *New York Herald Tribune,* envelope "*Herald Tribune* 1960," Center for American History; Detroit Telethon Interview.

19. Marilyn Bender, "Pat Nixon: A Diplomat in High Heels," *New York Times,* 28 July 1960, 31; *Life,* 26 September 1960; Martha Weinman, "First Ladies—In Fashion, Too?" *New York Times,* 11 September 1960, 32.

20. Harrison, "Mrs. Nixon Limns a Homey Picture."

21. Lillian Boyd to Pat Nixon, 18 September 1960, "Patricia Nixon—Re. News, Mag. Stories, Published Pictures," box 22, PPS 275, PRNC.

22. "The Important Women in Their Lives," *Newsweek,* 17 October 1960, 31.

23. Frank Richards to Pat Nixon, 30 July 1960, attached to Pat Nixon to Frank Richards, 29 October 1960, "23—Patricia Nixon—General—1960—R," box 13, PPS 275.

24. "Important Women," 32.

25. Mrs. Alice H. Sommer to Pat Nixon, 6 August 1960, attached to Pat Nixon to Mrs. Alice H. Sommer, 26 September 1960, "23—Patricia Nixon—General—1960—S," box 13, PPS 275.

26. "The Silent Partner," *Time,* 29 February 1960, 25.

27. For examples, see this book, chapter 2.

28. "Silent Partner," 25; Helen Erskine, "Dick and Pat Nixon: The Team on Ike's Team," *Collier's,* 9 July 1954, as quoted in Ambrose, *Nixon,* 350.

29. Ibid., 350; Lester David, *The Lonely Lady of San Clemente* (New York: Thomas Y. Crowell, 1978), 20, 115–116.

30. See various requests in appropriately marked folders in box 7, PPS 275, PRNC.

31. Pat Nixon to Bessie Newton, handwritten note on draft letter, Pat Nixon to Charles Revson, 27 April 1960, "Patricia Nixon Gifts, 1960 Early April," box 21, PPS 275, PRNC.

32. Pat Nixon, handwritten note on memo, Bessie Newton to Pat Nixon, n.d., "Pat Nixon January 11, 1960 National Hairdressers and Cosmetologists Luncheon," PPS 275, box 1. For the dress, see "FYI," 10 August 1960, "10—Patricia Nixon—1960—Requests for Pictures," box 6, PPS 275, PRNC.

33. Pat Nixon to Helene Drown, n.d., "1960," box 2, Helene and Jack Drown Collection, Nixon Presidential Library and Museum.

34. Richard Nixon to Tricia, 18 July 1960, "Tricia and Julie 1960: Letters to, Gifts, Misc.," box 2, PPS 275, PRNC.

35. Eisenhower, *Pat Nixon,* 189.

36. Pat Nixon to Helene Drown, n.d., "1960," box 2, Drown Collection.

37. Pat Nixon, handwritten notes on "FYI," 23 September 1960 and 29 August 1960, "9A—Tricia and Julie—1960 Invitations, Parties, Pictures," box 3, PPS 275, PRNC.

38. For Pat's calendar, see "Pat Nixon Monthly Calendars 1960–January 1961," PPS 275, box 1. For his travel, see the pertinent chapter in Nixon, *Six Crises.*

39. Eisenhower, *Pat Nixon,* 195.

40. Nixon, *Six Crises,* 386.

41. Ibid., 391–392.

42. Donaldson, *First Modern Campaign,* 152.

43. "Silent Partner," 25.

44. Eisenhower, *Pat Nixon,* 197.

45. Pat Nixon to Helene Drown, [November or December 1960], "1960," box 2, Drown Collection.

46. Eisenhower, *Pat Nixon,* 204.

47. Ambrose, *Nixon,* 626–627.

48. Richard Nixon to Styles Bridges, 12 January 1961, "EN 1961 Day files B," box 6, PPS 432, PRNC.

49. Pat Nixon to Helene Drown, [January 1961], "1961–1962," box 2, Drown Collection. In "1961" folder, box 1, PPS 278, there are several letters thanking Pat for inviting them to their last dinner party. They sent the guests engraved ashtrays as gifts.

50. Pat Nixon to Jo Haldeman, 16 January 1961, "EN 1961 Day Files H," box 6, series 432, PRNC; Pat Nixon to Mrs. Herbert Lecky, 9 January 1961, "Patricia Nixon Gifts," box 20, PPS 275, PRNC.

51. Pat Nixon to Judi Richards, 16 May 1961, "Patricia Nixon—California Invitations—1961 T&J, also TD's," box 1, PPS 278, PRNC. See more examples in this folder and box.

52. Ruth Montgomery, "Sad Pat Nixon Heads West," New York *Journal-American,* 10 June 1961, envelope "Pat Nixon 1960," Center for American History.

53. Eisenhower, *Pat Nixon,* 203.

54. Pat Nixon to Helene Drown, [January 1961], "1961–1962," box 2, Drown Collection.

55. Eisenhower, *Pat Nixon,* 203.

56. P. J. Everts to Pat Nixon, 11 July 1961, "Pat Nixon—Notes—1961," box 1, PPS 278, PRNC.

57. Eisenhower, *Pat Nixon*, 204.

58. Richard Nixon to Mabel Boardman, 17 July 1961, "Patricia Nixon—California Invitations—1961 T&J, also TD's," box 1, PPS 278, PRNC.

59. Program, University of Southern California seventy-eighth annual commencement, 8 June 1961, 4–5, "Patricia Nixon—Early—USC," box 2, PPS 265, PRNC.

60. Eisenhower, *Pat Nixon*, 205.

61. Ibid., 204.

62. Nixon, *Memoirs*, 232.

63. Ibid., 228; Ambrose, *Nixon*, 627–628.

64. For information about the meetings and his trips to the East Coast, see appropriate folders in box 11, PPS 432, PRNC.

65. Eisenhower, *Pat Nixon*, 204.

66. Ibid., 204; Ambrose, *Nixon*, 636–642.

67. Nixon, *Memoirs*, 237.

68. Richard Nixon to Tricia Nixon, 18 July 1960; Richard Nixon to Julie Nixon, 18 July 1960, "Tricia and Julie 1960: Letters to, Gifts; Misc.," PPS 275, box 2, PRNC.

69. Nixon, *Six Crises*, 11.

70. Nixon, *Memoirs*, 237–238.

71. Ibid.

72. According to author Fawn Brodie, Adela Rogers St. John overheard an argument between the Nixons in which Pat threatened to commit suicide if Dick ran for office again. The comment seems uncharacteristic of Pat. Fawn McKay Brodie, *Richard Nixon: The Shaping of His Character* (New York: Norton, 1981), 451.

73. Eisenhower, *Pat Nixon*, 205.

74. Patricia Nixon, "Crises of a Candidate's Wife," *Ladies' Home Journal*, November 1972, 118.

75. Eisenhower, *Pat Nixon*, 205–206.

76. Most accounts use Nixon, *Memoirs*, 239–240, as their source for the basis for their description of the scene. See Brodie, *Richard Nixon*, 454–455, and Ambrose, *Nixon*, 646–647. For Pat's side, see Eisenhower, *Pat Nixon*, 206.

77. Eisenhower, *Pat Nixon*, 206; Nixon, *Memoirs*, 240.

78. Eisenhower, *Pat Nixon*, 207.

79. Joan Sweeney, "Pat Nixon Launches Painful, Popular Task of Campaigning," *Citizen News* (Hollywood, California), 5 October 1962, "Action Package Publicity," box 1, PPS 275, PRNC.

80. Invitations, 22 September 1962, "Patricia Nixon—Schedule Committee"; "FYI," 12 October 1962, "Patricia Nixon—Schedule Interviews"; Bessie Newton to Bob Haldeman, 13 September 1962, "FYI—Newsroom," all in box 2, PPS 279, PRNC.

81. Ambrose, *Nixon*, 654.

82. "The Nixon/Gannon Interviews," University of Georgia, Athens, 13 September 1983, day 9, tape 1, 34:37, http://www.libs.uga.edu/media/collections/nixon/transcriptintro.html, accessed 20 May 2008.

83. Quote is from Ambrose, *Nixon*, 667. For discussion of this campaign, see Nixon, *Memoirs*, 237–245.

84. Ibid., 244.

85. Eisenhower, *Pat Nixon*, 209.

86. Daryl Lembke, "Pat Nixon Hits Smears," *Washington Post*, 16 October 1962, "Action Package Publicity," box 1, PPS 279, PRNC.

87. The controversy over Alger Hiss's guilt or innocence continued despite Hiss's imprisonment for perjury. Nixon's brother borrowed money from Howard Hughes using his mother's house as collateral. When he could not pay back the loan, his mother signed over the title, although Hughes never took possession. This issue had been played up during the 1960 campaign. Ambrose, *Nixon*, 662. The controversy over the house had to do with the Nixons getting their property at a cheaper price than similar properties in the area. Additionally, Teamster leader Jimmy Hoffa sold them the property. Ambrose, *Nixon*, 629.

88. Unsigned memo, "Per Pat Hitt," 26 May 1962, folder 17, box 61, White House Special File.

89. Campaign schedules, "Patricia Nixon Campaign Schedules," box 2, PPS 279, PRNC.

90. Nixon, *Memoirs*, 245–246.

91. Ibid., 246.

92. Eisenhower, *Pat Nixon*, 213–214.

93. Brodie, *Richard Nixon*, 451.

94. Ambrose, *Nixon*, 653–654.

95. Brodie, *Richard Nixon*, 424–425; Ambrose, *Nixon*, 652–653.

96. Eisenhower, *Pat Nixon*, 215–216; Nixon, *Memoirs*, 247–248.

97. For information about the house and remodeling, see "Houses—810 Fifth Ave. N.Y. 1963," box 1, PPS 280, PRNC. See also Brodie, *Richard Nixon*, 478–479; Eisenhower, *Pat Nixon*, 218.

98. Pat Nixon to Helene Drown, n.d. [3 September 1965], "1965," box 3, Drown Collection.

99. See chapter 1. He made the promise again after the 1960 loss. See Pat Nixon to Helene Drown, [January 1961], "1961–1962," box 2, Drown Collection.

100. See "1963 Trip Europe, Itineraries, Invitations, Etc.," box 1, PPS 280, PRNC for details of their stops in each city. See also Eisenhower, *Pat Nixon*, 217–219.

101. Nixon, *Memoirs*, 250.

102. Nunn interview.

103. Nixon, *Memoirs*, 248–249.

104. See itineraries for trip, "1963 Trip Europe, Itineraries, Invitations, Etc.," box 1, PPS 280, PRNC.

105. Nixon, *Memoirs*, 250.

106. Stephen E. Ambrose, *Nixon: The Triumph of a Politician, 1962–1972* (New York: Simon & Schuster, 1989), 27–28.

107. Nixon, *Memoirs*, 252–253; Ambrose, *Triumph*, 25; Eisenhower, *Pat Nixon*, 219.

108. Jacqueline Kennedy to Richard Nixon, as quoted in Nixon, *Memoirs*, 254–255. See Ambrose, *Triumph*, 32–33.

109. Brennan, *Turning Right*, 70–71.

110. James T. Patterson, *Grand Expectations: The United States, 1945–1974* (New York: Oxford University Press, 1996), 524–525, 530–533, 542–547.

111. Brennan, *Turning Right*, 71–81.

112. Ambrose, *Triumph*, 39–42, 45–50.

113. Nixon, *Memoirs*, 260.

114. Rick Perlstein, *Nixonland: The Rise of a President and the Fracturing of America* (New York: Scribner, 2008), 64; Ambrose, *Triumph*, 56–58.

115. Nixon, *Memoirs*, 268–271, 273–275, 282–283, 285; Ambrose, *Triumph*, 61–62, 68–69, 73–79, 91–92, 109–110, 126–127.

116. For Johnson's policies in Vietnam, see, among others, Paul Conkin, *Big Daddy from the Pedernales* (Boston, Mass.: Twayne, 1986), 243–286.

117. Maurice Isserman and Michael Kazin, *America Divided: The Civil War of the 1960s*, 2nd ed. (New York: Oxford University Press, 2004), 178, 188–194.

118. Ambrose, *Triumph*, 124–126. For a broader discussion of the rise of the issue of "law and order," see Michael Flamm, *Law and Order: Street Crime, Civil Unrest and the Crisis of Liberalism in the 1960s* (New York: Columbia University Press, 2005).

119. Nixon reviewed his pre-1968 activities in his *Memoirs*, 264–294.

120. Eisenhower, *Pat Nixon*, 218, 222, 224–225.

121. Pat Nixon to Helene Drown, n.d., [May 1965], "1965," box 3, Drown Collection.

122. Eisenhower, *Pat Nixon,* 225–226.

123. Ibid., 229–231.

124. Pat Nixon to Mamie Eisenhower, n.d., [March 1967], "Ni(1)," box 10, 1967 File Series, Mamie Doud Eisenhower Papers, Dwight D. Eisenhower Library, Abilene, Kansas.

125. Helene Drown to Pat Nixon, 21 February 1965, "1965," box 3, Drown Collection. See also Nunn interview.

126. Quote from Pat Nixon to Helene Drown, n.d., [6 February 1967], "1967," box 3, Drown Collection. For other examples, see Pat Nixon to Helene Drown, n.d., [May 1964], box 2A; Pat Nixon to Helene Drown, n.d., [May 1966], box 3; or Pat Nixon to Helene Drown, n.d., [March 1966], box 3, all in Drown Collection.

127. Eisenhower, *Pat Nixon,* 225.

128. Ibid., 222, 227.

129. Pat Nixon to Helene Drown, n.d., [1964]; Pat Nixon to Helene Drown, n.d., [November 1964], "1964," box 2A; Pat Nixon to Helene Drown, n.d., [February 1965]; Pat Nixon to Helene Drown, n.d., [November 1965], "1965," box 3, all in Drown Collection.

130. Eisenhower, *Pat Nixon,* 219.

131. Pat Nixon to Helene Drown, n.d., [November 1964], "1964," box 2A; Pat Nixon to Helene Drown, n.d., [9 February 1965]; Pat Nixon to Helene Drown, n.d., [December 1965], "1965," box 3, Drown Collection.

132. Pat Nixon to Helene Drown, [1961], "1961–1962," box 2, Drown Collection.

133. Pat Nixon to Helene Drown, n.d., [1964], "1964," box 2A, Drown Collection.

134. Pat Nixon to Helene Drown, n.d., [1964], "1964," box 2A, Drown Collection.

135. Pat Nixon to Helene Drown, n.d., [December 1965], "1965," box 3, Drown Collection.

136. Bessie Newton to Rose Mary Woods, "FYI," 15 May 1961, "1961—To California," box 11, PPS 432, PRNC.

137. Pat Nixon to Helene Drown, n.d., [May 1964], "1964," box 2A, Drown Collection.

138. Eisenhower, *Pat Nixon,* 232–233.

139. Nixon, *Memoirs,* 287–289.

140. Eisenhower, *Pat Nixon,* 227.

141. Pat Nixon to Helene Drown, n.d., [6 February 1967], "1967," box 3, Drown Collection.

142. Eisenhower, *Pat Nixon,* 231–232.

143. Ibid., 233–234.

144. Ambrose, *Triumph*, 152.

145. Eisenhower, *Pat Nixon*, 235–238; Flora Rheta Schreiber, "Pat Nixon Reveals for the First Time: 'I Didn't Want Dick to Run Again,'" *Good Housekeeping*, July 1968, 188.

146. Charlotte Curtis, "Pat Nixon: 'Creature Comforts Don't Matter,'" *New York Times*, 3 July 1968, 30; Mary Wiegers, "Pat Soft-Sells Lighter Side of the Nixons," *Washington Post*, 9 August 1968, C2.

147. Eisenhower, *Pat Nixon*, 238; Curtis, "Pat Nixon," 30; Marie Smith, "Mrs. Richard Nixon," *Washington Post*, 4 August 1968, G5.

148. Smith, "Mrs. Richard Nixon," G5.

149. Smith, "Mrs. Richard Nixon," G1 and Joy Miller, "Candidates' Wives: On the Handshake Trail," *Los Angeles Times*, 3 March 1968, N6.

150. Wiegers, "Pat Soft-Sells," C1.

151. Mary Wiegers, "Pat Nixon: On Cue for '68 Campaign," *Washington Post*, 28 October 1968, C1; Tom Wicker, "In the Nation: The Long-Distance Runner," *New York Times*, 28 May 1968, 46; Kandy Shuman, "Pat's Style: Sophisticated Simplicity," *Washington Post*, 1 June 1968, B7.

152. Wicker, "Long-Distance Runner," 46.

153. Wiegers, "On Cue for '68 Campaign"; Dick Schaap, "Pat Loves Everybody and Everybody Loves Pat," *Los Angeles Times*, 21 July 1968, A12.

154. Maxine Cheshire, "Very Interesting People," *Washington Post*, 1 February 1968, F1. She continued to use this term throughout the campaign. See, for example, Curtis, "Creature Comforts"; Mary Wiegers, "Pat Nixon: 'Volunteer,'" *Washington Post*, 8 October 1968, C1.

155. See this chapter, footnote 14.

156. "Important Women," 31; Schreiber, "Pat Nixon Reveals," 62.

157. Handwritten notes on back of itinerary, 10 October 1968, "1968 Camp Itineraries," box 7, Drown Political Materials.

158. Elizabeth Shelton, "Wives Corner Political Triangle," *Washington Post*, 20 February 1968, C1.

159. "For Pat, It's Win or Lose . . . Just Don't Drop Out," *Washington Post*, 24 April 1968, D1.

160. Gloria Steinem, *Outrageous Acts and Everyday Rebellions*, 2nd ed. (New York: Holt Paperbacks, 1984), 264–265.

161. Mary Wiegers, "The Same Pat Nixon—She's Polished," *Washington Post*, 27 May 1968, E1.

162. Mary Wiegers, "Volunteer"; Maggie Savoy, "Pat Nixon—Her Husband's

Indefatigable Running Mate," *Los Angeles Times,* 9 August 1968, E1; Lynn Lilliston, "1968: Year of the New Nixons," *Los Angeles Times,* 23 July 1968, G2. For a discussion of Nixon's views on activist women, see Brodie, *Richard Nixon,* 232–236.

163. Shelton, "Wives Corner Political Triangle"; Miller, "Candidates' Wives." For some of the schedules for the girls and David, see "Ni(3)," box 23, 1968 File Series, Mamie Doud Eisenhower Papers.

164. Schreiber, "Pat Nixon Reveals," 62.

165. Eisenhower, *Pat Nixon,* 240–241.

166. Nixon, *Memoirs,* 298.

167. Ambrose, *Nixon,* 144–145.

168. Kent G. Sieg, "The 1968 Presidential Election and Peace in Vietnam," *Presidential Studies Quarterly* 26, no. 4 (Fall 1996): 1062–1073.

169. Ambrose, *Triumph,* 137–140.

170. Nixon, *Memoirs,* 331–333.

171. Ibid., 331–332.

CHAPTER 4: BECOMING FIRST LADY

1. Julie Nixon Eisenhower, *Pat Nixon: The Untold Story* (New York: Simon & Schuster, 1986), 232–234.

2. Handwritten notes on back of itinerary, 10 October 1968, "1968 Camp Itineraries," box 7, Drown Political Materials, Helene and Jack Drown Collection, Nixon Presidential Library and Museum, Yorba Linda, California.

3. Eisenhower, *Pat Nixon,* 257.

4. Julie stated in her biography of her mother that the date had been set in December 1967. The date was not announced to the press until 24 November 1968. Eisenhower, *Pat Nixon,* 257. "Julie and David to Wed in N.Y. Church Dec. 22," *New York Times,* 24 November 1968, 7.

5. Richard M. Nixon, *RN: The Memoirs of Richard Nixon* (New York: Grosset & Dunlap, 1978), 358; Marie Smith, "Julie Nixon and David Setting Day," *Washington Post,* 14 November 1968, E1.

6. "Guests Invited to the Nixon Wedding," *New York Times,* 23 December 1968, 53.

7. "Ike Will See Julie Wed on TV," *Washington Post,* 19 December 1968, B1.

8. Eisenhower, *Pat Nixon,* 257–258.

9. Nixon, *Memoirs,* 360.

10. Richard Nixon, inaugural address, 20 January 1969, American Presidency Project, http://www.presidency.ucsb.edu/ws/index.php?pid=1941, accessed 24 October 2009.

11. For the Nixon–Kissinger relationship and foreign policy views, see Henry Kissinger, *White House Years* (Boston: Little, Brown, 1979); Robert Dallek, *Nixon and Kissinger: Partners in Power* (New York: HarperCollins, 2007), 740.

12. James T. Patterson, *Grand Expectations: The United States, 1945–1974* (New York: Oxford University Press, 1996), 829, 710–742; silent majority speech: http://watergate.info/nixon/silent-majority-speech-1969.shtml, accessed 31 October 2009.

13. Lady Bird Johnson, *A White House Diary* (Austin: University of Texas Press, 2007), 733–735.

14. J. B. West, *Upstairs at the White House: My Life with the First Ladies* (New York: Coward, McCann & Geoghegan, 1973), 357.

15. Nixon, *Memoirs,* 367–368.

16. Eisenhower, *Pat Nixon,* 242, 271–272.

17. Lydia Tederick (assistant curator, White House), telephone interview with author, 29 September 2010; West, *Upstairs at the White House,* 359; Eisenhower, *Pat Nixon,* 262–263.

18. Johnson, *White House Diary,* 725.

19. For discussions of earlier first ladies, see various chapters in Lewis L. Gould, ed., *American First Ladies: Their Lives and Legacies* (New York: Garland, 1996).

20. "The Main Idea Is I'd Like to Assist My Husband," *Christian Science Monitor,* 17 January 1969, 6.

21. West, *Upstairs at the White House,* 364.

22. Herbert S. Parmet, *Richard Nixon and His America* (Boston: Little, Brown, 1990), 543–561.

23. John Ehrlichman to Pat Nixon, 13 October 1969, "1969," PPS 285, box 1, Patricia Ryan Nixon Collection, Richard Nixon Library, Yorba Linda, California.

24. See, for example, John Ehrlichman to Connie Stuart, 10 March 1971, "People to People Project 1971 [2 of 2]," Porter Papers, box 10, no. 2, White House Central Files: Staff Member Office Files: Susan Porter. Richard Nixon Presidential Library and Museum, Yorba Linda, California, National Archives and Records Administration.

25. See, for instance, Mort Allin to H. R. Haldeman, 24 August 1971, "Parks to People, 1971 [1 of 2]," box 10, Porter Papers.

26. Karen Peterson, "Pat Tries to Pick Up the Pieces," *Chicago Tribune,* 6 February 1975, "East Wing Staff—Smith, Helen," box 50, Sheila Weidenfeld Files, Gerald R. Ford Presidential Library, Grand Rapids, Michigan.

27. Lenore Hershey, "Compassion Power: On Tour with Mrs. Nixon," *Ladies' Home Journal,* September 1969, 88; "Caring for Others Creates the Spirit of a Nation," *U.S. News & World Report,* 2 August 1971, 54.

28. "Boosting Volunteerism," *Time*, 27 June 1969.

29. Pat Nixon, "Remarks of Mrs. Nixon to Members of the Press on Departure for Trip to Volunteer Projects in Portland and Forest Grove, Oregon, and Los Angeles, California," 16 June 1969, White House Central Files: Staff Member Office Files: Gwendolyn King. Richard Nixon Presidential Library and Museum, Yorba Linda, California, National Archives and Records Administration.

30. "Traveling with Pat Nixon—A Different Type of Tour," *U.S. News & World Report*, 30 June 1969, 9; Hershey, "Compassion Power," 88.

31. Press release, 3 July 1969, Office of Press Secretary to Mrs. Nixon, "Miscellaneous," box 7, King Papers.

32. Coral Schmid to Constance Stuart, memo, 13 February 1960; Constance Stuart to Bernard S. Rensselear, memo, 8 June 1970, both in "Elder Citizens," box 7, no. 2, Porter Papers; Mrs. Julie Marr Robinson to Robert Benedict, 1 May 1970, "Teen Corps," box 12, Porter Papers.

33. "Pat Nixon's Answer to the 'Generation Gap,'" *U.S. News & World Report*, 16 March 1970, 40.

34. Ibid.

35. Marie Smith, "Pat's Volunteer Tour," *Washington Post*, 3 March 1970, B1.

36. Jim Tanck to Constance Stuart, 16 March 1970, attached to Constance Stuart to Bob Haldeman, 10 April 1970, "College Students," box 6, no. 1, Porter Papers.

37. Marie Smith, "Mrs. Nixon's Trip," 7 March 1970, *Washington Post*, C1; Marie Smith, "Peace, Protesters and Compliments," *Washington Post*, 4 March 1970, B3.

38. Todd Gitlin, *The Sixties: Years of Hope, Days of Rage* (New York: Bantam Books, 1987); Allen J. Matusow, *The Unraveling of America: A History of Liberalism in the 1960s* (New York: Harper & Row, 1984), 308–344.

39. Connie Stuart? to Coral Schmid, n.d., "College Volunteers," box 6, no. 2, Porter Papers.

40. "Pat Nixon's Answer to the 'Generation Gap.'"

41. Gwen King to Mrs. L. E. Matson, 27 September 1972, "Gwen King Carbon File, April, May, June 1972," box 1, King Papers.

42. "Travels with Pat," *Newsweek*, 16 March 1970, 35.

43. Constance Stuart to Bob Haldeman, 25 March 1970, "College Students," box 6, no. 1, Porter Papers.

44. Connie Stuart? to Coral Schmid, n.d., "College Volunteers," box 6, no. 2, Porter Papers.

45. Constance Stuart to Bob Haldeman, 10 April 1970, "College Students," box 6, no. 1, Porter Papers.

46. Mark Hamilton Lytle, *America's Uncivil Wars: The Sixties Era from Elvis to*

the Fall of Richard Nixon (New York: Oxford University Press, 2006), 352. For a discussion from the perspective of a participant, see Bill Ayers, *Fugitive Days: Memoirs of an Antiwar Activist* (Boston, Mass.: Beacon Hill, 2001), 191–193.

47. Patterson, *Grand Expectations: The United States, 1945–1974,* 829, 754–755; Lytle, *America's Uncivil Wars,* 353–356; Milton Viorst, *Fire in the Streets* (New York: Simon & Schuster, 1979), 507–543; Tim Spofford, *Lynch Street: The May 1970 Slayings at Jackson State College* (Kent, Ohio: Kent State University Press, 1988).

48. Thomas Byrne Edsall and Mary D. Edsall, *Chain Reaction: The Impact of Race, Rights, and Taxes on American Politics* (New York: Norton, 1991), 74–98. For discussions of the complicated and shifting meanings of race in the 1970s, see Eric Porter, "Affirming and Disaffirming Actions," in *America in the '70s,* ed. Beth Bailey and David Farber (Lawrence: University Press of Kansas, 2004), 50; Bruce J. Schulman, *The Seventies* (New York: Free Press, 2001), 53–77.

49. Melvin Small, *The Presidency of Richard Nixon* (Lawrence: University Press of Kansas, 1999), 161–177; Parmet, *Richard Nixon and His America,* 597–613. For the most thorough examination, see Dean J. Kotlowski, *Nixon's Civil Rights: Politics, Principle, and Policy* (Cambridge, Mass.: Harvard University Press, 2001).

50. Office of the Staff Director to Mrs. Nixon, press release, 22 February 1971; memo, n.d., "Chicago Postal Street Academy Meeting, 2/25/71, Mrs. Nixon," box 5, no. 2, Porter Papers.

51. Susan Hunsinger, "Post Office Delivers Dropouts, Too," *Christian Science Monitor,* 11 March 1971, 9; memo, n.d., "Chicago Postal Street Academy Meeting, 2/25/71, Mrs. Nixon," box 5, no. 2, Porter Papers.

52. Coral Schmid?, n.d., handwritten note, "Chicago Postal Street Academy Meeting, 2/25/71, Mrs. Nixon," box 5, no. 2, Porter Papers.

53. Coral Schmid to Constance Stuart, memo, 9 February 1970; Coral Schmid to Constance Stuart, memo, n.d.; Carol Reavis to Constance Stuart and Coral Schmid, memo, 1 April 1970; Constance Stuart to John Whitaker, 30 March 1970, all in "Environment [2 of 2]," box 7, no. 4, Porter Papers.

54. Constance Stuart to H. R. Haldeman, memo, 27 July 1971, "Parks to People Project . . . 1971 [1 of 2]," box 10, Porter Papers; Ed Coate to Coral Schmid, 8 April 1971, attached to Connie Stuart to Coral Schmid, n.d. [April 1971], "Environment [1 of 2]," box 7, no. 3, Porter Papers. See also Marlene Cimons, "Billing Split over Pat's Tour," *Los Angeles Times,* 16 August 1971, E2.

55. "Highlights of Mrs. Nixon's Duties, Projects and Accomplishments," n.d., "Volunteer Interviews," box 7, King Papers.

56. Marie Smith, "Children Cruise the Potomac with First Lady," *Washington Post,* 8 July 1969, D1.

57. "How the Nixons Have Changed the White House," *U.S. News & World Report,* 2 October 1972, 54–56.

58. Eisenhower, *Pat Nixon,* 262–264. See also "The Nixon Touch in the White House," *U.S. News & World Report,* 28 December 1970, 24–26; "How the Nixons Have Changed the White House," 54–56; "Mrs. Nixon's White House Restoration," "Projects and Activities—Information Packet," box 7, King Papers. For a description of Jackie Kennedy Onassis's visit to the White House, see Paul Healy, "Her Hospitality Shines Thru [*sic*] for Jackie," *Daily News,* 27 June 1974, "November 19, 2001, Supplements," Drown Collection.

59. India Edwards, *Pulling No Punches: Memoirs of a Woman in Politics* (New York: Putnam, 1977), 238.

60. Lucy Winchester to H. R. Haldeman, 14 February 1973, in Helen Thomas, *Dateline: White House* (New York: Macmillan, 1975), 149; Lucy Winchester to David Parker, 11 March 1974, "November 19, 2001, Supplements," Drown Supplements, Drown Collection.

61. For an example of her editing, see Pat Nixon to May Belle Dingle, draft, n.d., "Connie Stuart Letters," box 6, King Papers. The average is the number the staff gave out to interested citizens. Gwen King to David Baumgarten, 7 March 1972, "Gwen King Carbon File, January, February, March 1972," box 1, King Papers.

62. For examples, see recipe file, box 11; Gwen King to Lucille Simpson, 19 September 1972, "Gwen King Carbon File, September 1972," box 1; Gwen King to Robert Stein, 15 December 1972, "Gwen King Carbon File, December 1972," box 2; all in King Papers.

63. Gwen King to Jay Mallin, 14 December 1972, "Gwen King Carbon File, December 1972," box 2, King Papers.

64. See, for example, Gwen King to Stephen Porter, 2 August 1972, "Gwen King Carbon File, July, August 1972," box 1; Gwen King to Rhonda Sweet, 20 October 1972, "Gwen King Carbon File, October 1972," box 1; Gwen King to Anne Gallagher, 6 November 1972, "Gwen King Carbon File, November 1972," box 2; Gwen King to Wanda Schroeder, 12 December 1972, "Gwen King Carbon File, December 1972," box 2, all in King Papers.

65. Gwen King to William Honogach, 13 December 1972, "Gwen King Carbon File, December 1972," box 2, King Papers. For an example of a more personal request, see Gwen King to Mrs. Harrison Tucker, 17 May 1972, "Gwen King Carbon File, April, May, June 1972," box 1, King Papers.

66. See, for example, Gwen King to Alan A. Switzer, 6 December 1972, "Gwen King Carbon File, December 1972," box 2; Gwen King to Mrs. Florence Green, 13 October 1972, "Gwen King Carbon File, October 1972," box 1; Gwen King to John

Fedock, 12 April 1972, " Gwen King Carbon File, April, May, June 1972," box 1; Gwen King to Patricia Ayerra, 17 August 1972, "Gwen King Carbon File, July, August 1972," box 1; Gwen King to Loren F. Robb, 5 December 1972, "Gwen King Carbon File, December 1972," box 2, all in King Papers.

67. Constance Stuart to Marie Smith Schwartz, 26 March 1971, "New Projects," box 9, Porter Papers.

68. Constance Stuart to Bob Haldeman, 29 March 1971, "Constance Stuart March 1971," box 76, Haldeman Personal Files, Richard Nixon Presidential Library and Museum, Yorba Linda, California, National Archives and Records Administration.

69. Eisenhower, *Pat Nixon,* 312; "A Shy Tricia Nixon Emerges from Her White House Cocoon," *New York Times,* 10 May 1969, 18; Maxine Cheshire, "Mystery Boyfriend Tricia's Old Beau?," *Los Angeles Times,* 20 August 1969, E2; "Tricia, Ed Together," *Washington Post,* 1 January 1971, B5.

70. Thomas, *Dateline,* 175; Sarah Booth Conroy, "The Cox–Nixon Axis Connect N.Y., D.C.," *Los Angeles Times,* 11 June 1971, F4; Marlene Cimons, "Radiant Tricia Hears Father Tell June 5 Wedding Plans," *Los Angeles Times,* 17 March 1971, 1.

71. Cimons, "Radiant Tricia"; "For $19,000, You Can Have One, Too," *Washington Post,* 13 June 1971, 11; Judith Martin, "Triumph of Wedding Tradition," *Washington Post,* 6 June 1971, 127; "The Great Cake Controversy: No Retest, White House Decides," *New York Times,* 3 June 1971, 45.

72. H. R. Haldeman, *The Haldeman Diaries: Inside the Nixon White House* (New York: Putnam, 1994), 298.

73. Marlene Cimons, "Edward Cox Weds Tricia as Rain Drifts into Rose Garden," *Los Angeles Times,* 13 June 1971, O1; Nan Robertson, "Tricia Nixon Takes Vows in Garden at White House," *New York Times,* 13 June 1971, 1; "For $19,000, You Can Have One, Too."

74. Cimons, "Edward Cox Weds Tricia"; Haldeman, *Haldeman Diaries,* 299; Eisenhower, *Pat Nixon,* 314–315; Priscilla Kidder, as quoted in "The Pat Nixon I Know," by Jean Libman Block, *Good Housekeeping,* July 1973, 124.

75. Sarah Booth Conroy, "First Lady, and Wife First," *Washington Post,* 28 June 1993, B3.

76. Carl Sferrazza Anthony, *America's First Families: An Inside View of 200 Years of Private Life in the White House* (New York: Simon & Schuster, 2000), 180, 338; Ronald Kessler, *Inside the White House: The Hidden Lives of the Modern Presidents and the Secrets of the World's Most Powerful Institution* (New York: Simon & Schuster, 1995), 55.

77. "Mrs. Nixon Foreign Travel, 1969–1974," "Summary of First Family Activities, 1973–1974," box 19, Porter Papers.

78. "First Lady in the War Zone," *U.S. News & World Report,* 11 August 1969, 14.

79. "The Nixon/Gannon Interviews," University of Georgia, Athens, 27 May 1983, day 6, tape 2, 00:58:27 and 00:20:39, http://www.libs.uga.edu/media/collec tions/nixon/transcriptintro.html, accessed 20 May 2008.

80. "Stricken Peru Given $10-Million by U.S.," *New York Times,* 9 June 1970, 6.

81. Julie says it was her father's idea; Eisenhower, *Pat Nixon,* 291. However, Pat's press office claimed it was her own idea; Marie Smith, "Pat's Peru Trip," *Washington Post,* 25 June 1970, C4.

82. Malcolm W. Browne, "Mrs. Nixon Reaches Peru to Help Victims of Quake," *New York Times,* 29 June 1970, 1.

83. Eisenhower, *Pat Nixon,* 292–293.

84. "Pat Nixon's Gesture," translated from *La Prensa,* n.d., "Peru Report," box 7, King Papers.

85. "Mrs. Nixon in Peru," *Washington Post,* 3 July 1970, A26.

86. Julie describes the trip on pages 329–331 of her book. Nixon does not mention it in his memoirs. See also "The First Lady: Fellow Traveler," *Newsweek,* 10 January 1972, 19–20.

87. Eisenhower, *Pat Nixon,* 327–328. For examples of her editing prepared remarks, see "Suggested Remarks," and Press Guidance, n.d., "The Official Visit to Africa of Mrs. Richard Nixon, January 2–5, 1972 — Liberia," box 45, Porter Papers.

88. Press Guidance; "The First Lady: A New Pat," *Newsweek,* 17 January 1972, 33; "An African Welcome," *Ebony,* March 1972, 130.

89. Press Guidance.

90. "The First Lady: A New Pat," 33.

91. "A Medal for Mme. Nixon," *New York Times,* 9 January 1972, E3.

92. "The First Lady: A New Pat," 33; "African Welcome," 124–130; Eisenhower, *Pat Nixon,* 330.

93. "African Queen for a Week," *Time,* 17 January 1972; "Medal for Mme. Nixon."

94. Pat Nixon: Saludos to South America," *U.S. News & World Report,* 25 March 1974, 35.

95. Richard M. Nixon, "Asia after Vietnam," *Foreign Affairs* 46, no. 1 (October 1967): 111, 121, 122.

96. For Nixon's version of events, see Nixon, *Memoirs,* 1120, 544–580.

97. Briefing Paper, "Notes for Mrs. Nixon," 1972, "Visit of Richard Nixon President of the United States to the People's Republic of China February 1972 [1 of 2]," box 43, Porter Papers.

98. Eisenhower, *Pat Nixon,* 334; Helen Thomas, *Front Row at the White House* (New York: Scribner, 1999), 190.

99. Nixon, *Memoirs,* 569.

100. Thomas, *Front Row,* 190.

101. "The First Lady's Own Tour," *Time,* 6 March 1972.

102. Eisenhower, *Pat Nixon,* 336.

103. Richard Nixon, joint statement following discussions with leaders of the People's Republic of China, 27 February 1972, http://www.presidency.ucsb.edu, accessed 12 December 2009.

104. Nixon, *Memoirs,* 576–577, 580.

105. Parmet, *Richard Nixon and His America,* 623–624.

106. "Ladies' Day in Moscow," *Newsweek,* 5 June 1972, 37.

107. A.P. report, as quoted in "News Summary of Mrs. Nixon's Separate Activities in Moscow, Kiev, Tehran, Warsaw—May 22–27, June 1, 1972," "Mrs. Nixon," box 8, Porter Papers.

108. All in "News Summary of Mrs. Nixon's Separate Activities in Moscow, Kiev, Tehran, Warsaw—May 22–27, June 1, 1972."

109. Ibid.

110. Marlene Cimons, "The Emergence of New Pat Nixon," *Los Angeles Times,* 30 January 1972, E1. See also Lenore Hershey, "The 'New' Pat Nixon," *Ladies' Home Journal,* February 1972, 89–90+.

111. "Redoing Pat," *Time,* 24 January 1969.

112. "Pat's Wardrobe Mistress," *Time,* 12 January 1970.

113. Hershey, "The 'New' Pat Nixon," 89–95; "First Lady with a Style All Her Own," *U.S. News & World Report,* 2 June 1969, 17.

114. Cimons, "Emergence of a New Pat Nixon."

115. Judith Viorst, "Pat Nixon is the Ultimate Good Sport," *New York Times Magazine,* 13 September 1970, 139.

116. Viorst, "Good Sport," 27–28; Block, "The Pat Nixon I Know," 72.

117. Jessamyn West, "The Unknown Pat Nixon," *Good Housekeeping,* February 1971, 124, 128.

118. Thomas, *Front Row,* 241.

CHAPTER 5: THE EMBATTLED FIRST LADY

1. Jeffrey P. Kimball, *Nixon's Vietnam War* (Lawrence: University Press of Kansas, 1998); Bruce J. Schulman, *The Seventies* (New York: Free Press, 2001); James T. Patterson, *Restless Giant: The United States from Watergate to Bush v. Gore* (New York: Oxford University Press, 2005), 448.

2. Vietnam war casualty statistics, National Archives, http://www.archives.gov/research/vietnam-war/casualty-statistics.html, accessed 26 May 2010.

3. Kimball, *Nixon's Vietnam War,* 98, 118–119, 131–135, 137–139, 185–193, 202–213, 263–337.

4. James T. Patterson, *Grand Expectations: The United States, 1945–1974* (New York: Oxford University Press, 1996), 829, 735–736; Herbert S. Parmet, *Richard Nixon and His America* (Boston: Little, Brown, 1990), 755, 575–576, 581–585; J. Anthony Lukas, *Nightmare: The Underside of the Nixon Years* (New York: Viking Press, 1976), 32–39.

5. Marie Smith, "Peace, Protestors and Compliments," *Washington Post,* 4 March 1970, B3.

6. Julie Nixon Eisenhower, *Pat Nixon: The Untold Story* (New York: Simon & Schuster, 1986), 291.

7. Connie Stuart? to Coral Schmid, n.d., "College Volunteers," box 6, no. 2 and Connie Stuart to Coral Schmid, n.d. [April 1971], "Environment [1 of 2]," box 7, no. 3, both in White House Central Files: Staff Member Office Files: Susan Porter, Richard Nixon Presidential Library and Museum, Yorba Linda, California, National Archives and Records Administration.

8. Dorothy McCardle, "Singer's War Protest Startles Nixon Dinner," *Washington Post,* 29 January 1972, A1.

9. H. R. Haldeman, *The Haldeman Diaries: Inside the Nixon White House* (New York: Putnam, 1994), 404.

10. "The Main Idea Is I'd Like to Assist My Husband," *Christian Science Monitor,* 17 January 1969, 6; Office of the Press Secretary to Mrs. Nixon, "Remarks of Mrs. Nixon to Members of the Press on Departure for Trip to Volunteer Projects in Portland and Forest Grove, Oregon, and Los Angeles, California," 16 June 1969, White House Central Files: Staff Member Office Files: Gwendolyn King, Richard Nixon Presidential Library and Museum, Yorba Linda, California, National Archives and Records Administration.

11. Sara Evans, *Personal Politics: The Roots of Women's Liberation in the Civil Rights and the New Left* (New York: Random House, 1979); Ruth Rosen, *The World Split Open: How the Modern Women's Movement Changed America* (New York: Penguin Books, 2000), 94–140.

12. Rosen, *World Split Open,* 63–93.

13. Ibid., 296–302, 320–322.

14. Lenore Hershey, "The 'New' Pat Nixon," *Ladies' Home Journal,* February 1972, 126; Patricia Nixon, n.d., "Mrs. Nixon's Equal Rights Statement," box 7, King Papers; Rosen, *World Split Open,* 90–91.

15. Haldeman, *Haldeman Diaries,* 367–368.

16. Isabelle Shelton, "Pat Is Pressed," *Evening Star* (Washington, D.C.), 19 September 1972, "Miscellaneous," box 7, King Papers.

17. H. R. Haldeman with Joseph DiMona, *The Ends of Power* (New York: New York Times Books, 1978), 73–74; Deborah Hart Strober and Gerald S. Strober, *The Nixon Presidency: An Oral History of the Era,* rev. ed. (Washington, D.C.: Brassey's, 1994), 36–37; J. B. West, *Upstairs at the White House: My Life with the First Ladies* (New York: Coward, McCann & Geoghegan, 1973), 362–363.

18. John Ehrlichman, *Witness to Power: The Nixon Years* (New York: Simon and Schuster, 1982), 81. Much of this concern arose during Nixon's first year in office. For an example of Haldeman's memos concerning these issues, see Haldeman to Lucy Winchester, 16 and 17 July 1969, "Memos/Lucy Winchester (July 1969)," box 51, Haldeman Personal Files, Richard Nixon Presidential Library and Museum, Yorba Linda, California, National Archives and Records Administration.

19. Melvin Small, *The Presidency of Richard Nixon* (Lawrence: University Press of Kansas, 1999), 31–58.

20. Parmet, *Richard Nixon and His America,* 543–545, 560–561.

21. Ehrlichman, *Witness to Power,* 18–19, 39–40.

22. Haldeman with DiMona, *Ends of Power,* 46–52; Richard M. Nixon, *RN: The Memoirs of Richard Nixon* (New York: Grosset & Dunlap, 1978), 337.

23. Haldeman with DiMona, *Ends of Power,* 58; Small, *Presidency of Richard Nixon,* 43–44; Lungren and John C. Lungren Jr., *Healing Richard Nixon: A Doctor's Memoir* (Lexington: University Press of Kentucky, 2003), 76–81; Sally Quinn, "Haldeman: No-Nonsense Guardian of Keys to the Kingdom," *Washington Post,* 27 October 1972, B1.

24. Melvin Small posits that Nixon might have wanted to demote Woods to keep her from bothering him with small details. See Small, *Presidency of Richard Nixon,* 44. Lungren suggests that Haldeman's Christian Science background might account for his treatment of Nixon's doctor. See Lungren and Lungren, *Healing Richard Nixon,* 76.

25. Small, *Presidency of Richard Nixon,* 44; Lungren and Lungren, *Healing Richard Nixon,* 76–78; Ronald Kessler, *Inside the White House: The Hidden Lives of the Modern Presidents and the Secrets of the World's Most Powerful Institution* (New York: Simon & Schuster, 1995), 56–57.

26. Eisenhower, *Pat Nixon,* 240–241, 299, 361–363; Ehrlichman, *Witness to Power,* 81.

27. Haldeman, *Haldeman Diaries,* 58, 350–351; Eisenhower, *Pat Nixon,* 332.

28. Ehrlichman, *Witness to Power,* 57; Quinn, "Haldeman"; Susanna McBee, "Pat Nixon and the First-Lady Watchers," *McCall's,* September 1970, 77.

29. Constance C. Stuart exit interview, 15 March 1973, Nixon Presidential Li-

brary and Museum, Yorba Linda, California, http://www.nixonlibrary.gov/virtual library/documents/exitinterviews/stuart.php, accessed 6 January 2010.

30. Karen Peterson, "Pat Tries to Pick Up the Pieces," *Chicago Tribune*, 6 February 1975, "East Wing Staff—Smith, Helen," box 50, Sheila Weidenfeld Files, Gerald R. Ford Presidential Library, Grand Rapids, Michigan.

31. McBee, "Pat Nixon and the First-Lady Watchers," 144.

32. See, among others, Constance Stuart to Coral Schmid, n.d., "New Projects," box 9; or Constance Stuart to Bob Haldeman, 25 March 1970, "College Students," box 6, no. 1; or Connie Stuart to Gwen, Coral, Helen and Martha, n.d., "Chicago Postal Street Academy Meeting, 2/25/71, Mrs. Nixon," box 5, no. 2, all in Porter Papers.

33. Constance Stuart to H. R. Haldeman, 27 July 1971, "Parks to People Project . . . 1971 [1 of 2]," box 10; Constance Stuart to Coral Schmid, Penny Adams, and Carol Reavis, 13 May 1970, "College Students," box 6, no. 1; John Ehrlichman to Connie Stuart, 10 March 1971, "Parks to People Project . . . 1971 [2 of 2]," box 10, no. 2, all in Porter Papers; Lucy Winchester to David Parker, 11 March 1974, "November 19, 2001 Supplements," Drown Supplements, Helene and Jack Drown Collection, Nixon Presidential Library and Museum.

34. Penelope A. Adams exit interview, 26 September 1973, Nixon Presidential Library and Museum, http://www.nixonlibrary.gov/virtuallibrary/documents/exit interviews/adams.php, accessed 6 January 2010.

35. Haldeman, *Haldeman Diaries*, 88, 119; W. Dewey Clower to Dwight Chapin, 9 November 1971, "Haldeman Memos David Parker, Nov. 1971," box 7, Nixon Presidential Contested Materials Collection: White House Special Files (WHSF), Richard Nixon Presidential Library and Museum, Yorba Linda, California, National Archives and Records Administration.

36. H. R. Haldeman to Constance Stuart, 5 November 1971, "Constance Stuart, November 1971," box 87, Haldeman Personal Files; Sally Quinn, "Bill Schustick: 'Yo, Ho, Ho's' at the White House," *Washington Post*, 5 November 1971, B1.

37. Constance Stuart to H. R. Haldeman, 15 November 1971, "Constance Stuart, November 1971," box 87, Haldeman Personal Files.

38. Harry Dent, memorandum for the president, 9 July 1969, "Harry Dent: Memos to the president—1969 3/3," WHSF, Staff Member Office Files (SMOF); Dwight Chapin to H. R. Haldeman, 5 April 1972, "Haldeman–Chapin Memos, Jan.–Feb. 1972," box 46, WHSF, SMOF; Haldeman, *Haldeman Diaries*, 489.

39. Jon M. Huntsman to Bill Carruthers, Dwight Chapin, Connie Stuart, and Mark Goode, 1 March 1971, and Constance Stuart to the Staff Secretary, 8 March

1971, "Constance Stuart March 1971," box 76, Haldeman Personal Files; Haldeman, *Haldeman Diaries*, 477.

40. Ehrlichman, *Witness to Power*, 57–58; Strober and Strober, *Nixon Presidency*, 36–37.

41. Eisenhower, *Pat Nixon*, 299–300.

42. Dwight Chapin to H. R. Haldeman, 24 July 1970, "[1970—First Family Scheduling]," box 46, WHSF, SMOF. For other examples, see H. R. Haldeman to Dwight Chapin, 20 July 1970, "HRH July–Aug. 1970 Staff Memo A—Chotiner," box 6; Dwight Chapin to William Codus and David Parker, 20 September 1972, "Presidential and First Family Scheduling [1 of 2]," box 46; Connie Stuart to Herb Klein, 2 December 1970, "HRH—Staff memos P–S December 1970," box 6, WHSF, SMOF.

43. Chuck Stuart to Harry Dent, 19 July 1969, "Harry Dent: Main Staff Memos, no. 2," box 5, WHSF, SMOF.

44. Dwight Chapin to H. R. Haldeman, 24 July 1970, "[1970—First Family Scheduling]," box 46, WHSF, SMOF.

45. Joseph B. Treaster, "Tricia Nixon, Surrounded by Republican Candidates, Drops into Danbury State Fair," *New York Times*, 4 October 1970, 29.

46. H. R. Haldeman to Dwight Chapin, 22 July 1970, "HRH July–Aug. 1970 Staff Memo A—Chotiner," box 6, WHSF, SMOF.

47. David Parker to H. R. Haldeman, 10 September 1971, "Projects—Julie Eisenhower [3 of 3]," box 11, Porter Papers.

48. Parmet, *Richard Nixon and His America*, 620–627; Small, *Presidency of Richard Nixon*, 245–250.

49. Small, *Presidency of Richard Nixon*, 250–258. For a harsher view of these "dirty tricks," see Rick Perlstein, *Nixonland: The Rise of a President and the Fracturing of America* (New York: Scribner, 2008), 583–584, 592–594, 627–631, 633, 635.

50. Tricia Nixon Cox to Mr. Carter, 11 May 1972, "Tricia—May [1972] Letters," box 54, King Papers.

51. Richard Nixon to H. R. Haldeman, 6 June 1972, folder 14; Richard Nixon to Tricia and Julie, 24 July 1972, folder 15, both in box 50, President's Personal File, WHSF, SMOF.

52. Dwight Chapin to H. R. Haldeman, 18 September 1972, "Haldeman–Chapin Memos, Jan.–Feb. 1972," box 46, WHSF, SMOF.

53. Dwight Chapin to William Codus and David Parker, 20 September 1972, "Presidential and First Family Scheduling [1 of 2]," box 46, WHSF, SMOF.

54. Richard Nixon to H. R. Haldeman, 28 January 1972, folder 11, box 50, President's Personal File, WHSF, SMOF; "On the Campaign Trail with Wives of the Candidates," *U.S. News & World Report*, 2 October 1972, 28+.

55. "African Queen for a Week," *Time*, 17 January 1972.

56. "Pat Nixon Backs Julie on Dying for S. Vietnam," *Los Angeles Times*, 19 September 1972, A12; Charles T. Powers, "Pat Nixon on the Campaign Trail," *Los Angeles Times*, 24 September 1972, D1; Ken Ringle, "Pat Nixon Campaigns Like First Lady," *Washington Post*, 27 September 1972, A1; James T. Wooten, "Enter Now the Leading Man," *New York Times*, 24 September 1972, E1.

57. Isabelle Shelton, "Pat Is Pressed," *Evening Star*, 19 September 1972, "Miscellaneous," box 7, King Papers; Helen Thomas, "Mrs. Nixon Backs Viet Regime," *Washington Post*, 19 September 1972, A6; Nan Robertson, "Mrs. Nixon, on 7-State Tour, Shuns Politics," *New York Times*, 23 September 1972, 14.

58. Haldeman, *Haldeman Diaries*, 506.

59. 18 September 1972, *Presidential Daily Diaries, 1969–1974*, CD-ROM, Nixon Presidential Library and Museum.

60. Haldeman, *Haldeman Diaries*, 178, 363–364, 467.

61. Nixon, *Memoirs*, 687; "The Nixon/Gannon Interviews," University of Georgia, Athens, 9 February 1983, day 3, tape 3, http://www.libs.uga.edu/media/collections/nixon/transcriptintro.html, accessed 20 May 2008.

62. Ehrlichman, *Witness to Power*, 56.

63. Haldeman, *Haldeman Diaries*, 178, 363–364, 467.

64. Roger Ailes to H. R. Haldeman, 4 May 1970, http://www.nixonlibrary.gov/virtuallibrary/documents/donated/050470_ailes.pdf, accessed 6 January 2010.

65. Richard Nixon to Pat Nixon, 5 February 1969, "Memos, Feb. 1969," President's Personal File, box 50, WHSF, SMOF; Richard Nixon to Pat Nixon, 5 February 1969, "1969, Feb., RN," box 2, WHSF, SMOF.

66. Strober and Strober, *Nixon Presidency*, 35; 5 February 1969, Presidential Daily Diaries.

67. Kessler, *Inside the White House*, 38–39.

68. Haldeman, *Haldeman Diaries*, 119; Strober and Strober, *Nixon Presidency*, 36–37.

69. UPI reporter Helen Thomas begins her chapter on Nixon with anecdotes about his sense of humor, or lack thereof. Helen Thomas, *Thanks for the Memories, Mr. President* (New York: Scribner, 2002), 81–86.

70. Ehrlichman, *Witness to Power*, 56. See also Kessler, *Inside the White House*, 96.

71. Strober and Strober, *Nixon Presidency*, 37. See also Lester David, *The Lonely Lady of San Clemente* (New York: Thomas Y. Crowell, 1978), chap. 15, for a complete listing of various incidents. For news accounts of the presidential appearance at the Grand Ole Opry, see Carroll Kilpatrick, "A Night at the Opry," *Washington*

Post, 17 March 1974, A1; Rudy Abramson, "High-Spirited Nixon Plays Piano, Yo-Yo at Grand Ole Opry," *Los Angeles Times,* 17 March 1974, 1.

72. David, *Lonely Lady,* 186–192.

73. The president's official diary records the president's moves throughout the day. Scanning through any of the years shows the presidential couple eating together on a regular basis. See Presidential Daily Diary.

74. "The Nixon/Gannon Interviews," 10 June 1983, day 7, tape 3.

75. Nixon, *Memoirs,* 89; David, *Lonely Lady,* 189.

76. Nixon, *Memoirs,* 507.

77. Stanley I. Kutler and Richard M. Nixon, *Abuse of Power: The New Nixon Tapes* (New York: Free Press, 1997), 383; Nixon, *Memoirs,* 569; Haldeman, *Haldeman Diaries,* 363–364.

78. Patrick Buchanan to Spiro Agnew, 26 September 1970, "H. R. Haldeman Misc. Materials, 1970," box 6, WHSF, SMOF.

79. Ibid., 220, 296, 350–351; Constance Stuart to Bob Haldeman and Dave Parker, 7 October 1971, "Eisenhower Theater, October 18, 1971, JNE," box 7, no. 1, Porter Papers.

80. Ehrlichman, *Witness to Power,* 56.

81. Haldeman, *Haldeman Diaries,* 63–65. When Helene Drown read an excerpt from Ehrlichman's memoirs, she wrote to him and lambasted him for "stoop[ing] so low as to write what you know is untrue." Helene Drown to John Ehrlichman, 21 January 1982, "1980– 1985," box 4, Drown Collection.

82. Robert Dallek, *Nixon and Kissinger: Partners in Power* (New York: Harper-Collins, 2007), 362.

83. Haldeman, *Haldeman Diaries,* 58, 88, 119, 207, 477, 367–368.

84. Seymour Hersh, "Kissinger and Nixon in the White House," *Atlantic Monthly* 249 (May 1982): 45.

85. Robertson, "Mrs. Nixon, on 7-State Tour, Shuns Politics."

86. See various letters and memos in "November 1972," "CVH—April 1973," and "CVH—July 1974," box 54, King Papers.

87. Constance C. Stuart exit interview.

88. Constance Stuart to H. R. Haldeman, 9 June 1970, "HRH—Staff Memos May/June 1970, N–Z," box 6, WHSF, SMOF.

89. Maureen Drown Nunn, interview by author, 16 August 2008, Richard Nixon Library.

90. Envelope, "Christmas Tags," "Misc. Notes and Tags," box 3, Drown Collection.

91. There are innumerable books about the Watergate scandal. For a good gen-

eral overview, see, among others, Stanley I. Kutler, *The Wars of Watergate: The Last Crisis of Richard Nixon* (New York: Knopf, distributed by Random House, 1990); Lukas, *Nightmare;* Theodore H. White, *Breach of Faith: The Fall of Richard Nixon* (New York: Atheneum, 1975). See also memoirs of participants, including Ehrlichman, *Witness to Power;* Haldeman with DiMona, *Ends of Power;* Charles Colson, *Born Again* (Peabody, Mass.: Hendrickson, 1976).

92. "His Defense Is an Offense; Evidence Is Yet to Come," *New York Times,* 18 November 1973, 223; "Text of Statement by Nixon, Aides' Letters," *Los Angeles Times,* 30 April 1973, 2; "Transcript of President's Broadcast Address to the Nation on the Watergate Affair," *New York Times,* 1 May 1973, 31; "Nixon on Transcripts: 'Entire Story Is There,'" *Washington Post,* 30 April 1974, A8; "The Text of President's Talk from Oval Office," *Los Angeles Times,* 9 August 1974, A1.

93. Nixon, *Memoirs,* 963–964.

94. Nan Robertson, "Mrs. Nixon, on Her Own, Begins Campaign Swing," *New York Times,* 19 September 1972, 109.

95. Nixon, *Memoirs,* 845–846; Eisenhower, *Pat Nixon,* 366–368.

96. See Lukas, *Nightmare,* 357–361, for a discussion of the Nixons' tax problems.

97. Maxine Chesire, "Kings, Princes, Foreign States, Jewels and the 'Gifts Unit,'" *Washington Post,* 14 May 1974, C1; "Mrs. Nixon Turns Over Saudi Arabian Gems," *Los Angeles Times,* 14 May 1974, 2; Donnie Radcliffe, "A Story 'For the Birds,'" *Washington Post,* 16 May 1974, B7.

98. "White House Luncheon," *Washington Post,* 8 May 1973, B3; Jeannette Smyth, "I Have Complete Faith," *Washington Post,* 18 May 1973, B3; Dorothy McCardle, "A First for a First Lady," *Washington Post,* 27 July 1973, B3.

99. "Pat 'Happy and Proud,'" *Washington Post,* 16 August 1973, A16; "Wife Expresses Love, 'Great Faith' in Nixon," *Los Angeles Times,* 29 January 1974, A16.

100. Mary Lou Loper, "First Lady Brings Out the New," *Los Angeles Times,* 2 April 1973, G3; Tom Zito, "Teacher of the Year," *Washington Post,* 19 April 1973, B9; Jeanette Smyth, "With Flags Waving," *Washington Post,* 21 September 1973, B2; Henry Mitchell, "A Nixon Relives History," *Washington Post,* 2 May 1974, B4.

101. Smyth, "With Flags Waving"; "Serenity in Crisis," *Washington Post,* 24 October 1974, B3; "Wife Expresses Love, 'Great Faith' in Nixon"; "In Support of the President," *Washington Post,* 9 May 1974, B2.

102. "Pat Nixon to Attend Rites in S. America," *Los Angeles Times,* 23 February 1974, A5; "Pat Nixon Greeted Quietly in Caracas," *Los Angeles Times,* 12 March 1974, 3A; Donnie Radcliffe, "Winging Her Way Back Home," *Washington Post,* 16 March 1974, B1.

103. Kilpatrick, "A Night at the Opry."

104. "Wife Expresses Love, 'Great Faith' in Nixon"; Kilpatrick, "A Night at the Opry"; "President Not Planning to Quit, Mrs. Nixon Says," *Los Angeles Times,* 11 May 1974, 20.

105. Marlene Cimons, "First Family Agonizes on the Sidelines," *Los Angeles Times,* 2 May 1973, H1.

106. "Christmas 'Escape,'" *Washington Post,* 20 December 1973, B3.

107. Donnie Radcliffe, "Pat Nixon: A Full Partner in the American Dream," *Washington Post,* 9 August 1974, A47; Rex Reed, "Celebrity Smoking: Who Does and Who Doesn't?" *Washington Post,* 21 July 1974, M5.

108. Kessler, *Inside the White House,* 41. Woodward and Bernstein's accusation of alcoholism will be addressed in chapter 6.

109. Gwen King to Helene Drown, 14 February 1974, "November 19, 2001, Supplements," Drown Collection; Helene Drown to Olie Atkins [*sic*], 12 August 1974, "November 19, 2001, Supplements," Drown Collection; Mamie Eisenhower to Pat Nixon, 2 January 1974 and 6 August 1974, "Eisenhower Correspondence, 1973–1974, Aug. 7," box 1, Post-Presidential Series 268, Special File, Patricia Ryan Nixon Collection, Nixon Presidential Library.

110. Brigid S. Flanigan to Marlene Malek et al., 11 January 1974, "Re.: Meetings," box 5, no. 3, Porter Papers; Helene Drown, speech, attached to Jack Drown to Richard Nixon, 28 April 1986, "Drown," box 2A, Drown Collection; "White House Luncheon," *Washington Post,* 8 May 1973, B3; Donnie Radcliffe, "Of Ladies—First and Senate," *Washington Post,* 14 May 1974, C4; McCardle, "A First for a First Lady."

111. See correspondence in the King Papers for the pertinent months to get some idea of the numbers of letters. See also Margo Harakas, "Media Role Demanding," (South Florida) *Sun-Sentinel* [September 197?], "East Wing Staff—Smith, Helen," box 50, Shelia Weidenfeld Files, Gerald R. Ford Presidential Library; "Mrs. Nixon Sends Cards of Thanks," *Los Angeles Times,* 24 November 1973, 22.

112. "Release of Tapes Displeased Pat," *Washington Post,* 20 May 1974, A23; Eisenhower, *Pat Nixon,* 380.

113. "President Not Planning to Quit, Mrs. Nixon Says"; "Lunching with Friends," *Washington Post,* 22 May 1974, C3.

114. Julie Eisenhower to Pat Nixon, March 1974, telegram, "Mrs. Nixon's Visit to Venezuela and Brazil, March 1974," box 57, WHSF, SMOF; Eisenhower, *Pat Nixon: The Untold Story,* 399–400.

115. Helen Thomas, *Front Row at the White House* (New York: Scribner, 1999), 263.

116. Donnie Radcliffe, "Family Isolated during the Final Hours," *Washington Post,* 9 August 1974, A7; Eisenhower, *Pat Nixon,* 419–430.

CHAPTER 6: PEACE, AT LAST

1. See, for example, Bradley Graham, "At Home in San Clemente," *Washington Post*, 11 August 1974, A1.

2. Julie Nixon Eisenhower, *Pat Nixon: The Untold Story* (New York: Simon & Schuster, 1986), 432.

3. Robert Sam Anson, *Exile: The Unquiet Oblivion of Richard M. Nixon* (New York: Simon & Schuster, 1984), 24–25.

4. "Release of Tapes Displeased Pat," *Washington Post*, 20 May 1974, A23; "President Not Planning to Quit, Mrs. Nixon Says," *Los Angeles Times*, 11 May 1974, 20.

5. "Nixon Relaxes with Family and Friends," *Los Angeles Times*, 12 August 1974, A12; "Nixon Has a Picnic with Tricia and Husband," *Los Angeles Times*, 15 August 1974, 2; Eisenhower, *Pat Nixon*, 432–433.

6. Mamie Eisenhower to Helene Drown, 15 November 1974, "1974—Aug. 1979," box 4, Helene and Jack Drown Collection, Nixon Presidential Library and Museum, Yorba Linda, California; Eisenhower, *Pat Nixon*, 432; Anson, *Exile*, 87.

7. "Nixon Subpoena Still Not Served," *Washington Post*, 26 August 1974, A7.

8. "Text of Ford's Proclamation," *Los Angeles Times*, 9 September 1974, B15; John Herbers, "No Conditions Set," *New York Times*, 9 September 1974, 73.

9. Eisenhower, *Pat Nixon*, 433.

10. Ibid., 431.

11. "Nixon Called Ill by Eisenhower," *Los Angeles Times*, 13 September 1974, A11. See also Stuart Auerback, "Nixon's Health and Pardon," *Washington Post*, 17 September 1974, A15; Howard Seelye, "Son-in-Law Cox Apparent Source of Reports of Nixon Being 'in Pain,'" *Los Angeles Times*, 12 September 1974, A20; Ann Blackman, "David Recalls Final Days in White House," *Los Angeles Times*, 5 September 1974, A1.

12. Anson, *Exile*, 60–62.

13. Lawrence K. Altman, "Doctor Says Nixon Has a New Attack of Phlebitis in Leg," *New York Times*, 14 September 1974, 61; "Doctor Says Nixon Feared Hospital Stay," *New York Times*, 15 September 1974, 54; Helen Thomas, "Tkach Says Full Pardon Didn't Lift Nixon Spirits," *Washington Post*, 16 September 1974, A3.

14. John C. Lungren and John C. Lungren Jr., *Healing Richard Nixon: A Doctor's Memoir* (Lexington: University Press of Kentucky, 2003), 21–39.

15. Ibid., 83–100.

16. Eisenhower, *Pat Nixon*, 433–435.

17. Richard M. Nixon, *In the Arena: A Memoir of Victory, Defeat, and Renewal* (New York: Simon & Schuster, 1990), 23.

18. Trude B. Feldman, "The Quiet Courage of Pat Nixon," *McCall's*, May 1975, 74.

19. Ibid., 115.

20. Stephen E. Ambrose, *Nixon: Ruin and Recovery, 1973–1990* (New York: Simon & Schuster, 1991), 447–454; Henry Silver and Evelyn Silver, "Who Is the Owner of Presidential Papers?" *Los Angeles Times,* 25 September 1974, D6; J. F. ter-Horst, "Ford's Pity for Nixon Fades with Tapes Case," *Los Angeles Times,* 17 November 1974, 11; William Safire, "The Second Comeback?" *New York Times,* 13 October 1975, 25.

21. Anson, *Exile,* 112–115.

22. Julie Eisenhower to Helene and Jack Drown, 2 June 1975, "1974—Aug. 1979," box 4, Drown Collection; Anson, *Exile,* 171–187.

23. Anson, *Exile,* 122–133; Ambrose, *Nixon,* 488–493.

24. Bob Woodward and Carl Bernstein, *The Final Days* (New York: Simon & Schuster, 1976); Ambrose, *Nixon,* 494–495; "Price of 'Final Days' Is Raised $1 to $11.95," *New York Times,* 11 April 1976, 45; " 'Final Days' Sets a Paperback Record," *New York Times,* 13 April 1976, 27.

25. Woodward and Bernstein, *Final Days,* 164–166.

26. Julie Nixon Eisenhower, "My Mother," *Newsweek,* 24 May 1976, 13.

27. Helen McCain Smith and Elizabeth Pope Frank, "Ordeal! Pat Nixon's Final Days in the White House," *Good Housekeeping,* July 1976, 83, 127–133.

28. Victor Lasky, "The Woodstein Report," "1975–1976 Lasky Article," box 8, Helene and Jack Drown Collection, Nixon Presidential Library, Yorba Linda, California; Deidre Carmody, "Book on Nixon's Last Months in Office Challenged on Methods and Accuracy," *New York Times,* 3 April 1976, 14. For another editorial view, see Phil Kerby, "The Novelizing of Nixon's 'Final Days,' " *Los Angeles Times,* 7 April 1976, C5.

29. Jessamyn West, "The Real Pat Nixon," *Good Housekeeping,* February 1971, 70, 124.

30. Ambrose, *Nixon,* 498.

31. Eisenhower, *Pat Nixon,* 447–453; Lungren and Lungren, *Healing Richard Nixon,* 159–162.

32. Nunn interview; Eisenhower, *Pat Nixon,* 450.

33. Ibid., 457.

34. Lungren and Lungren, *Healing Richard Nixon,* 162; Anson, *Exile,* 141; Eisenhower, *Pat Nixon,* 447; "Still More Pain for the Nixons," *Time,* 19 July 1976; Joyce Brothers, "Pat Nixon's Hidden Story," *Good Housekeeping,* October 1976, 80–84.

35. Nick Thimmesch, "The Unsinkable Pat Nixon," *McCall's,* April 1979, 142.

36. Lester David, *The Lonely Lady of San Clemente* (New York: Thomas Y. Crowell, 1978), 9–10.

37. Joann Barrett, "Pat Nixon's Happiest Night," *Good Housekeeping*, May 1978, 153.

38. Eisenhower, *Pat Nixon*, 456–457.

39. Ibid., 457–458; Winzola McLendon, "Pat Nixon Today," *Good Housekeeping*, February 1980, 172.

40. Eisenhower, *Pat Nixon*, 458–459.

41. Lester David, "Pat Nixon's Golden Years," *McCall's*, October 1986, 138.

42. Carl Sferrazza Anthony, "Richard Nixon's Tribute to His Beloved Pat," *Good Housekeeping*, July 1994, 176.

43. See, for example, "Pat Nixon, RIP," *National Review*, 19 July 1993, 20; "Love Bears All Things," *Newsweek*, 5 July 1993, 65; Beth Brophy, "Devoted Wife," *U.S. News & World Report*, 5 July 1993, 14; "Forged of Hidden Steel," *People*, 5 July 1993, 38.

44. Carl Anthony, "Pat Nixon, Stealth Feminist?" *Washington Post*, 27 June 1993, C2.

45. Elaine Tyler May, *Homeward Bound: American Families in the Cold War Era* (New York: Basic Books, 1988), 183–207.

BIBLIOGRAPHIC ESSAY

Until very recently, anyone doing research on a topic connected to Richard Nixon had to contend with the ramifications of Nixon's battle for control over his papers. The National Archives and Records Administration (NARA) housed his presidential papers at its facility in College Park, Maryland, while his personal papers and those of some of his associates resided in his presidential library in Yorba Linda, California. Scholars trying to develop a complete picture of the administration had to scramble between the two places, hoping nothing fell through the cracks. With the conclusion of the legal battles and negotiations, NARA trucked most of the papers across the country during spring 2010.

Included in the thousands of documents are the Patricia Ryan Nixon Collection. These papers, divided into seventeen different series, include both personal items, such as mementos from her childhood and letters from and to her brothers, and political material. Notes and itineraries from her trips during the prepresidential years and souvenirs from official functions provide evidence of her participation in her husband's political career. Although the boxes contain many carbon copies of responses to constituent mail and considerable political ephemera, they also reveal important information about Pat's life as wife, mother, friend, and political being before and during her years as first lady. For example, one box includes Pat's reflections on her first trip as second lady to the Far East.

Another invaluable source for understanding Pat Nixon is the Helene and Jack Drown Collection, also housed at the Nixon Library. Helene and Pat met while they were both teachers at Whittier High School. The two couples became fast friends and shared a lifelong interest in politics. The correspondence between Helene and Pat gives researchers a glimpse into Pat's world in her own words. Except for a brief stint at diary writing during the vice presidential years, Pat did not leave a written record of her thoughts and feelings. Her letters to Helene, her closest friend, provide researchers with Pat's perspective and her personality. She could be herself with Helene, and the letters show her sometimes biting sense of humor as well as her frustrations and tolerance. Unfortunately, as the two women began telephoning more in the mid-1960s, the number of letters declines precipitously.

The papers of East Wing staffers, particularly Susan Porter (appointments secretary) and Gwendolyn King (director of correspondence), offer less personal information but are important in exploring Pat's role as first lady. The Porter papers contain memos discussing her various projects and expose the tensions existing between East and West Wing personnel. The King papers include carbons of correspondence from the first lady to constituents as well as some communication between Mrs. Nixon and her staff. The papers of Lucy Winchester (social secretary), particularly the first box, contain further evidence of the difficulty experienced by members of Mrs. Nixon's staff in dealing with the president's people. In addition, the National Archives conducted exit interviews with staff members. These are available online through the Nixon library (http://www.nixonlibrary.gov/virtual library/documents/index.php). Of particular importance for understanding how Pat ran her side of the house were interviews with Constance Stuart and William Codus.

The White House special files, staff member files, and office files of Richard Nixon's aides also contain information about Pat Nixon. These collections provide further examples of Pat's work as first lady, her husband's vision of her role, and his staff's attitudes toward the first lady, her projects, and her staff. Of particular value are the personal files of H. R. Haldeman and the notes of John Ehrlichman. Both men played important roles in the administration and oversaw the operations of both West and East Wings. The president's daily diaries show his movements throughout the day and include listings of his phone calls. The diary reveals the time Dick and Pat spent in one another's company on any given day.

As a result of a change in the law, NARA sent all materials in the central and special files of a personal or political/personal nature (that is, having to do with campaigns) to the Nixon Library beginning in 1994. These files, cataloged as "returned materials," are available for research and contain information regarding Pat's role in the various campaigns.

The library also houses Nixon's papers from his prepresidential years. This category covers not only the vice presidential years, but also the time period that Nixon dubbed the wilderness years. Material from the transitions to California and New York as well as campaign information from the 1962 gubernatorial race are included in this classification. Obviously these collections focus primarily on Richard Nixon, but diligent researchers might find some material concerning attitudes toward Pat's involvement in campaigns or her husband's decisions about his political career.

Pat's interactions with other first ladies provide insight into her personality and the difficulty of the job itself. Pat's first experience with a first lady came from her acquaintanceship with Mamie Doud Eisenhower when Richard served as vice president under President Dwight Eisenhower. The affection the two women shared is evident in Mamie's papers housed in the Dwight D. Eisenhower Library in Abilene, Kansas. Pat's relationship with her successor, Betty Ford, was much briefer and more formal. The papers of Sheila Weidenfeld, Mrs. Ford's press secretary, detail some of the transition difficulties between the staffs of the Nixon and Ford administrations. The papers of Lady Bird Johnson, housed at the Lyndon B. Johnson Library in Austin, Texas, have not yet been fully processed. Lady Bird's diary, however, has been published as *A White House Diary* (Austin: University of Texas Press, 2007), and details their common efforts to effect a smooth transition in 1969.

There are several oral history collections related to Pat Nixon, some of which are especially important to understanding her life before her marriage. The Richard Nixon Oral History Project at California State University, Fullerton, includes interviews with many of Pat's childhood friends. The interviewers also spoke with individuals who knew Dick as a young man and who knew the two as a couple. In addition, Alice Martin Rosenberger collected reminiscences of people in the Whittier area, particularly former students, who had known Pat. She presented these to Pat as a birthday surprise in 1986. The volume, *Collection of Sixty Interviews for Pat Ryan Nixon,* is available in the Whittier Public Library. The Whittier College Oral History Collection, including over 300 interviews with individuals ranging from family members to political associates, should be available online soon.

Other oral histories detail Pat's life after her marriage and during her years as first lady. The previously mentioned exit interviews, available through the Richard Nixon Library Web site, are helpful in understanding the workings of the White House staff. In 1983, Richard Nixon sat down with his former aide, Frank Gannon, and discussed his life and career. These interviews, during which the former president talked about his relationship with his wife, are also available online (http://www.libs.uga.edu/media/collections/nixon/transcriptintro.html). Although his words must be used carefully, the president does address issues concerning his marriage and his feelings about his wife. Deborah Hart Strober and Gerald S. Strober's *The Nixon Presidency: An Oral History of the Era*, revised edition (Washington, D.C.: Brassey's, 1994), includes a few comments by Nixon staffers about the West Wing staff's view of the Nixons' relationship.

Because Pat spent much of her adult life in the public arena, journalists chronicled her shifting roles. The Center for American History in Austin, Texas, has a good collection of articles about her early career through the 1960 campaign. Although Pat distrusted the press and tended to rely on a set of standard answers to questions, she occasionally revealed more than she intended. As an example, scholars should examine Jessamyn West's "The Unknown Pat Nixon" (*Good Housekeeping*, February 1971). As Dick's cousin, West had her own stories to add to her formal interview with Pat. The memoirs of journalists who covered the White House offer a different perspective of Pat Nixon. Particularly useful are the books by Helen Thomas, who worked for UPI throughout the Nixon years (*Front Row at the White House* [New York: Scribner, 1999]; *Thanks for the Memories, Mr. President* [New York: Scribner, 2002]; and *Dateline: White House* [New York: Macmillan, 1975]). Thomas developed a personal relationship with Pat that did not interfere with her journalistic integrity. In contrast, Robert Pierpoint's *At the White House* (New York: G. P. Putnam's Sons, 1981) describes a completely different Pat Nixon, one who fit the traditional stereotype of the first lady.

There are two biographies of Pat that should serve as a starting point for any research concerning her. The earlier, Lester David's *The Lonely Lady of San Clemente* (New York: Thomas Y. Crowell, 1978), was based on interviews David conducted with various persons connected to Pat, including old friends, East Wing staffers, and journalists. As the title indicates, the author portrays Pat as a victim and martyr rather than a woman fully engaged in her own life. The second biography is Julie Nixon Eisenhower's *Pat Nixon: The Untold Story* (New York: Simon & Schuster, 1986). Benefiting from Julie's insider information, the book offers a more positive picture of Pat than David's monograph. Eisenhower paints her mother as a strong woman who was unfailingly faithful to her husband and his vision for America.

Although there are few biographies of Pat, she is included in volumes covering the first ladies and first families. In his *Upstairs at the White House: My Life with the First Ladies* (New York: Coward, McCann & Geoghegan, 1973), J. B. West, who served as chief usher for decades, discusses the Nixons' initial days in the White House. Because he retired soon after the inauguration, his interaction with Pat was limited. In a similar vein, Ronald Kessler collected stories from various men and women who worked in and around the White House in *Inside the White House: The Hidden Lives of the Modern Presidents and the Secrets of the World's Most Powerful Institution* (New York: Simon & Schuster, 1995). The anecdotes humanize Pat, even if the image is not always flattering.

Considering that Pat's papers were only opened recently, scholars researching Pat's role as first lady have done a good job of trying to expose the real woman behind the stereotypes. Historian Betty Boyd Caroli's *First Ladies* (New York: Oxford University Press, 1987) includes a discussion comparing the three presidential wives of the 1960s. Caroli recognizes that Pat had strengths that were never acknowledged by a media more focused on her overbearing husband. Carl Sferrazza Anthony, who has written extensively on first ladies and presidential families, wrote the chapter on Pat in Lewis L. Gould, ed., *American First Ladies: Their Lives and Legacies* (New York: Garland, 1996). Anthony does a wonderful job of treating Pat as a well-rounded individual both in that short work and in his other books, such as *America's First Families: An Inside View of 200 Years of Private Life in the White House* (New York: Simon & Schuster, 2000), which includes the Nixons along with other White House families. In Gil Troy's *Mr. & Mrs. President: From the Trumans to the Clintons* (Lawrence: University Press of Kansas, 1997), Pat becomes a strong woman used by her husband for his political ends. In fact, those old images die hard, as evidenced by Kati Marton's *Hidden Power: Presidential Marriages that Shaped Our Recent History* (New York: Pantheon, 2001). Marton reverts to the image of Pat as a silent victim of her husband's ambition.

Any investigation of Pat's life must include her husband's perspective as well. Pat is a supporting character in all of Richard Nixon's memoirs beginning with *Six Crises* (Garden City, N.Y.: Doubleday, 1962), continuing with *RN: The Memoirs of Richard Nixon* (New York: Grosset & Dunlap, 1978), and concluding with *In the Arena: A Memoir of Victory, Defeat, and Renewal* (New York: Simon & Schuster, 1990). Dick portrays Pat as loving and supportive, even when she disagreed with him. Although she is definitely not a victim in these monographs, she often seems more a caricature than a real human being. Despite the self-serving aspects of these books, the importance of the relationship between Dick and Pat is readily apparent.

The memoirs of some of the men associated with the Nixon administration reinforce the struggle Pat faced during the White House years. Haldeman's diary, *The Haldeman Diaries: Inside the Nixon White House* (New York: Putnam, 1994), is of particular importance in understanding the perspective of the West Wing. His memoir, written with Joseph DiMona, *The Ends of Power* (New York: New York Times Books, 1978), as well as that of John Ehrlichman, *Witness to Power: The Nixon Years* (New York: Simon and Schuster, 1982), must be read with a cautious eye, however. Written in the years after their incarcerations for Watergate-related crimes, the memoirs are bitter. Both men remember Pat in dismissive terms at best and with insulting characterizations on occasion. If the Haldeman and Ehrlichman books attempt to attack Pat, Henry Kissinger's book about his days in the Nixon administration, *White House Years* (Boston: Little, Brown, 1979), almost ignores her. In fact, she is a bit player in his version of the drama. When he does write of her, she becomes the victim/saint rather than active participant. A variation on the theme appears in John Lungren's memoirs of his days as one of Nixon's doctors (John C. Lungren and John C. Lungren Jr., *Healing Richard Nixon: A Doctor's Memoir* [Lexington: University Press of Kentucky, 2003]). Lungren describes Pat in glowing terms that echo the saintly image of other authors. He does, however, also include a more human side in his chapter on her stroke.

Some biographies of Richard Nixon mention his wife and discuss his relationship with her in a positive light. Earl Mazo, who wrote one of the earliest books about Nixon, *Richard Nixon: A Political and Personal Portrait* (New York: Harper, 1959), became a family friend and treats Pat with respect even as he helps to create her "wonder woman" image. Jonathan Aitken had access to Nixon's private papers and interviewed many people close to Nixon. His book, *Nixon: A Life* (Washington, D.C.: Regnery, 1993), accepted Nixon's version of his life with Pat. Stephen E. Ambrose's multivolume biography of Nixon (New York: Simon and Schuster, 1987–1991) draws heavily from Julie's biography of her mother for information regarding Pat. Consequently, Pat appears as less of a victim in the Ambrose version of events. Similarly, in Robert Sam Anson's *Exile: The Unquiet Oblivion of Richard M. Nixon* (New York: Simon & Schuster, 1984), Pat is treated with respect. Anson's monograph is one of the few to give Pat credit for a vital role in fighting with and for Nixon during the postresignation years.

Other biographers turn her into another casualty of her husband's political ambition. Gary Wills, in *Nixon Agonistes: The Crisis of the Self-Made Man* (Boston: Houghton Mifflin, 1970), characterizes her as a woman driven to become obsessively self-controlled and prone to occasional verbal attacks on her husband. Bob Woodward and Carl Bernstein, in *The Final Days* (New York: Simon & Schuster, 1976), created the most thoroughly victimized characterization of Pat. Their portrayal of Pat as stereotype remained firmly entrenched even as Nixon's image began to be rehabilitated years later. Fawn McKay Brodie, in *Richard Nixon: The Shaping of His Character* (New York: Norton, 1981), repeats many of the stories of Dick's mistreatment of Pat and uses them to psychoanalyze Nixon. Completing the victimization of Pat, journalist Anthony Summers, in *The Arrogance of Power: The Secret World of Richard Nixon* (New York: Viking, 2000), stated that Nixon physically abused his wife on several occasions. The sensational accusations, which are based on hearsay and rumors, run counter to all reliable evidence. In the 1990s, Nixon revisionism emerged among historians. Herbert Parmet's *Richard Nixon and His America* (Boston: Little, Brown, 1990) and Tom Wicker's *One of Us* (New York: Random House, 1991) led the way in looking beneath the dirt of Watergate to explore other aspects of the Nixon administration. Pat's image, however, did not get revised in these volumes. She remains a behind-the-scenes political wife. Both Irwin Gellman in *The Contender, Richard Nixon: The Congress Years, 1946–1952*

(New York: Free Press, 1999) and Melvin Small in *The Presidency of Richard Nixon* (Lawrence: University Press of Kansas, 1999) acknowledged Pat's participation and importance to Dick's career. Because their focus was on Dick, the Pat revisionism was limited. For a less positive view of Nixon but a slightly enlarged role for Pat, see Rick Perlstein's *Nixonland: The Rise of a President and the Fracturing of America* (New York: Scribner, 2008). Perlstein casts Pat, in the role of dutiful wife and mother, as an essential character in the creation of Nixon's America.

INDEX